THE NAKED ISLAND

THE NAKED

ISLAND

BY RUSSELL BRADDON

DOUBLEDAY & COMPANY, INC., GARDEN CITY, N.Y., 1953

FIRST PUBLISHED, 1953, IN THE UNITED STATES

LIBRARY OF CONGRESS CATALOG CARD NUMBER: 52-13375

Printed in the United States
At the Country Life Press, Garden City, N.Y.

AUTHOR'S NOTE

This book is written as one man's fear of things that lie ahead. It is also written as one man's tribute to the Britishers' capacity for living fearlessly and gently.

It is especially a tribute to two men—Padre Noel Duckworth and Major Kevin Fagan—who lived more fearlessly and more gently than all others.

It is dedicated to a Welshman called "Mush." R.B.

BOOK ONE

1 THE FOURTEENTH STEP 11
2 INSANITY IN THE FAMILY? 13
3 FIVE-BOB-A-DAY BUTCHERS 23
4 "NOW IS THE HOUR" 29
5 "BAD DAMES" 32
6 "HOW TO LIVE IN MALAYA" 38
7 "HULLO, JOE" 46
8 "BATTLE STATIONS" 55
9 AIRBORNE INVASION 60

BOOK TWO

1 OUR FIRST GAOL 113
2 "SHANGRI-LA" 121
3 "PUDU'S GROWING PAINS" 125
4 HOW TO BE A P.O.W. 141
5 TOJO NUMBER TEN 146
6 THE PHONY CAPTIVITY 166
7 SINGAPORE INTERLUDE 170
8 BORE-HOLES 177

BOOK THREE

1 "BRING YOUR PIANO" 187
2 KANEMOTOSAN 200
3 "ULCERS AND BUSHIDO" 205

BOOK FOUR

1 A HOME TO BE BUILT 243
2 THE AERODROME 253
3 THEATRE 263
4 "HARRY THE HAWK" 265
5 THE FOURTH YEAR 270
6 ON OUR RETURN 275
7 THE HIROSHIMA INCIDENT 281
POSTSCRIPT 284

1

1 THE FOURTEENTH STEP

There were twenty-two steps altogether from the courtyard of the gaol up to the cells. I had got into the habit of counting those steps. Made them seem shorter, or easier. Anyway I had got into the habit of counting. And at the fourteenth I stopped, done. Because I could go no further, I lowered myself onto the step above me and took stock of my surroundings.

At the foot of the stairs, barely visible in the gloom, sat the sentry —steel-helmeted, knees wide apart, rifle and bayonet across his knees. Silent, unintelligent, unfriendly. Beyond him a small courtyard about thirty yards square. Round the courtyard ran a high prison wall—sheer and made unscalable by five or six rows of loose-piled bricks balanced twenty feet up on its top.

Above my head, all along the balcony which ran from the top of the stairs round three sides of the ancient block of cells, the darkness was restless with the small sounds of men who slept neither comfortably nor well. And at my feet, also on the staircase, lying doubled up over three or four steps, sprawled a half-naked soldier—an Argyll, I recognized from his cap which, last of his possessions, he wore even at night.

I had passed him on the way down to the latrines. Then, he had writhed on the stairs with the griping pains of dysentery; and, having lost all control of his bowels, his legs were fouled and his pride outraged.

"Anything I can do, Jock?" I had asked him.

"Och, man, leave me alone," he had exclaimed. I regretted my intrusion. That was the trouble nowadays; one was never alone, not even on a prison staircase in the early hours of the morning.

"Sorry," I muttered, and, stepping over him, continued on down to the sentry.

"Benjo-ka?" I asked him.

"Benjo hei," he grunted. Permission granted, I crossed the twenty feet of maggot-ridden mud to the latrine. Soon I returned. In accordance with instructions, I thanked the sentry.

"Aringato," I said, to which he replied, disinterestedly, *"Okayga."*

I had walked to the stairs; climbed them slowly; passed the young Argyll (without speaking) and then stopped—exhausted—at the fourteenth step.

I looked at the sprawled figure again. Even in the gloom I could see fair hair under the black cap with its check colours: sturdy legs: one hand clenched tightly over the back edge of the step on which my feet rested: head on one side and a clean-cut jaw.

A Scot of the best type. I hoped no one would come down the stairs and see either of us at that moment. I decided then that, since I too was incapable of moving, I could now decently address him.

"How are you doing, Jock?" I asked. He didn't answer. He didn't seem resentful of the intrusion, however, so I persisted, with a feeble attempt at humour:

"Toss you for who carries who up the rest of the stairs," I said—and again he didn't answer.

I knew then what had happened: knew without looking. The Argyll was dead. Within a week of arriving in the gaol, the first man in our seven hundred had died—not of wounds, not in battle, but from exhaustion and privation.

Weaker then ever, I leant back. This was something I could not easily understand. Death in war was an unpleasant event which must befall many—not oneself, naturally: but many others, even one's friends. One regretted the fact, but one did not bewail it.

But this—this death due to lack of food and drugs, both of which were plentiful—this was something against which one could not steel oneself. A week, I thought, and one dead already. A young, sturdy Scot. There must be lots of weeks to go yet before we would be out. A year probably, I thought. That was if they didn't shoot us as they'd said they would. Then, more honestly, I added to myself, "four years, more likely." It didn't bear thinking about.

I looked at the Argyll. He was about my age, perhaps a little younger, perhaps twenty. I reflected that only recently I had taken the activity and the fleetness of foot and the exuberance of youth entirely for granted. I reflected that only a fortnight ago I should never have considered mounting these stairs any other way than two at a time. Now, one by one, counting idiotically, I had crawled up: and—finally—had bogged down altogether at number fourteen.

In the dark, on the stairs, resting my elbows on my knees, my forehead on my fists, I gave myself over to misery. I found myself retracing in my mind the sequence of events which had led me, so inevitably, to this staircase between the punishment cells and the courtyard of Pudu Gaol, Kuala Lumpur, onetime administration centre of British Malaya.

2 INSANITY IN THE FAMILY?

It was that brass band I blamed most. Day after day, with unremitting fervour, it had played martial airs outside the Sydney Recruiting Office in a jolly attempt to convince young Australians that war was just one long march by Sousa. Thousands of volunteers (the theory was)—hypnotized by the blare of brass—would pour, in a Hamelin-like procession, into the Australian Imperial Forces.

Once before, months earlier, I had volunteered, only to be told to go away and get my mother's consent, and finish my university course. Accordingly, I had obtained my mother's consent and passed my exams. and become a Bachelor of Arts. This, to my limited intelligence, did not appear an excessively helpful contribution to the Empire's war effort, so, at the beginning of 1941, I had returned to the Recruiting Office, determined this time to enlist and kill many Germans. And there, outside the small wooden hut (which, in the middle of the grandeur of Martin Place, and immediately above the gentlemen's lavatory, was so typical a product of the military mind), stood the scarlet ranks of a brass band playing martial airs.

Irritated, I stopped short on the corner of Martin Place and Pitt Street. If I was going to join up, I was going to join up of my own accord. I was *not* going to be wafted into the Army on the end of any conductor's baton, however magnificent his moustache or innumerable his campaign ribbons. Stubbornly, taking care not to walk in step with the march that stirred the depths of the city, I strolled away up the hill, crossed Castlereagh Street, crossed Elizabeth Street, caught the Bondi tram and went for a swim.

Next day, punctually after my morning lectures, I ran from the University Chambers, wherein the Law School was housed, down to the Recruiting Office in Martin Place. And there, once again, the sun glinting on the silver of epaulettes and the gold of instruments, was the band! Again I went for a swim. Every day for a week the band was there and every day for a week, while others joined up and were consigned to Syria and Darwin and England, I went swimming.

Then at last the band vanished, and in I marched, into the small hut in the middle of Martin Place, immediately above the gentlemen's lavatory. The same recruiting sergeant greeted me in the same bluff and congenial manner as he had when first I was interviewed by him—a manner that had all the roguish humour of a commercial traveller and all the sincerity of a pawnbroker.

"Hullo there, laddy," he said, "going to join our Army?" I nodded. "How old are you, laddy?" he asked. I said, "Twenty," and he said, "Tell it to the Marines, laddy, tell it to the Marines. Eighteen years ago you wouldn't even have been a gleam in your father's eye, now would you, eh?" Realizing that the sergeant was the possessor of a particularly hammy wit, I didn't answer. I simply placed on the table before him a form signed by my mother—the form which rendered minors eligible for enlistment.

"Mother's signed this, laddy," he observed astutely, "why not your father?"

"Died eight years ago," I told him. At this the sergeant appeared embarrassed and started pounding his pockets one after the other in the frenzied manner of all smokers who know quite well that they have no cigarettes but wish to give the impression that this is a fact they have only just discovered. Finally, with an air of childlike candour, which was most unbecoming, he turned to me and said: "Wouldn't it, eh?—clean out of smokes! Got a cigarette to spare, laddy?" I said I was sorry, I hadn't. "Got the makings?" he persisted, and his brown face, with its short ginger moustache, assumed an air of pleading even less pleasing than the one of candour.

I said I didn't smoke. Making the best of it, he laughed abruptly and—inevitably—remarked, "Don't smoke: don't drink and don't go out with bad women." He then turned to the private who was the clerk in the office, and, abandoning all pretence of pleading, said peremptorily, "Give us a fag, Snowy," and Snowy, with considerable ill-grace, passed him over a cigarette. The sergeant then slapped all his pockets again one after the other so, rather wearily, Snowy also tossed over his matches. The sergeant lit up, inhaled deeply, blew a cloud of smoke out of the hut door towards the gentlemen's lavatory and then—tiring for the moment of swelling His Majesty's Forces—stepped out of the office into the sunlight of Martin Place.

"Be back in half an hour, Snow," he said, tossing him his matches. "You, laddy," he added, "you come back at two and we'll have transport for you over to Victoria Barracks." Another cloud of smoke and he was gone.

"That bastard," observed Snow, with detached calm, "is the greatest cold bite in the A.I.F.!" And, having delivered himself of this verdict, he, too, turned his back on me and began gloomily going through a vast pile of Army forms. Ignored by all in this my latest attempt to fight the Germans, I followed the sergeant's example and stepped out into the sunlight of Martin Place. Probably, I thought, I would go for a swim——

All of these trivial incidents were to control my destiny. As I stepped out of the hut, I was hailed by a boyhood friend who, looking most surprised, said, "You joining up?" and when I nodded, asked, "What unit?"

"God knows," I told him—it didn't seem important anyway.

"Well, what branch of the Army?" he asked.

"What do you mean, what branch?" I demanded. It had frankly never occurred to me that armies had branches. As far as I was concerned, impelled by one's sense of duty, or by whatever other motive it was, one just joined the Army and killed Germans.

"Well," he explained, "infantry, artillery, A.S.C., sappers—what branch?"

"I don't know," I assured him, "they haven't told me. Infantry, I suppose." This appeared to shock him greatly. The infantry, apparently, were not at all a good thing. The infantry were just footsloggers—the P.B.I. "You'd better come up and see Dad," he told me: and so, being an obliging youth, I went up and saw Dad.

Dad was a solicitor, who asked all sorts of penetrating questions about my future military plans, none of which, to his unconcealed dismay, I could answer. Finally, he made the fateful decision.

"You'd better join your father's old unit," he said firmly. "I know the C.O. I'll write him a note and get him to apply for you. Then when you go out to Victoria Barracks, you'll be requisitioned."

"I'll be what?" I asked.

"Requisitioned," he said. Whatever it was, I didn't like the sound of it. But I had been well brought up, and he was an old friend of the family, so I merely repeated the word "requisitioned," noting mentally that it was very uncouth, and said politely, "Thank you, sir," and left. Thus, though fortunately at that moment I was blissfully unaware of the fact, was my entire future settled by the playing of brass bands, the sudden desire of a recruiting sergeant for a smoke rather than an immediate recruit, and the firm pulling of strings by an old friend of the family the better to procure that heart-warming procedure known as "requisitioning."

Arrived at Victoria Barracks, all did not go smoothly—not at all smoothly. We recruits (there were about a dozen of us that day) had been greeted with overwhelming *bonhomie* by yet another sergeant, a middle-aged man with less charm than stomach—the latter being firmly girt up by a pair of vast trousers and yards of webbing belt. He had a ready line of patter. "Just this way, son," he had said. "You'll be right, me boy . . . just sit here and we'll have you fixed up before you can say Jack Robinson." . . . "Now you boys, get to know one another." . . . And finally—presumably to hasten the process of getting to know one another—"Just come this way and strip off."

So we all went that way and stripped off and for the next three quarters of an hour remained stripped off, whilst the Army lost all interest in us. We just stood round surreptitiously comparing sun tans and birth marks, until finally, six feet of complete disinterest, in the shape of a medical orderly, emerged from behind a turf guide and summoned us, one by one, to be weighed and measured. Next, in to the doctors for an examination.

2 INSANITY IN THE FAMILY?

Doctors were a tribe for whom I had never had much time. The one before whom I now stood filled me with no confidence at all. He had the outward appearances of a publican and the delicate hands of a navvy. He confirmed my worst fears about the profession in general and himself in particular by thrusting an inquisitive finger against what is euphemistically termed one's lower abdomen and saying, "Cough."

If that, I thought to myself, is where he imagines I get a sore throat, no wonder he had to join the Army! I stood silent and contemptuous.

Irritably he looked up from the inquisitive finger and my lower abdomen. "I said 'Cough,'" he told me. I nodded. "Well then," he ordered, very abruptly indeed, "Cough!" With no great conviction, I coughed.

"Uh-huh," he said, and removed the finger and averted the gaze and wrote something down on a form which I tried very hard to read but with no success at all.

"Now," he said in a businesslike manner, "some questions." I prepared myself for questioning.

"What diseases have you had?" This, I thought, at least displayed a pleasantly paternal interest in my past, so, even though it appeared quite irrelevant to the business of killing Germans, I answered him briskly, saying, "Measles and whooping cough."

He looked most disappointed. "No chicken pox?" he queried. I denied the chicken pox.

"No mumps?" I denied the mumps. I also denied broken limbs, missing teeth and interesting scars. The doctor became quite patently bored and attempted a different gambit.

"Do you throw fits?" he asked hopefully. I denied that I threw fits.

"Mother or father throw fits?" he persisted. I said, "No." His face clouded with despondency but he pressed on: "Any insanity in the family at all?" he demanded desperately—"grandparents or anything?" Again I said no: whereupon—quite disgruntled—he wrote down on the form that I didn't throw fits, that my mother and father didn't throw fits and that my grandparents were sane. Meantime I stood by, still quite naked, and listened to the other naked recruits also being interrogated about the state of their grandparents' sanity. I suddenly had a terrible desire to assure this doctor who looked like a publican that actually both my parents had the D.T.s and that my great-grandmother had been as mad as a cut snake. These reveries were, however, completely disrupted by a curt order to bend over. All around the room at that moment recruits were bending over—and very unsightly it was, too.

"Why?" I asked.

"Because," said the publican, with quite unwarranted impatience, "I want to see if you've got piles."

"I haven't," I told him firmly—and remained vertical.

"Bend over," he bellowed. "You can't expect me to take your word for it—got to see for myself."

"You didn't want to see my grandparents," I argued.

"I am not," he hissed, "examining your grandparents for piles. Now bend over."

"You asked me," I pointed out, "whether my grandparents were cracked. I said, 'No.' You didn't say, 'Show me your uncracked grandparents!' Now, you ask, have I got piles and I say, 'No,' and you say, 'Bend over.' It doesn't make sense."

With a look of undisguised hostility, he straightened up in his chair.

"All right," he capitulated, "you have *not* got piles. Now, for God's sake," and he said the words very slowly and with not much good will, "go away. Go next door," and, dismissing me, he pointed to the far room. So off I marched in naked dignity, whilst behind me the publican sat writing furiously all over my medical form.

The next room turned out to be occupied by an orderly, by one of my fellow recruits—a huge, amiable and incredibly sun-tanned Life Saver who rejoiced in the nickname of Tarzan—and finally by a most impressive array of bottles. There were milk bottles, ink bottles, oyster bottles, beer bottles—bottles of every description.

Pressing an ink bottle into my hand, the orderly said, "Fill this," and, at the same time, passed Tarzan a milk bottle. I gazed curiously at my bottle—Swan's Blue Black, I noticed.

"What with?" I demanded, at which the orderly looked quite incredulous and Tarzan flung me, over his vast brown shoulder (a brown made all the more striking by the white gleam of his buttocks), a patronizing grin. The orderly explained what with, and simultaneously Tarzan proudly produced his milk bottleful, so that I could even see what with. This was a facet of Army life for which I was wholly unprepared. In fact so far all the facets were facets for which I had been wholly unprepared.

"Can't be done," I said.

"Why not?" demanded the orderly.

"Don't feel like it," I explained.

"Don't give me that, mate," said the orderly, disagreeably. "Now come on: fill it up and I'll test it for sugar."

Although the prospect of being tested for sugar struck me as (so far) the only interesting event of the entire day, I had, reluctantly, to refuse. I had to confess, sadly, that at that moment I was as dry as the Sahara: utterly arid, in fact. There was not the smallest possibility of Messrs. Swan's ink bottle being even dampened. At this, the orderly looked most ill done by. Tarzan, however, intervened on my behalf.

"The kid's nervous," he said. "Turn on the tap. A running tap'll fix him up."

The orderly, though obviously aggrieved, was a good-natured lad and turned on a tap. He, Tarzan, and two newly arrived recruits watched my reactions with absorbed interest. I remained arid. I was *not* nervous, but definitely I was arid.

Warming to his task, the orderly went into the closet in the corner of the room and gave the chain a lusty pull. There were loud rushing water noises, but I remained arid.

Tarzan and the other two recruits turned on all the rest of the taps in the laboratory and at once the room filled with the sound of falling water—but I was unmoved. Three more recruits entered and one of them—a young ex-milkman—suggested whistling. It worked with his spaniel pup, he said. Soon the whole building resounded to watery splashes and sibilant and insinuating whistles, as the entire medical staff and a dozen potential soldiers united in bringing to its successful conclusion Operation Ink Bottle. But finally, when it became obvious that my bottle (the milkman's spaniel notwithstanding)—now the cynosure of twenty pairs of eyes—was doomed to remain empty, everyone admitted failure. Taps were turned off; cisterns slowly refilled and became silent: even Tarzan desisted from a particularly seductive line of whistle.

There was only one thing to do. I dressed and went out and drank three chocolate milk shakes. I then returned and filled my bottle with consummate ease, and was thereupon tested for sugar—which turned out to be not interesting at all, and I still can't remember whether I have it or not, though one of them I know to be an extremely bad thing.

This done, we were hustled down to the main hall in the barracks to take the oath, which is the final act of enlistment. The recruiting sergeant was ponderously jovial as he herded us along.

Like children repeating the alphabet, we mumbled out the phrases of the oath as they were gabbled at us by an individual whose voice glowed with all the warmth and patriotic fervour of a manual of Military Law. And at the second upon which the last word of the oath fell from our lips, the recruiting sergeant, his *bonhomie* shed with all the speed of a heavy coat upon the arrival of a heat wave, started screaming: "All right now, you blokes—git fell in. C'mon, c'mon. Shake a leg or you'll be doing some spud-bashing—you're not civvies any longer, you know." And straight away, to the accompaniment of his hysterical screams of "Left, right, left, right" and of mutinous backchat from ourselves, we ambled off.

"Pick it up there, pick it up," screamed the sergeant. "Left . . . Right . . . Left . . ." But the small squad of recruits only burst into a squall of abuse and, sturdily ignoring all his instructions, straggled along looking remarkably un-military.

"Silly old bastard," Tarzan remarked during a comparative lull.

"What's that you said?" bellowed the sergeant, bringing us to a violent halt.

"I said," stated Tarzan with awful calm, "silly old bastard." And, to remove all doubts, the milkman added: "He meant you!"

Uproar ensued. Everyone enjoyed themselves enormously. Colourful Australian phrases filled the air with lurid insubordination. And into the midst of this chaos exploded an overwhelming and humourless bellow which informed us in incontrovertible tones that we were in the Army now, not a bloody rabble! It blasted us straight on to the end of the vaccination queue. It was our first experience of a sergeant major.

"Stick by me, kid," said Tarzan, "I'll look after you." Three minutes later a woman doctor pricked the huge man's sun-tanned arm with her needle. Uttering a small sigh, Tarzan swayed dizzily on his feet and crashed, all six feet four of him, to the ground in a faint.

"Mug lair," commented the milkman dispassionately as he surveyed the prostrate giant. He held out his arm to the woman doctor. I followed suit. Then—bereft of my protector, who still lay unconscious—I was marched off with the rest of the squad to the sleeping quarters. Marched off to the accompaniment of howls from all sides of "You'll be sorry, rookie, you'll be sorry," and to the recruiting sergeant's frenzied shouts of, "You're in the Army now. Come on there: pick it up. Left, right, left, right." I wasn't at all sure that this bedlam was what I'd bargained for. Certainly it gave no indication of my ever killing Germans.

Our sleeping quarters turned out to be the pigpens of the Royal Agricultural Showground of Sydney. These had been whitewashed with nice clean whitewash and contained all the usual fittings for sleeping and hanging clothes and storing toothbrushes that most concrete pigpens do. Two men moved into each pen, presumably working on the refreshing military principle that two adult males equal one prize pig.

My companion was the ex-milkman. He was about nineteen, was very little more than five feet in height, sported a green shirt, brown slacks, a thin white belt with a silver buckle stamped "1940" on its front and "Made in Japan" on its back, and he had no teeth at all.

"Don't like them drills," he explained, "so I got 'em all whipped out. Bloke at Newtown done it for a quid."

I had a brief and shocking vision of the dental gentleman at Newtown whipping out thirty-two teeth for a quid. Meantime, the victim of this atrocity, apparently quite unmoved, asked me my name. Glad of the change of conversation, I said: "Russ, what's yours?" and he said, Cyril, only his friends called him Mick. "You call me Mick," he added sociably.

There was a bellow at the doorway—our old friend the recruiting sergeant. "Right," he roared, "five volunteers wanted for a job." And while men scattered in every direction or hid behind the walls of their pens he detailed them off, pointing with a stubby nicotine-stained finger, "You . . . you . . . you . . ."

"Meet you in the dyke," Mick hissed, and fled. Heading for the opposite door, and ignoring the frenzied shouts of the sergeant as he called after me, "Hey you . . . that fair-haired bloke!" I too fled, and a few seconds later met Mick in the latrines.

"Nice place you've got here," I told him, as I surveyed the row of thunder-boxes and appreciated the skill with which a long line of military minds had thus contrived to deny the ex-civilian even this his last and most trusted place of privacy.

Mick grunted indifferently. "Glad you tricked old Mud-Guts," he said. "Heard him screaming for you."

I asked had he himself had any difficulty in escaping the sergeant. Mick gave his white belt a contemptuous tug.

"The day that mug cops me," he declared, "I'll take a running jump at meself," and having thus confidently disposed of the sergeant, he added: "Where to now? Can't stop here all day." And, having not the least inclination to dispute this statement, I suggested a swim. Mick agreed readily.

"See you back at the sty," he said. Without more ado we proceeded, independently, back to our pen. There I took my trunks out of the small suitcase I'd brought with me.

"Aw, Jesus," said Mick, "I haven't got any togs." "Hire some down there," I suggested. Mick shook his head. "Can't," he explained, "got no dough."

"That's all right," I told him. "I've got twelve bob. That should see us through. Come on, let's go." For a second Mick looked quite embarrassed at this offer, and then grinned a completely toothless grin.

"You got a mate with you?" he queried. I said I hadn't.

"What say we stick together then?" he suggested. I said I thought it was a good idea.

"Right," concluded Mick, "let's go for a swim."

We waited only long enough to discuss what we should do with our toilet gear and spare clothes, finally deciding to leave them all together in my bag in the pen, and headed out of the barracks.

"Leave pass?" demanded the guard at the gate.

"Don't be bloody ridiculous," Mick told him, his expression outraged at this liberty, and off we sailed to Bondi.

After the last of the day's sun, we returned penniless and happy to the barracks. There the earlier problem of where we should stow our gear we found had been settled forever. Someone had stolen the lot—suitcase and all. Also the possibility of our sticking together was abruptly disposed of by the sergeant, who slouched over and asked: "You Braddon?" and, when I nodded, said, "Well, report to the office: you've been requisitioned by the artillery."

"What about Mick?" I demanded.

"Never 'eard of him," replied the sergeant. "Who's Mick?"

I pointed at the ex-milkman—said, "This bloke."

"Miserable little runt, aren't you?" observed the sergeant, looking him up and down.

"Least I can see me boots over me guts," replied Mick with spirit.

"Now cut that out, mate," rebuked our warrior of the orderly room, "you just git down to the cookhouse double smart or you'll find yourself on a charge. And you, Braddon, you report to the office." He thrust his stomach out an extra foot to emphasize both his point and his authority.

For a moment Mick glared mutinously. Then he shrugged. "Better do what the bastard says," he concluded. He held out his hand and said, "Good-bye, mate, don't do anything I wouldn't do," and, having shaken hands, off he went. With a final defiant tug at the white belt, the short, small-waisted figure with its brown pants and green shirt vanished out of the doorway. It was the last time I ever saw him.

Feeling quite forlorn, I made my way to the office to investigate this "requisition." Maybe now, I thought, I'll do something about the Germans.

3 FIVE-BOB-A-DAY BUTCHERS

At the office I found four other men who had also—one gathered from their comments—been requisitioned to the artillery. Three of them were as young as myself, the fourth was a man of about fifty who had, he said, given his age as thirty-five. He had been a sergeant in the 1914–18 war; he seriously considered that nothing had really happened since the Battle of Passchendaele; and he couldn't get into this war quickly enough. These veterans of 1914 who were rejoining in 1940 were known as Ratty Diggers—"ratty" because it was thought by Australia's disrespectful youth that, having survived one war, they should have had enough sense to avoid another.

"Your name Braddon?" the Ratty Digger asked me, and when I admitted that it was, he announced, "Braddon's here now, sir," and a major at a desk looked profoundly bored at this piece of information, whilst the ex-sergeant stood rigidly at attention like a dog pointing.

"Shall I take charge, sir?" asked the Ratty Digger eagerly. With weary indifference the major nodded. Thereupon we were issued with ten pounds of butter and eating-irons and bundled into a truck which, with frenzied speed, was driven out to one of Sydney's racecourses. This, we were informed, it was our duty, as artillerymen, to guard.

For five days we lived in a tent on the racecourse, which was high with rank grass and covered with mushrooms. Then, at the end of the fifth day, when we had received no stores, no arms and no order of any kind from the Army: when the Ratty Digger, relying upon his status as a 1918 vintage sergeant, had assumed all the airs and graces of a full-blown colonel and become quite intolerable: when all the mushrooms on the racecourse had been fried in our ten pounds of butter and consumed: and, finally, when no enemy had made even the smallest attempt to seize the racecourse, which we had been determined to defend to the death, if necessary, with our knives and forks—then we grew very mutinous and rang up the major at Victoria Barracks.

He seemed most surprised to hear my voice and asked where we were. I told him the racecourse. Still more surprised, he said what were we doing there: so I told him guarding it. He asked what with, so I told him, "Knives and forks and a Ratty Digger," and he said, "Now, now, soldier, enough of that. I'll send a truck for you," and rang off without even saying good-bye.

Quite soon the truck arrived and we returned to Victoria Barracks. There we were equipped with uniforms that didn't fit and boots that didn't bend and two pairs each of the most obscene-looking long woollen underpants. So ended my first military operation against the Germans.

As soon as the ungracious business of the kit issue had been concluded, we were ordered to proceed to Central Station, report to the R.T.O. and catch a train to Liverpool. None of us had the smallest idea what this R.T.O. was except the Ratty Digger. He wasn't going to tell us unless we asked him, and we had no intention of gratifying him by asking. Swinging packs onto shoulders, we prepared to depart.

Then at the last moment—to our unqualified joy—the Ratty Digger was withdrawn from the party. The remaining four of us made our way alone and with great nonchalance to Central. There, adopting a tone of complete familiarity, I demanded the R.T.O. It was only with difficulty that I concealed my surprise when the R.T.O. turned out to be merely a nondescript little man with some pips on his shoulders who gave you railway tickets if you had enough forms signed by sufficient people.

Armed with the little man's tickets, we boarded the electric train to Liverpool and arrived there forty-five minutes later. We found the town swarming with both militiamen and Free French troops—and with ladies anxious to pick up either—but no one at all concerned with us. We were, by that time, however, developing considerable initiative in these matters. We knew that we had to get to the camp of the 2/15th Field Regiment at Holdsworthy. We therefore walked the town till we found one of the regiment's trucks and then clambered aboard. We sat in it for an hour till its crew returned, then we drove out with them to Holdsworthy, having refused to be evicted by them.

In a surprisingly short time, although no one in the regiment had expected us or been warned of our arrival, we were given a meal (in which good Australian beef had miraculously been transformed into the most noisome stew), a cup of hot cocoa, a palliasse on which to lie, and a tent in which to sleep. For the first time I felt that I was really in the Army and wondered what the subsequent days of training would bring.

Very quickly I found out. They brought weeks of rookie training from an N.C.O. whose knowledge of textbook soldiering was as intimate as his language was bawdy. There were endless lectures on the art of stripping down both rifles and machine guns. The same N.C.O. could strip and remount a Lewis machine gun blindfold and with heavy gloves on. He could also play the piano blindfold and with heavy gloves on. He would do either at the drop of a hat and of the two operations he was proudest of the latter, though the former was infinitely the more artistic.

The weeks drew on. At the behest each dawn of a redheaded sergeant major whom I detested, I peeled about one million pounds of potatoes and disposed of about one million gallons of urine which was collected in latrine pans outside each hut each night and was especially prolific on beer nights.

I got lumps under my arms from my vaccination and lumps in the groin from my inoculations. I learnt that a Short Arm Parade had nothing to do with small arms, side arms or shouldering arms and that, at its best, it could only be described as Presenting Arms. I learnt how to hook up all the pieces of webbing with which we had been issued till they formed the one uncomfortable harness, and I learnt how to crawl out the back fence of the camp so that I could go absent without leave till my pay expired under the strain.

I heard sufficient foul language in five days to deter me from ever using anything but the King's English for the next five years (though not enough to blind me to the fact that on occasions the Australian uses his "bloodies" and "bastards" with a rhythmic grace of which I—in my more orthodox style—could never be capable). I absorbed the principles and practice of field gunnery almost with pleasure, although I never ceased to be irritated by the instructor's maxim (which he repeated with infantile pleasure) that "A gunner doesn't walk: he doesn't run—he FLIES." And I never learnt to salute officers whom I regarded as dopes with the smallest degree of conviction. Moreover one day I was paid. The possibility of being paid in the Army had frankly never occurred to me. Five shillings a day it was.[1] I was most surprised.

Finally I learnt to keep quite level an eyebrow which had a deplorable tendency to rise most noticeably whenever I observed any of the innumerable follies of Army administration and which had already, after only two months' service, earned me three charges for "dumb insolence."

The last of these occasions had been when a gun crew, of which I was a member, practised gun drill round a non-existent gun. We

[1]This amount earned us the title of "Five-bob-a-day butchers" from a pacifist Labour member who had never seen military service of any kind (and consequently was made a high-ranking member of the wartime Labour Cabinet).

wound imaginary elevating gear: levelled imaginary clinometres: hunched imaginary shells into imaginary breeches—taking care (by clenching one's fist) that one's fingers were not amputated by the slamming of imaginary breech blocks. All this we had done with the most admirable composure, although I had never been good at this playing at soldiers.

Then we were ordered by the "gun's" officer to drag our imaginary gun with imaginary dragropes. Still our composure was beyond reproof. Next we were ordered to coil our imaginary dragropes, hang them on the front of the imaginary gun shield, hook up our non-existent gun and ammunition limber to our non-existent tractor and leap aboard—with drilled precision—onto the non-existent tractor's non-existent seats.

All this we did with the external composure and ardour of lunatics playing their demented games. Six men in the middle of an empty parade ground stood resting their bottoms on nothing as if convinced that they were seated in a 30-hundredweight truck, to which was attached a Mark IV eighteen-pounder and its limber—not a trace of derision on any one face.

Then it happened. The officer, obsessed with the excitement of this exhilarating manoeuvre, screamed at us: "Sit at attention there. When you mount your tractor you sit at attention!"—and up shot my eyebrow. In that non-existent truck with its six petrified passengers, the only thing that moved was my eyebrow—and immediately I was on a charge. Same old thing. Dumb insolence. I resolved thenceforward to keep the offending feature horizontal.

And having thus acquired both a knowledge of gun drill and a sense of discipline, I was transferred into Battery Headquarters to learn the more precise art of ranging the guns onto their targets.

I moved into a galvanized iron hut which, in those winter months, was so freezing at night that its occupants fairly refrigerated. Requests for extra blankets were met with the restatement of a summertime regulation, which limited blanket issues to three. Our quartermaster sergeant devoted his entire life to the cause of issuing nothing if possible and as little as he decently could if it were not. Consequently, we got no extra bedding from him and everyone retired to sleep at nights dressed in every single article of his clothing issue, not excluding the two pairs of obscene-looking long woollen underpants.

I soon came to like most of the men in the hut. They were an assorted bunch, certainly, but likable. Four of them had enlisted together (with yet a fifth, who, being a sergeant, dwelt elsewhere) from an accountants' firm—Piddington, Magee, Shackle, Robinson. Of them only Piddington was to survive. Magee and Robinson died in Thailand on the Japanese railway, Shackle died on the Sandakan March in Borneo. Then there were the two Icetons—Johnny and Bluey, who was called Bluey, in the Australian fashion, because he had red hair. They had not known each other before their Army days and had met in the regiment quite by chance. They became inseparable friends. Johnny was to be killed at Parit Sulong: Bluey lost an arm in an action the day before.

Wimpey, who slept opposite me, was small and quiet and never washed. Ponchard, his mate, was seldom in camp, being more or less permanently A.W.O.L. This tendency he was unable to curb even in Thailand when in 1943 I saw him wandering in the jungle, apparently mad and miles from his own camp.

Ronnie Welsh, stocky, dark-haired, played a delightful game of football and in battle proved that he had no fear and had never known it. He was a bombardier and a man whom I respected wholeheartedly. His fellow bombardier, Rosenberg (a solicitor of nearly forty), was a pleasant soul with a passion for slide-rule computations—which took him hours—and for shaving with a cut-throat razor and no mirror—which he did in a matter of seconds. He, too, died in Thailand.

Hugh Moore, who had been at the university with me, was to share in many of the unpleasant events which subsequently befell me. Clift, though a gunnery officer of the 1914 war and the only man in the regiment who combined a fluent knowledge of the Malayan language with a high speed on the morse key, was to languish as a gunner (his talents quite wasted) for the duration.

These were the men whose company I was to share for the next few months. They were friendly and generous to an incredible degree.

There were, of course, others whose names now escape me—others, like the two friends who, whenever the price of rabbit skins became high, gave up soldiering for weeks on end while they trapped rabbits instead. Rabbit trapping had been their civilian occupation. Theirs was an economic delinquency, not one of discipline—they could *not* resist high prices for rabbit skins! The C.O. treated them with understanding, knowing that as soon as prices dropped they would be back, amiable and conscientious as ever.

Finally, there were the drivers—always grumbling: always in trouble: and always ready to lend a hand (after a reasonable period of protesting) in any difficulty.

Thus, for months we trained. The regiment had been formed for fifteen months and had become extremely efficient. It wanted now to put its efficiency to some purpose overseas. For months more nothing happened.

But in July the regiment was given its final embarkation leave and everyone went home to say good-bye before departing overseas for the serious business of war.

4 "NOW IS THE HOUR"

My own farewells turned out to be completely unsatisfactory. Having determined to have no fuss, and my family having determined likewise, no one mentioned the subject of my impending departure until the actual second when I left. Then, with everything unsaid, I found myself kissing my mother good-bye in the garage, both of us incapable of speech, whilst the dog rushed round and round, barking hysterically and asking for its ball to be thrown.

I got into the family car—a cantankerous little brute known as the Bug, whose reliability had been in no way increased by the occasion when my stepfather had involved it in an argument with a petrol wagon—and drove off. As I ran down the hill, I saw my mother staring after me, dry-eyed and smiling hard—no doubt pondering deeply on this absurd culmination to twenty years of parental devotion. For my part, I was neither dry-eyed nor smiling and had, at the bottom of the hill, to halt the Bug for five minutes lest I added a tram to my stepfather's toll of petrol wagons. Then I drove to my stepfather's office and he drove me on to Brisbane interstate station, where the leave train waited. Tactfully he talked in quiet tones all the way and never once looked at me.

When we parted on the station, he said, "Your young sister's waiting to wave as you go past her school. Don't miss her." I nodded. "And don't worry about your mother," he added, "I'll look after her." I could have kissed him. Instead I nodded mutely again, shook his hand and clambered into the train.

Every compartment was full except one, in which sat five sailors. Taking the last seat near the corridor, I joined the Navy. Almost at once the train started and I began peering across two sailors and out the far windows, looking for my sister's school.

The sailor at the outside window looked at me curiously for a few seconds.

"Expecting to see someone, Dig?" he asked. I told him: "Yes, my young sister."

"Better sit here," he suggested, and as I moved over he jogged his neighbour—already fast asleep in the best nautical manner—and said, "Move up, Nobby," so Nobby moved into my seat, where he at once fell asleep again, and the sailor moved into Nobby's seat and watched me with unconcealed interest. I stared out at the embankments flashing by.

Far sooner than I had expected, the school came into sight. There was Pat, waving furiously, and along with her most of the school—also waving. Then they were gone as the train, with a speed most unwarranted for the Queensland Railways, thundered on. I gulped heavily. The sailor looked at me sympathetically and broke an awkward silence by commenting, "Pretty good roll up that. Thousands of Sheilas waving you good-bye. What you got that I haven't got?"

Feeling rather less desolate, I hastened to reassure him. "Nothing, Jack," I told him, "they couldn't have known the fleet was in!"

The rest of the twenty-four-hour trip to Sydney was spent in that state of acute discomfort which the authorities deliberately contrive for all troop trains, so that their passengers will be delighted finally to get back to their camps. For the whole time, the Navy proved themselves excellent company and—with the conspicuous exception of Nobby, who slept an unbroken sleep in the luggage rack—completely belied their reputation as "The Silent Service." We parted at Central Station, Sydney, and I returned to camp.

For the first time after any leave it was found that *no one* was

A.W.O.L. Only final leave could have achieved that miracle with the A.I.F.

A week later, a week of intense security during which no one was allowed to leave the camp—the Army's method of preventing spies from getting any information—we *"embussed."* This hideous word was the invention of some military genius and meant simply that we got aboard trucks—a procedure for which we had rehearsed most assiduously during the entire previous seven days, it being deemed by officialdom a difficult one.

Having *"embussed,"* we travelled the few miles to Liverpool railway station. There we *"debussed"* and *"entrained."* The train then chugged erratically down to Darling Harbour, where we *"detrained"* and *"embarked."* Except for the technical terms involved and the amount of baggage to be carried at each change, the entire operation proceeded with a smoothness which, for the Army, was quite startling. Everyone got aboard and no spies had observed us embussing, or debussing, entraining or detraining, nor even embarking. Everything had been done with a maximum of secrecy.

Thus it was that, still shrouded in security, we stole furtively down Sydney Harbour towards the Heads—accompanied by no fewer than a hundred small craft bearing friends and relatives and large placards with "Good luck, Bill Smith, of the 2/15th" or "Whacko Bluey of the 2/29th" or "Bon Voyage 8th Div. A.I.F."—the navigators and passengers of these small craft having presumably obtained their extremely accurate information by crystal gazing. We knew, of course, that all the spies in Australia were both unobservant and unintelligent, so, without any anxiety, we waved wildly to our friends below in their yachts, launches, rowing boats and canoes, and steamed slowly out to sea.

As the last of the accompanying launches began to fall away, the whole ship broke out into "The Maoris' Farewell"—traditional song of Australians departing their country. Several thousand voices caught up the melody: voices in the small craft joined them: voices from the foreshores joined in again. With the sun behind us, behind our celebrated Harbour Bridge, we passed out of Sydney Harbour—it was a moving scene. The 8th Division were off to the wars.

5 "BAD DAMES"

The voyage from Sydney, on the east coast of Australia, to Fremantle, on the west, was uneventful except for the unfriendly state of the sea in the Great Australian Bight. Black, arctic waters raged at us and no one was very happy. Some, in fact, like Bombardier Rosenberg of the slide-rule computations and the mirrorless shaving, laid themselves down to die. Indeed, Rosie's case was the cause of acute amusement to all except Rosie, because with typical caution and forethought he had equipped himself with anti-seasickness pills sufficient for months of travelling. Observing some small waves just out of Sydney's Heads, however, his nerve had failed him and he had devoured the lot before we had even turned the bottom of Australia. Devoid of both pills and nourishment, utterly without hope, he abandoned himself to the sea and his Maker and longed for death.

Instead of death, however, came Fremantle—sunny and vastly hospitable. At once everyone, even Rosie, revived and went ashore for a last night out on Australian soil. The cause of "security" was greatly enhanced by a flood of telephone calls, telegrams and letters from western Australia across to the Eastern States, telling everyone who cared to listen that the Eighth Division was on its way to the Middle East, to Darwin, to Malaya, to Cape Town, even to England. One could only feel acute sympathy for the spies who listened—everyone was making categorical statements about our destination, statements which grew steadily more vehement as the intake of Swan beer increased, and no two statements ever seemed to agree.

The wiser ones, however, pointed out, with considerable logic, that in the holds of our ships were vehicles; and that those vehicles were all painted bright yellow; and that bright yellow was a natural camouflage in desert. By morning, when the entire division had transshipped into three Dutch vessels, this view had prevailed over all others and everyone wrote off urgent letters cancelling all previous orders to those at home and assuring them that we were destined for the Middle East. One hopes profoundly that the spies steamed open and read all these letters because, of course, we at once departed from Australia—complete with our bright yellow trucks—and headed for the dark green jungles of Malaya.

The Dutch vessels were not nice. I cannot remember which deck it was on our particular ship to which we were consigned, but, working on the principle that decks are lettered alphabetically and that the one *farthest* from the keel is A, I should say that we were on about Z+3.

Certainly we crawled down multitudinous steps into the bowels of this abominable boat until eventually there were no more steps to descend, and on our left we observed the galleys, whilst, on our right, low-roofed and reeking with the fumes of cooking and diesel oil, we observed our quarters. These contained rows of wooden benches at which one ate: two feet above them rows of hammocks in which one slept: adjoining them a large Dutch lavatory, and a small Dutch bathroom, outside which one queued interminably.

Confronted with these appalling facilties for bathing, only Wimpey, who never washed at all, remained unmoved. Not even the unconscious humour of the Dutch notice on the bathroom—a notice which, in letters of gold, announced that the bathroom was for "Bad Dames"—not even this could disguise the fact that it was a very small and inadequate bathroom. When, on inspection, it was discovered to be not only small and inadequate, but also totally devoid of the advertised bad dames, comment became very unfavourable indeed. Worse, however, was to come. The lavatories were equipped with a quaint continental device called a *sanitaire douche*. This was a jet of water which dealt the unwary occupant a fiendish blast in the bottom when he succumbed (as we all succumbed) to the temptation of pressing a button which seemed to protrude from the marble wall for no apparent reason. This provided us in the first hour of our voyage with much ribald amusement. But when, after an hour, it was discovered that Dutch plumbing did *not* cater for toilet paper but *only* for the *sanitaire douche*, and when, as a result, the entire system had choked and our Z+3 deck had become some ten inches deep in the overflow—then even Wimpey became vociferous.

That night no one on Z+3 had the smallest intention of attempting sleep in an atmosphere redolent with the ship's cooking, the ship's engines and the ship's sewage. In spite of fierce orders that every man must stay below, all of us made our way stolidly up the multitudinous steps for the starlit freshness of an open deck at sea.

Admittedly, this deck was prominently labelled "Out of Bounds: For Officers Only," but that matter was simply solved by removing the offending sign and casting it—with a phosphorescent plop—into the Indian Ocean. Thereupon, hundreds of men proceeded quietly and contently to bed themselves down.

Not for long, however, was there quiet. The orderly officer, outraged by this violation of the sanctity of the vacant deck which was for officers only, came storming round demanding that we should return at once ("forthwith" was the word he used) to Z+3.

From all sides rose a bedlam of abuse. "Go away, you silly bastard. . . ." "Get back to your mess, you great galah. . . ." "Drongo . . ." "Stop your noise, I'm trying to get to sleep." With great spirit and complete unanimity three or four hundred men spoke their minds and this was something which the officer was not prepared to tolerate. Switching on his torch, he aimed it in the direction of the most outspoken group and said to his sergeant: "Take their names." But there were to be no names taken that night. The ship was under full blackout orders. Not even the silliest private on that deck would have lit so much as a cigarette. It had remained for the orderly officer to turn on a powerful torch.

A lean figure pounced on the offending light. Amid a roar of "Douse that bloody torch," it was hurled away, and a faint splash indicated that it had joined the "Out of Bounds" notice. Then the lean figure spoke to the orderly officer most earnestly: "Get out, you mug," he said, "or you'll go over after your torch." Three seconds later the deck was inhabited by Other Ranks only, so, without further comment, we settled ourselves down to sleep.

But even as we did there came a second interruption. A clatter of boots on the stairs intruded upon the peaceful quiet. Steadily it plodded up towards the deck. Up and up, hundreds of stairs. And then, at last, a head appeared rising slowly and deliberately out of the stair well. Rosie! After hours of calculations—doubtless on his slide rule—Rosie had decided that Z+3 was a social, physical and mathematical impossibility. He was now going to join us on "Officers

Only." On the second stair from the top he halted, surveying the cool darkness outside with evident satisfaction. It was exactly as he had planned. Things were always as Rosie planned. Then came the unplanned . . . as he moved to step forward his hobnailed boot slipped on the brassed edge of the top stair and abruptly, delightfully, he plunged precipitously backwards and out of sight.

To the accompaniment of maniacal peals of laughter from all sides, he crashed down the stairs—his progress marked by the wild clatter of eating-irons, slide rules, seasick pills, razors and water bottles (for Rosie went nowhere unprepared and was constantly aware of the possibility of our ship being sunk). Then suddenly, as we laughed, we became aware of the fact that below the clatter had ceased and there was only silence. Instantly all laughter stopped. Someone said, "Christ, he's killed himself," and then silence—silence of the kind that is usually termed "pregnant"—fell again.

And from this silence, deep down from the reeking entrails of that horrible vessel, rose the cultured tones of the ex-solicitor who was now a bombardier. Rosie expressed the sentiments of us all. With awful clarity and a legal precision, he intoned his verdict. "You bloody bastard," he said, "you bloody bastard of a bloody Dutch bloody ship." Rosie was a man not much given either to bad language or to violent emotion: yet seldom was I to hear the great Australian adjective and the great Australian noun combined with such lyrical and irresistible effect.

And so we steamed steadily northwards: the weather grew steadily warmer: the food steadily fouler· our sleeping up on deck more and more of a *fait accompli*. But the daytime was the time during which the Army enjoyed itself most.

It organized us into long sessions of physical training to which no one objected particularly—there always being a sneaking suspicion at the back of one's mind that, somehow, sometime, P.T. might do one some good—but the periods of drill on three-inch mortars that followed the P.T. were regarded by artillerymen (trained for fifteen months on eighteen-pounders) with a vague distrust: whilst the long lectures (delivered to us by the redheaded sergeant major, who at Holdsworthy had specialized in detailing latrine duties) on the horrors of tropical diseases were openly disliked.

The redheaded sergeant major had once been in Darwin and consequently regarded himself as an ultimate authority on all tropical complaints from malaria to schistosomiasis. Tinea, however, was his forte. On tinea he could—and did—wax lyrical for hours on end. Tinea, he told us, crept! All over you. Awful it was. And consequently we were all paraded one day to have our feet examined for tinea. The smallest crack in the skin between one's toes was regarded with manifest horror and one was at once consigned to the lepers' queue for treatment—before it crept.

The queue was cunningly held in a narrow alley in the hottest part of the ship so that—having waited one's turn for several hours—one would then know better than to have cracks between one's toes in the next war. When at last one did reach the head of the queue, one's toe (the offending digit) was painted liberally with a bright green paint which stung considerably but had not the least effect on the crack. This continued for four days until everyone lost interest in tinea, including the redheaded sergeant major.

Mortar drill, however, continued with unabated fury and the fact that we were leaving home waters was brought home even more forcibly to us when one day, in the midst of this drill, a shout went up from the submarine lookout of "flying fish." Having never seen a flying fish, and being naively excited at the prospect, I at once abandoned the mortars and rushed to the side of the ship. Awful disillusionment! These flying fish, which I had always understood to be exotic kaleidoscopic monsters some six feet long, which winged their way vigorously through portholes so that they landed, colourful and flapping, on one's bunk—these flying fish turned out to be colourless, graceless and quite unexciting. About nine or ten inches long with transparent wings, they skimmed, like a cross between a grasshopper and a herring, with pedestrian stolidity from wave to wave. Quite sad, I returned from the ship's rail to the exhilarating occupation of pretending to drop mortar bombs down the spout of a mortar and hurriedly slamming back over its muzzle a leather cover to prevent the inside of this dreary piece of ironmongery being exposed to the sea air and consequently going rusty.

And thus the days of P.T., medical parades, kit inspections and mortar drill followed one another—days which, in spite of the Army's attempts to keep us occupied, managed nevertheless to be exciting because ahead lay uncertainty.

5 "BAD DAMES"

As we steamed closer to the equator, the conversation reverted more and more frequently to the possibility of Japan's entering the war (because, as soldiers in Malaya, our only opportunity of seeing active service would be against a Japanese invader).

Rosie dealt our hopes a rather devastating blow. With all the dogmatism of the confirmed bachelor in his late thirties (not to mention the stubborn Jew and the successful lawyer), Rosie declared: "Of course, Japan won't come into the war. Why should she when she can stay out and make a profit from both sides like the Turks and the Spaniards?"

And Rosie was an intelligent and well-informed man, too, one had to recognize that. And even if the Japanese were reckless enough to disregard Rosie's opinion, a war with Nippon gave no indication of being very exciting, if one listened to what the intelligence officer said in his lectures. Apparently the Japanese were very small and very myopic and thus totally unsuited either physically or optically to tropical warfare. Nor was this all. They had aeroplanes made from old kettles and kitchen utensils, guns salvaged from the war against Russia in 1905 and rifles of the kind used by civilized peoples only in films about the Red Indians. Also, they were frightened of the dark.

Regretfully we resigned ourselves to a war without battles where our sole function was to guard the Empire's greatest source of tin and rubber. Meantime the floating septic tank which was both the pride of the Dutch merchant marine and our transport made its way steadily towards Singapore through the incredible beauties of the Sunda Strait—soon to be the graveyard of the gallant handful of Dutch, American and Australian vessels of war who flung themselves at the throat of a Japanese fleet.

Singapore, I was surprised to find, when I looked at a map, was a small diamond-shaped island at the bottom of a leg called Malaya. Sprawling sideways beneath it were Sumatra, Java, Timor and New Guinea—the four joined in a long chain by innumerable smaller islands. And New Guinea, at the eastern end of the chain, sat square on the northernmost tip of Australia.

Even to my completely non-military mind, it seemed most advisable that Malaya (at the Asiatic end of this chain which contained most of the world's rubber and tin, and much of its tea, quinine and oil; and which led directly to Australia) should be securely held.

One felt relieved to hear that the key point of Malaya was that small diamond-shaped island which was universally known as the impregnable fortress of Singapore.

6 "HOW TO LIVE IN MALAYA"

Into this impregnable fortress we steamed early one morning. It was August 15. Four years later—to the very day—the war in the Pacific was to end. Very few of the two infantry battalions and the regiment of artillery who waited on the steaming decks that August 15 were to see this fourth anniversary of their arrival in Singapore. Two thirds of them were to die in a last-ditch battle on the west coast of Malaya: of the remainder, many were to fall under the scythe of cholera on the Thailand railway.

But, for the moment, all this lay in the future, and so we stood, young and full of hope and unaware, on the decks of our three transports. "Stood" is a magnificently inadequate word for an Army operation which had commenced in the early hours of the morning (when, carrying all our equipment and wearing rolled greatcoats round our necks in a horse collar of incandescence, we were fallen-in in a tight-packed, sweating parade), and, at noon, still continued. By then it had become a sweating, tight-packed, bad-tempered parade. A few of the more cunning ones had flopped to the deck in a feigned faint and were carried to the spaciousness below: the rest of us stood up there, sullen, but far from silent.

Then, at noon, the order to disembark was given and we filed off the ship in a long khaki column. Filed down towards wharves seething with native labourers who managed, with a maximum of shouting and gesticulation, to do a minimum of work—which, in that heat (to us almost overwhelming), we couldn't help but think most sensible.

Once ashore, and away from such fearful non-military contraptions as steamships, normal routine reasserted itself and, with great speed, we clambered aboard waiting lorries. About such nautical matters as coming down a gangway, the Army becomes deeply perplexed: but, given a lorry, it knows exactly what to do. And so we boarded our trucks and sped off through the city of Singapore.

Driving through Singapore for the first time was an experience. There were the vivid colours of tropical flowers in parks: the incredible stenches of fish drying on the pavements—each fragrant morsel the target of a million flies: the bamboo poles slung out from each side of the street, on which was suspended much native washing rather indifferently laundered: and in the streets, everywhere, contemptuous of death and traffic laws alike, a bedlam of fowls, rickshaws and natives, through which all vehicles careered as fast as possible.

Turning right, we sped into a less chaotic thoroughfare and were touched (though surprised, since our journey had been so secret) to observe, slung from one side of it to the other, a huge banner bearing the words, "Welcome to the A.I.F." Our driver, a youthful English private, grinned.

"What's the joke?" we asked. He pointed down the road over which the banner hung.

"That's Lavender Street," he told us. Not finding this enigmatic remark either particularly humorous or informative, we dropped the subject. It was a week before we discovered that Lavender Street is one of the world's most notorious streets of brothels. Obviously, our security had been as superb as the reputation which went before us was high!

We were deposited a few miles out of Singapore City near some very substantial-looking English barracks. Immediately God indicated His extreme displeasure at our arrival in Neesoon by deluging us in a fierce downpour of lukewarm rain. Carrying our mountainous kit bags and still wearing our horse collars of rolled greatcoats, we staggered through mud and rain to our new camp. It stood on the side of a hill in a rubber plantation. Rows of tents. And through the tents cascaded a torrent of brown water draining off the slope.

Drenched and enervated, we made our way to the tents—four men to each one—deposited our gear inside and, stripping off, at once commenced digging drains round our new home. Immediately the rain stopped: the sun blazed: the earth steamed and the orderly officer arrived.

This gentleman had been thoroughly coached in the art of avoiding malaria and, in accordance with his vast knowledge on the subject, at once ordered us all to redon our shirts, roll down our sleeves and tuck our pants into our socks. Thus, he said, the malarial mosquito would find no flesh exposed into which to sink his infested fangs. Apparently the malarial mosquito and the military authorities had arrived at an agreement whereby—for the purpose of biting—the neck, face and wrists were, to all anopheles, strictly out of bounds. For the next ninety minutes we dug in vicious tropical sunshine, clad as no one else in the whole of Malaya was clad at that hour.

By nightfall we were delighted to crawl on to the native-style beds (wooden frames with a webbing of fibre cords to support one—the whole thing revelling in the name "charpoy"), with which we had been issued. Under our nets we listened to the peevish buzz of mosquitoes and the curious insect noises of the rubber plantation. A moon came out so brilliantly that under it the guy ropes cast clear-cut shadows and one could easily read one's Malayan-English dictionary. And so, having observed idly that "*come*" was "mari" and that "*go*" was "pigi," I fell asleep—our first night's sleep with the "A.I.F. Abroad."

Next morning we were swiftly initiated into a new way of life. We were told that, heat being a constant factor in the tropics, greatcoats were no longer necessary (a fact of which we had ourselves been acutely conscious for at least twenty-four hours) and accordingly these were exchanged for a completely useless garment called a "slicker." This was a crescent-shaped waterproof which, when draped as it was intended to be draped, contrived to make the wearer sweat like a pig, whilst, at the same time, letting in all the rain.

Next we were told that the soil of Malaya was infested with hookworm; that this hookworm was ubiquitous; that it entered the body through the soles of the feet and worked its way remorselessly round one's blood stream into one's bowels and that there it became the cause of a "slow lingering death." This slow lingering death instantly befell anyone who so much as set a bare little toe onto the earth and was quite incurable. Prevention was the only cure, we were assured: and, the better to prevent this ghastly fate, we were thereupon all issued with wooden clogs on which to clip-clop down to showers and back. And if anyone asks, "Why not wear shoes or sand shoes down to the showers and back?" the answer is quite simple. Those who wore shoes all the time got tinea. And tinea—as we had learned from the redheaded B.S.M.—crept! And when tinea crept one was almost as badly off as when one had contracted the slow, lingering death. So the entire regiment hobbled round most inexpertly on clogs for weeks on end and every man fell off them and onto the hookworms so often that at the end of that time it was very surprising to learn that, so far, no one at all had died.

Next we were issued with sheets—unprecedented luxury for Other Ranks. Indeed, the officer who arrived to conduct this issue was heard to remark loudly to the quartermaster sergeant in pained surprise: "What! Sheets for the gunners?"—and was consequently never called anything else but "What, sheets for the gunners" for the rest of his military career. Nevertheless, in spite of the officer's astonishment, sheets we got—and nothing brought home to us more forcibly than this the fact that now we were in an entirely different theatre of war.

Perhaps "nothing" is too strong. The M.O.'s parade, where he informed us that 96 per cent of Malayan women had V.D., was not without its impact. When he amended his statement two days later to 99.9 per cent, we were even more impressed.

In spite of this unendearing fact, however, we were instructed at all times to act towards the locals in a dignified and friendly fashion, so as to win the respect of the Malays. We were, moreover, to take care not to offend against any Malayan ethics or codes of behaviour —as a demonstration of which we were at once ordered to parade in the open rubber, naked, for a mass examination for V.D.! Ten yards away from this parade (which was not in the least dignified and which flatly contravened the Asiatics' modest aversion even to bathing in the nude) worked a large party of Tamils, men and women. As the first few men, protesting violently, went through the elegant ritual of the Short Arm Parade, the hundreds behind them reacted swiftly to the Tamil women's giggles and menfolk's outraged stares. They jacked up! That was the last Short Arm Parade to be held in public in Malaya. One had to learn these points of behaviour. We quickly realized that at the moment no one knew anything, and that the best thing we could do was to learn as we went along.

Meantime, our cooks revelled in this golden opportunity to be really cussed and prepared us hot meat and vegetable stew for seventeen consecutive meals—by which time no one any longer troubled even to collect the stuff. Accordingly, orders were issued requiring every man to attend meal parades. Nothing, however, was done about the food, the officers of our regiment being just as afraid of the venomous old men who were our cooks as we were—so, with typical British compromise, we attended the parades, drew no food, and proceeded straight from the mess hut to the NAAFI canteen, where we bought fried eggs from the native staff.

Our growing pains were not yet finished. Clothing still remained a pain in the neck to soldiers and authorities alike. But finally, when the authorities produced a strait-jacket-like coat, which buttoned tightly up to the neck, and Bombay bloomers (a hideous garment, neither short nor long, which touched the body nowhere and deprived the male body of all grace and dignity), the men took matters into their own hands and ordered tailored slacks, open-neck shirts and shorts from the local natives. These were delivered almost on the same day and the A.I.F. at once became as immaculate and impeccably dressed a body of men as ever stepped out on leave.

Leave itself was the cause of some trouble in those days. The Argylls had held undisputed sway in Singapore for many years and delivered an uncompromising note to all Australians, advising them not to encroach on Scottish territory—in other words: "Keep out of Singapore, or else . . . !" That, of course, was all that was required. On the first available leave day every free Australian on the island went into the city. There they were met by every free Argyll, and great and bloody were the battles—until the provosts arrived, whereupon both sides, furious at this gratuitous display of officious intervention, ceased battle and fell upon the common foe. Thus round the Great World and the Happy World and the main streets of Singapore did the volunteers from the Dominions first join hands with the professional soldiers from the Homeland.

Establishing friendly relationships with the garrison troops from Britain was not difficult—beer, fights, football matches and the Union Jack Club soon settled that. But establishing friendly relationships with the trading civilians and planters from Britain—that turned out to be impossible.

After three weeks in Malaya we had none of us, we ordinary

soldiers, spoken to a white woman (except the volunteers at the Anzac Club, who only had time to ask, "One lump or two?" as they poured one's tea). To address a European woman or girl—or, in many cases, man—anywhere in Singapore (whether it was a shop, a cinema or in the street) was to incur the most calculated snub.

This was something we found impossible to combat and impossible to understand. Whilst one expected no gratitude for having been posted to Malaya, presumably to defend these quaint people, and whilst one expected no automatic hospitality (although one was very homesick and greatly longed for it), one nevertheless *did* expect civility. And civility was precisely what one did not, at any time, from any quarter, get.

My first sally into Singapore shocked me considerably. Having lost myself most successfully in the heart of the city, I turned to the first white people I set eyes on—two women, extremely well dressed; one beautiful, the other pleasant-faced—and asked for directions: "Excuse me, madam," I said, "but how do I get to the Union Jack Club? I'm lost!"

Madame, in fact, mesdames, drew themselves up to their full height: the pleasant-faced one announced to the beautiful one in tones of pure vinegar: "Good God, these soldiers are everywhere—let's go to the club for a drink," and, thereupon, hesitating long enough only to look at me as if I'd been contemplating rape, both Beauty and Pleasantry swept off. I remained lost.

To extricate myself, I got into a rickshaw and said, "The Union Jack Club, please." We jogged for miles and finally took a familiar right-hand turn. Suddenly I realized where I was—Lavender Street, the street of brothels. It was useless protesting to the rickshaw coolie. It didn't matter where in Singapore you boarded a rickshaw or where you asked to go—they always took you to Lavender Street.

But in this they were not without their wisdom. Practically every reputable hotel and eating establishment in Singapore had been put "Out of Bounds to O.R.'s," so that Lavender Street was the solution to most men's eating problems. The girls were quite reasonable and once one explained that one wanted food, not a 99.9 per cent chance of contracting V.D., they left one alone in peace to eat. Nevertheless, the enforced company of other soldiers or taxi girls or prostitutes on all leaves for the next four months before the Japanese invasion was not the happiest solution in the world to the problems of lonely troops stationed many thousands of miles from home. I was *not* very amused when one day, in the levelling atmosphere of a gaol into which the Japanese had thrust us all, I asked an English planter why this vicious policy of ignoring and ostracizing the ordinary soldier had grown up.

"But, my dear good fellow," he said, "with all due respect to yourself—*it was because you chaps were always hanging round in the brothels!*"

Now that the war is over, one wonders whether Malayan Europeans are not again just as contemptuous of the garrison troops who protect them as ever they were. In 1941, however, we Australians were not pleased. A storm of criticism went home in letters and evoked a storm of protests from Australia to family friends who were civilians in Malaya—which, in their turn, evoked hundreds of offers of hospitality to the fortunate few. And, once properly accredited and introduced, very lavish was the hospitality extended to these few. But to the many, who had no family or business contacts with Europeans in Malaya, the ban remained—most especially on the British troops who (having been there longer and having less pay) deserved it least.

For my part, I received, from friends of my mother's, four invitations to go at any time to various estates on the mainland. From my grandmother I received two letters of introduction—one to the governor of Singapore (this I considered hardly suitable, so I gave it to a rickshaw boy in the fond hope that he would use it) and another to the daughter of one of her greatest friends. This woman, my grandmother told me, always dined on Sundays at Raffles. "Go to Raffles and send this note in to her," the letter said, "but don't go by taxi because the native taxi drivers are Muslims and not afraid to die."

How well my grandmama knew Malayan taxi drivers. So I took a rickshaw on my last Sunday leave in Singapore—we were due to go upcountry the next week—and said firmly, "Raffles." And when I observed the boy, even more firmly, to be trotting off in the direction of Lavender Street, I leaped out of his rickshaw and, standing in front of him, bellowed: "*Pigi, Raffles* [Go to Raffles]." And as I climbed back into the seat, I added a thunderous: "*Lacas* [quickly]!" Astounded at my fluent command of the language, and not realizing that I had thus expended two thirds of my total Malayan vocabulary, the boy meekly obeyed. Quite soon we were there. Having struck a hard bargain and paid the rickshaw off, I climbed the steps, ignored the "Out of Bounds" sign and entered the luxurious coolness of Singapore's most expensive hotel.

"Sir," the doorkeeper protested, and pointed at the "Out of Bounds" sign.

"Nuts," I told him—it was a word to which he was apparently not accustomed, for he relapsed into an uneasy silence whilst I straightened my slacks and saw that my hair was no untidier than usual. This done, I handed him my grandmother's letter. "Do you know this lady?" I asked, pointing at the address. "Yes, sir."

"Would you take the letter to her, please, and ask her if she can spare a minute—I'd like to see her if I may." "Yes, sir," said the doorkeeper—and vanished. After a few minutes, I tired of hanging around. I was thirsty and decided to get a drink. I walked into the lounge, sat down and ordered a long squash. And as I did so, a tall, fair-haired woman, thirtyish and remarkably good-looking, strolled coolly into the room and sat down nearby.

"Boy," she called. The drinks waiter came running. "Tell that soldier," she said in the clear, ringing tones of the very rich when talking about the very poor, whom they fondly imagine to be deaf, "that he's out of bounds in here and ask him to leave."

Obediently the "boy" pattered over. "You're out of bounds, sir," he said diffidently.

"Well, that's O.K. by me," I told him.

"But the lady . . ." protested the boy.

"Tell the lady," I answered rudely, "to go to hell."

The boy pattered back and relayed a mealymouthed version of my original. Promptly she reacted. Turning round to look at me for the first time—which she did with unconcealed distaste—she instructed the boy: "Go outside and call the Military Police," and then, as the boy was about to leave, added: "and while you're out there, bring in the Mr. Braddon who brought this note—ask him if he'll have a drink with me in here."

The opportunity was too good to miss. I walked over to her: "I'm Braddon," I said, "and I wouldn't drink here or anywhere else with you. And when this war with Japan starts and you go screeching off on the first evacuation ship to Australia, I sincerely hope that none of my family will either."

With that, feeling like Garrick on one of his best exits, I left. At the door she caught me.

"Mr. Braddon," she began . . .

"Gunner Braddon," I interrupted.

"I'm awfully sorry," she continued, "must you go? Where are you going?"

"Lavender Street," I told her, "the Green Cat. Down there the women are bitches and they know it. I think I prefer it that way."

At that moment a provost arrived and so I—rather precipitately—left. Left her to explain why she'd summoned him. I just sat in my rickshaw as it headed down past the Great World towards the street of brothels and wondered why wars had to be so unpleasant. It was almost four years later that I heard that the fair-haired lady to whom I had carried my letter of introduction in Raffles was drowned when one of the *last* evacuee ships left Singapore Harbour. Apparently she had been very brave. During most of that four years, of course, Raffles was a Japanese brothel.

7 "HULLO, JOE"

The next week we moved out of the tented camp in the rubber plantation, off the island, over the Johore Causeway which links Singapore to Malaya, and one hundred and fifty miles upcountry to a small village called Tampin. There we were installed in cool, airy, wooden huts: and there we stayed, very pleasantly, for almost the rest of the year.

In this period we painted our bright yellow trucks a sombre shade of jungle green and resigned ourselves to the indignity of being a mortar regiment instead of a field artillery unit. There being no hope of our receiving the guns we had been so long trained to use, we settled down grimly to adapt artillery principles (designed for ranges up to thirteen thousand yards) to the firepower of three-inch mortars (whose range is *six* hundred). This initial disappointment overcome, however, the regiment set to in their task with violent energy and achieved as much success in the art of deploying their weapons swiftly and effectively, in country mainly composed of plantations, as the regulations permitted. Led by a vehement Sultan of Johore, various Malayan owners had succeeded in having imposed a fine of five dollars upon any soldier who in any way damaged any rubber tree—however slightly and even though it was in the pursuit of his training. Nothing could have been more calculated to interfere with mobility and efficiency (in these predominantly rubber-growing areas) than this regulation. But then one could never accuse the promoters of this regulation of being at any time the smallest bit interested in either the mobility or the efficiency of the military forces of Malaya.

On the other side of the picture, however, there was much that was delightful and praiseworthy.

We were well paid, well clothed, given sufficient leave in the nearby towns of Seremban and Malacca, and we were magnificently healthy—a fact which was to save thousands of Australian lives in the long days of the captivity to come.

As well as our work there was every encouragement to indulge in sport—with the result that I played rugby, hockey and tennis and swam to my heart's content. Moreover, so thorough were the precautions taken by our authorities, and so constant was the stress they placed upon hygiene—both personal and communal—that the dreaded tropical diseases (about which our redheaded sergeant major had spoken so luridly) remained just as unknown to us in Tampin as they had been when he first addressed us. Thus, sick parades became almost exclusively the province of those who had hurt themselves playing football or received stings from Malayan wasps (which are extremely bad-tempered) or from Malayan vines (which can be treacherously deceptive). By November of 1941 we were a hardened unit, immune to the tropic heat, accustomed to the strange ways of the jungle, confident of our own ability to hit hard if the occasion arose. Our only fears were that the Russian front would not hold fast for the hundred days which American experts said was the minimum Allied requirement if Germany were not to sweep the world: and that, in the event of action, our mortar ammunition might, over the past few months, have been affected by the damp. To dispel the first fear, we ploughed through endless press and B.B.C. communiqués. To avert the second, we moved all our ammunition from one place to another, round and round the camp. Taking its temperature, wiping its bottom and dusting its top with all the loving care of a mother with her first child. As events turned out, we need not have worried about either—the Russians held on for three years and most of the mortar bombs we so jealously saved from the ravages of moisture were used by the Japanese against our own forces.

Not only in the matter of our health did our authorities excel themselves. They also encouraged the Australian troops—always easy-going souls—to make friends with the local inhabitants, the Malays. Thus, in Tampin and Malacca and Seremban, there were always swarms of children round every Australian soldier. Kids who clamoured for pennies and cigarettes and, when they got them, dutifully took the money home to mum and smoked the cigarettes with all the nonchalance of old men. The vision of Malays which remains longest in the soldier's mind is that of children, mere infants of four or five, running beside one, grabbing a finger of one's hand (a hand that swung almost higher than their own heads) and demanding pennies—whilst, from the cigarettes that hung from the corners of infant mouths, they inhaled and breathed out tobacco smoke with all the abandon of the chain smoker. That and their worldly whispers of "You want my sister, tuan. My sister very clean. Only two dollars, tuan"—and the little face would gaze up, in this sordid business of soliciting, with exactly the same baby air of pleading as when they asked for pennies.

Between the Malays and ourselves there sprang up a jovial familiarity which can best be summed up in the invariable greeting that passed between us—"Hullo, Joe." All Malays, to us, were Joe. To the Malays, all Australians were Joe. This greeting—accompanied by a cheerful "Thumbs Up"—was never omitted. Had the officers of the Eighth Australian Division been saluted as assiduously as the Malays of the State of Negri Sembilan were "hullo-Joe'ed," they would have died of shock. Whether we were in convoy, on a single truck, on a route march or on leave, when you passed a native, you grinned, and he grinned, and you both raised the right thumb and said, "Hello, Joe." There was a warmth in this relationship of ours with the locals which partly compensated for, and partly arose out of, the fact that it was the only social relationship open to us. Forbidden, on pain almost of death, to visit or take out our own Australian nurses at Malacca, and ostracized by the vast majority of Europeans on the peninsula, we turned the full force of our frustrated conviviality upon the Malays. And they responded nobly.

Two complications from this fraternization were feared. One was that in the process we might divulge information as to our strength and numbers. The other was that the 99.9 per cent chance of V.D. might, in some cases, be translated into a 100 per cent fact. On both these scores the powers-that-were feared needlessly.

On the subject of our strength and numbers, it is certainly a fact that the locals (taxi dancers, small boys, traders and shopkeepers alike) questioned us enthusiastically. Those Malays who are not curious are dead. The questions were inevitable. Also, no doubt, there were the odd fifth columnists anxious to accumulate information against the day when they could sell it (for the native does nothing for nothing) to the invader. We, however, told them nothing. In spite of the fact that our common sense told us that any native who cared could come up the road, count us on parade, count our vehicles in the car park, and count our mortars in the rubber when we trained; and count our bombs on the innumerable occasions when we shifted them to dryer ground—in spite of that, we told them nothing.

And, although our common sense told us that when natives delivered the vegetable ration and saw our ration figures; and when natives cleaned the camp's many drains; and when natives did the entire regiment's laundry—in the course of which they ascertained the exact number of men in each and every hut in the camp—although our common sense told us that when they did all these things it was rather improbable that they were unaware of our strength, *still* we told them nothing.

And when *they* told *us*, which they did with a great air of friendly triumph, we looked quite wooden-faced . . . and admitted nothing. Meanwhile, our Recreation Hut was plastered with notices informing us that "The Enemy Listened"; imploring us not to talk, and assuring us that if we did not talk, no one would ever know anything. Only we ordinary soldiers thoroughly appreciated the fact that, on the contrary, everyone in the district knew everything, but that so long as we remained in the district to defend it, that knowledge could do us no harm.

The second official fear—that V.D. would be contracted—was equally groundless. As far as we were concerned, taxi girls were there only to be danced with; the ordinary Malay women were there for the same reason as the rubber trees—they grew there! And they received no more attention than rubber trees, except that their coloured saris and, on occasions, their remarkably beautiful eyes and teeth made them rather more soothing to the optic nerve.

And so life in Tampin proceeded. Mortar drill and manoeuvres during the day: football or hockey matches twice a week: a walk down to the village each night. There some danced with the taxi girls—not many dances, because they cost twenty-five cents each: some practised their Malay and grew fairly fluent: some bought native ornaments in silver and pewter and sent them home: and always there were the swarms of children—the shrill screams of "Pennies," "Cigarettes," "You want my sister, tuan?" and "Hullo, Joe."

The highlights of our village life were the occasional visits of a native-owned cinema unit (which specialized in showing, at one sitting, all fourteen chapters of particularly improbable Hollywood serials) and of native circuses. At the latter, the entire regiment gasped at two Chinese, who dived through a ring of razor-edged knives—all pointing inwards—and gaped, in awe-struck silence, at a ballet of five native women, all of whom were most noticeably pregnant. Both films and circuses, performed in a tent, were punctuated by the shrill screams of native audiences and by the overpowering aroma of urine, owing to the delightful Malayan custom of relieving oneself where one sits.

And in the tranquillity of these village interludes—for there is no hour anywhere which is more refreshing than the first cool ones of the Malayan evening when the swallows and starlings settle down on the telephone wires, wing to wing for miles, to sleep till the dawn rouses them to their shrill flight—it was almost impossible to believe that a few thousand miles away the Old World was reeling, still less that in French Indo-China, China proper and Japan millions of troops waited for the order which would shatter this village peace for four long years.

And yet there were signs of danger. When an artillery regiment can only be equipped with three-inch mortars, and when no tanks or armour are ever seen, and when only a few comparatively slow

Brewster Buffalo planes ever ascend into the skies, and when there are virtually no automatic weapons at all and not even enough ammunition for issue to guards on sentry duty at bomb dumps—then it is obvious that all is not entirely well.

This malaise became steadily more widespread—nowhere more so, apparently, than in our own high command. Manoeuvres with full complements of trucks and equipment, the men wearing gas masks and steel helmets, became the order of the day: doubled guards the order of the night.

Even some of the natives sensed the tension and, as a symbol of it, there arrived on our doorstep one day a small naked brown child, doe-eyed, white-toothed, delightful. As with all our small visitors, he was fed till his tummy was quite round and then told firmly to "*pigi* [go home]!"

Next morning he was found asleep in the mess hut: still naked, still delightful, but his tummy quite flat and his eyes rather frightened. So we enquired and found that his parents had suddenly left Tampin. Left in a panic that they hadn't been able to explain. And now the small brown child was an orphan. Without more ado, the regiment adopted him.

For the next few weeks his brilliant smile and his sturdy refusal to wear any clothes, his insatiable appetite and his refreshing air of complete innocence and confidence, made him a universal favourite. As we came back from training each day, he would be waiting at the gates. As each truckload of men came in, the dark eyes would swing solemnly up to them and he would hold up a minute thumb and say, "Hullo, Joe." And they, for their part, would gravely salute him and reply, "Hullo, Little Tinea," which was what they called him, because, like the affliction after which he was named, Little Tinea was always all over the place.

When the war came to Tampin and his soldier foster parents were sent to fight elsewhere, it is said that Little Tinea was killed by the bombs. I don't know. I rather hope he was; for there was no place for children such as he in the arms of the soldiers of Nippon.

That moment, however, had not yet quite arrived. Though the tension increased and senior staff officers appeared more and more often, looking less and less happy, war was still not with us.

Nevertheless, the threat of it was sufficient to make life exceedingly uncomfortable. Guard duty became a chore which, as well as daytime duties, befell one almost every second night because of the doubled sentry order and the increased number of posts. In an effort to offset the tedium of these guards, they were transformed into ceremonial affairs with glittering boots, razorlike creases in tailored slacks, and highly polished belts.

The Australian, however, does not derive much pleasure from such spit and polish parades: and when—owing to the frequency of surprise visits by senior staff officers—a special ceremonial guard was kept constantly at the alert, to appear in place of the actual guard on duty at any moment should a V.I.P. arrive on the horizon, our cup of displeasure was full.

It is worth noting that at a time when there were only three weeks left in which to prepare to meet the invasion which swiftly encompassed our total destruction, our regiment still had a man hiding all day behind a bush at the corner of the camp and the main road, so that whenever he saw a staff car approaching he could blow a whistle. When he blew his whistle the routine group of men on guard duty in the guardhouse hid. They were replaced (amidst much panic by the orderly officer) with a Special Glittering Guard, who would at once fall in and present arms—thereby greatly impressing the visiting staff officer, and, no doubt, giving the Japanese much cause to doubt the possibility of their ever achieving a victory in Malaya.

For weeks this madness persisted. The Brigadier Commanding Artillery appeared and, as his contribution to the speeding up of the war effort, examined all the dixies in the cookhouse with an eagle eye and declared that they were dirty! This was quite true, had been true for months, and remained so till our most veteran cook died as a prisoner of those whom his dirtiness had not deterred some three years later. To the Special Glittering Guard the C.R.A. spoke words of praise. He even asked their sergeant gravely—did they practise rifle drill in their spare time? The sergeant replied, equally gravely, "Yes"—at which God should, in fairness to Ananias, have struck him dead, and the temporarily deposed Scruffy Guard (hiding in a truck across the road) became convulsed with laughter.

Later, Air Chief Marshal Sir Robert Brooke-Popham appeared; and he, too, was delighted with the Special Glittering Guard. He spoke a few words to each man and asked him what he had done in his civilian days. Regrettably, not a man told the truth. Solicitors said they had plumbed: a carpenter said that he trained choirboys, and gave the Air Marshal a very lewd look: a hardened journalist fluttered his eyelashes and announced in effeminate tones that he was a ballet dancer. By the time the Air Marshal had made his way as far as me, all the more reasonable occupations having gone, I could only, in answer to his query, say: "Mortician, sir," which he said was very interesting.

In the course of the next few days, there were several false alarms and millions of false rumours. One effect of these was that a sufficient number of .303 bullets was unearthed to enable each member of the mounting guard to place five in his magazine—so long as the duty sergeant had remembered to collect them from the guard which was about to be relieved.

This innovation had some refreshing consequences. One was that few guard mountings took place without a detonation (someone always contrived—whether accidentally or not—to leave a bullet in the breech of his rifle and this, of course, was fired off in the course of the elaborate ritual of "clearing arms"). The instant reaction to any such detonation was for all onlookers to gaze swiftly at the orderly officer, and immediately upon ascertaining that he still lived, there would be a howl of "Missed him, you silly bastard"—whereupon many names would be taken and charges would next day be preferred for "conduct prejudicial . . ."

But a second and much pleasanter consequence came on the sentry beat itself. In an effort to make guards more alert, the orderly officer had taken to making surprise visits to all posts over the last few weeks. In fact, quite a lot of officers, on their way back from parties, had taken to attempting to surprise the sentries. It had become a sort of game for them. For us it was becoming very tedious.

I had first noticed it when I stood guarding the mortar-bomb dump with Cliffie one night. Cliffie spoke excellent Malay and (as mentioned before) was the speediest signaller in the regiment and a 1918 artillery officer. Therefore, as we stood back to back, I urged him, now that the war seemed to be coming closer to us, to apply for a commission again because none of our officers spoke any Malay; very few of them could signal at all, let alone fast, and still fewer of them had had battle experience. Cliffie replied sadly that his application had been in for months and appeared to have gone and got itself lost!

And it was at this moment that I observed an officer weave an erratic course from F Troop's lines towards the Officers' Mess—a course which took him (in brilliant moonlight) within forty yards of our dump. I pointed this phenomenon out to Cliffie and we both followed the gentleman's course with all the interest of those who are very bored and are, therefore, prepared to watch anything. At the Officers' Mess we were even more interested to see him bear right and vanish into the bush below our dump, where he could be heard crashing round in a rather furtive fashion.

"What the hell do you think he's doing, Cliffie?" I asked, and Cliffie said he didn't know, he'd go and have a look. So Cliffie made his way towards the bush—whereupon the officer leapt out and, as Cliffie said, "Good evening, sir," shouted: "Got you!"

It appeared he had stalked us and caught us completely unawares! Nothing could dissuade him. That sort of thing happened all the time—*until* we got live ammunition for our rifles on guard. Then, owing to the determination of one man, all surprise visits stopped.

This man, a gunner called Caldwell, was a lean, conscientious and stubborn soldier. He had spent all his life farming and he stood no nonsense from anyone. The military claptrack of "Halt, who goes there?" . . . "Advance one pace and be recognized" . . . "Password and Reply" . . . was too much for Gunner Caldwell. When he heard anyone coming—and he had very good ears—he shoved a bullet firmly and audibly up the spout, clicked off his safety catch and bellowed, "Stop or I shoot." And if, after that, he saw or heard so much as an eyelash moving, he shot! When the second duty officer on two successive guards had been despatched into the jungle in frantic haste by a volley of bullets from the redoubtable ex-farmer, the practice of stalking sentries ceased, as the vernacular was, forthwith.

8 "BATTLE STATIONS"

By the beginning of December, 1941, the Germans having moved firmly into most of western Russia and the Japanese having insinuated themselves slyly into much of Southeast Asia—Manchuria and French Indo-China, anyway—the atmosphere in Malaya became tenser. Everywhere training was accelerated; gas masks were inspected almost daily; lectures were delivered on the Japanese and their habits, their methods of warfare and how to defeat them.

Someone circulated a rumour that on the Siam frontier of Malaya we had exactly one million Sikhs; but, although one had oneself seen two convoys of these troops heading north, no one who was not half-witted believed the report. In the interests of security, however, one refrained from comment.

The intelligence officer spoke to us at great length on three subjects. First, the frequent use made by the Japanese of crackers with which to frighten their enemies—especially at night. Second, the use that the Japanese would make of gas. Third, a quaint element in battle termed "justifiable war risk." This term apparently embraced anything in an action which anyone might order you to do, at any time—however silly or useless—and at once seemed to commend itself most favourably to all our superiors, who used it thenceforth incessantly.

It is regrettable to have to relate that the Japanese never in my experience resorted to crackers—apparently working on the old-fashioned principle that mortar bombs were better: that they used no gas—which was perhaps as well when one recollects that in answer to a question: "How do you decontaminate a twenty-five-pounder gun?" the intelligence officer had replied, "Take it to pieces: scrape all the paint off it, and then boil it in a petrol drum!"; and that, once the war started, practically the only order ever issued to an army only too anxious to indulge in a spot of *justifiable war risk* by engaging the enemy was "Withdraw"!

Nevertheless, it was upon the basis of these three principles that our training continued. As we made corduroy mats (which we knew from experience to be quite valueless as a track for Army vehicles in heavy mud—although that was their purpose): and as we ran up and down the road wearing gas masks and steel helmets, the better to prepare ourselves for the coming battle, we could only feel profound relief that at least we were extremely fit. Little knowing how prophetic his words would be, Cliffie one morning (as we doubled for the tenth time up and down the road outside Regimental Headquarters) snatched off his steaming gas mask and snarled: "Well, probably we won't be able to do the Japs much harm: but at least the bastards'll have to chase us all the way to Singapore before they'll ever catch us." Two months later that was exactly what the Japanese did.

Irksome though these worthless preparations were, however, our authorities still had the wisdom to allow the occasional respite of sport. And so it happened that one afternoon we went to Malacca to play the Army Service Corps rugby football. The A.S.C. fed us nobly and then annihilated us on the field. I marked a winger who seemed many feet taller than myself and ran with his knees high. To stop him was both difficult and painful. But when our own back line moved off and Shearer passed to Hingst, and Hingst—beautiful footballer—passed to me, that same opponent at once crushed me to the ground with appalling ease. However, we enjoyed the carefree atmosphere of this regimental game, after the strain of the few weeks before, and accepted our defeat quite happily.

The match over, we showered, dried thoroughly, flung talcum powder over most of the accessible portions of our respective anatomies—an efficient preventative against the tinea that crept—and then, dressed in cool, clean clothes, moved into the town of Malacca to dance, or eat, or sit in the cinema, according to one's mood. It was perhaps as well that at that moment no one realized that Shearer and Hingst, not to mention half a dozen other members of our team, would never throw a football again.

At about half past ten—just when our revels in Malacca were reaching their height—the alarm was sounded! Provosts rushed round blowing whistles: officers (wearing tin hats, revolvers and an urgent expression) appeared everywhere in trucks, saying, "Get back to your camp at once," and then vanishing again before one had time to clamber aboard: and everywhere the rumour flashed round, "It's war." It was not a nice feeling. Abruptly the revels ceased. The taxi girls, abandoned, sat silent and lonely at their tables. The cinemas emptied: the cafés vomited a stream of khaki soldiers all heading for camp. No one having thought of sending in transport for these hundreds of men, they quickly set about securing their own. Cabs, rickshaws and passing cars were hailed and swiftly loaded. Very soon a motley convoy headed out of Malacca towards Tampin—some fifteen miles away.

As I passed over the bridge just outside the town (in a cab which I shared with a young lieutenant, a gun sergeant and Johnny Iceton), I noticed a rickshaw pursuing a particularly erratic course. On further examination, it proved to be Piddington—he who was to be the only survivor from an office of five who had joined the regiment. Piddington with Magee and Robinson (two others of that five) had—upon the alarm—boarded a rickshaw. Midst many protestations, the rickshaw boy had at last set out for Tampin. At the bridge he had tired—having covered only two of the fifteen miles—so now Piddington, who had had a good evening, pulled the rickshaw in which (in drunken splendour) rode Magee . . . and Robinson . . . and the rickshaw boy.

"Want a lift, Piddo?" I shouted, telling the cab driver to pull up.

"Lift?" demanded he aggressively. "Whaffor? Nothing wrong with these. Much better than those taxis. Very unsafe Malayan taxis. Remember what your grandmother said?" And with that he jogged off shouting:

"Fares, please, fares, please—move right down the centre there. No standing on the platform," so I told our driver to carry on.

"How much to take to Tampin, tuan?" he enquired threateningly.

"A smack in the kisser if you *don't*," replied Johnny Iceton succinctly, whereupon we at once moved off and quickly repassed the rickshaw.

We completed the trip without further excitement, except that the young lieutenant suddenly decided that someone should keep a lookout for enemy aircraft. He was a bit of a dope but harmless enough, so we allowed him to perform this vital function himself, which he did with enormous enthusiasm, standing on the front seat with his head and shoulders out of the sun roof and his revolver in his hand. Meanwhile, the Malay driver hurtled through the darkness whilst Johnny surveyed our air lookout with a frankly jaundiced eye; the gun sergeant sang about forty-nine choruses of "Bless 'Em All" in the revised version, and I wondered to myself whether it was really possible—wars being nowadays so much bigger and better than they had ever been before—to survive one.

We arrived at the camp shortly before midnight to find it seething—seething with extra guards, rumours and official indecision. Since no one would tell me what to do, I went to my hut and cleaned my rifle. On almost every bed others sat doing the same thing. The bed beside mine—Hugh Moore's—was empty. He was in hospital with fever and I wondered how all this would affect him and when he would rejoin us.

I had just finished with the pull-through when an N.C.O. came in and issued us with five rounds each of ammunition. Johnny Iceton looked at him in incredulous amazement. "What," he queried, "five rounds for every man in the regiment?" The N.C.O. nodded.

"Well, then," said Johnny firmly, "it bloody *must* be war," and with that we all went to bed and swiftly to sleep.

Next day, to set upon the situation the seal of official acknowledgment that here was a crisis, we were issued with many special orders. First: "*No* native will be allowed to enter the camp for any purpose without his pass." The camp's squad of native workers had been issued with these passes months earlier when we had arrived. They had all, long since, lost them. Of this rather human weakness, however, the orders took no notice at all. We were, the order continued, to challenge *all* natives. We were, moreover, to challenge them in Malay. We were to say: "*Berenti jika-lau tidak sayah* something or other" which I now forget—and which most men forgot the second they heard it. This gabble meant, "Halt: if not I shoot!"

"Finally," the order concluded, "if the challenged native does not halt, you must shoot!" With decided distaste, we marched to our posts. What ensued was chaos.

Upon being challenged, the natives would just shrug cheerfully, scratch their legs and spit betel-nut juice and assure us that their passes were lost. The fierce gabble (the one which meant that if they did not then immediately halt one would shoot them), they greeted with wide smiles, revealing a mouth full of gold-capped teeth and an agreeable certainty that one was talking nonsense. They would then march straight under the muzzle of one's outstretched and indignant rifle and, giving the inevitable greeting of the up-pointed thumb and the "Hullo, Joe," would pass confidently into the camp. One was then confronted with the inhuman necessity of blowing their heads off from behind or of sparing them and endeavouring to do better with the next. At the end of the day, the men of the regiment compared notes. Everywhere one heard the same question: "How many boongs did you manage to halt today, mate?" and everywhere one heard the same answer, "Sweet F.A. How about you?" If it was necessary to the winning of the Malayan campaign that native workers, whom we knew as well as our regimental comrades, be either halted for identification or shot, then upon that very first day of the crisis, the war was lost!

Other signs of official reaction came equally swiftly. One must carry one's rifle and one's five rounds of ammunition everywhere. When men in the latrines were charged for attending to the demands of nature without the protection of firearms, it was realized that this order was not one with which to trifle.

Next we must again move, count, wipe and take the temperature of every mortar bomb in the two regimental dumps, in spite of the fact that this extraordinary performance had only a few days earlier been completed for the thousandth time.

Also, we must all look at, and have a vague notion how to operate, the three tommy guns to each battery of three hundred men which had been lavishly issued to us as our total automatic firepower against the cracker-throwing Japanese. We accordingly looked—and someone even rashly enquired could he fire one? He was, of course, savagely reprimanded and informed that as there was practically no ammunition available for any of these guns he most certainly could not.

Next, one Bren carrier arrived for each battery—nasty, inadequate vehicles with small protection from the ground and none at all from above (as the enemy were quick to demonstrate). These, with one armoured car, were to be our total mobile reply to the Japanese and their tanks.

Finally, the regiment was presented with some twenty-five-pounders. Beautiful English guns, still thick with the grease that had been plastered on them to protect them on their journey from factories in Britain. There were not sufficient of them, it was admitted: but they were a delightful piece of mechanism and the eyes of many a gunner, long dulled by the prosaic ugliness of our three-inch mortars, shone again as he glanced down the barrel, over the shield, on to the dials and controls and right back past the breech block to the spade. Guns again instead of stovepipes—it was a nice feeling. Quickly each gun was cleaned by volunteers of its protective grease and polished till it was spotless. In their few minutes of spare time, men came from all over the camp and practised their drill. Had the C.R.A. appeared at that moment and asked, "Tell me, Sergeant: do the men practise in their spare time?" then the answer could, truthfully this time, have been "Yes."

So the second day of the crisis passed. Passed with spirits as high as spirits can be only when men are in good health, are confident of themselves and one another and—though under no illusions about the insufficiency of all their weapons, from aeroplanes to bullets—are anxious to test themselves against this mysterious element known as "The Enemy."

The enemy meantime appeared to dally; so we, perhaps to deter him, perhaps to prepare for his onslaught, or perhaps for both, were ordered to proceed at once to battle stations.

9 AIRBORNE INVASION

The movement of the entire regiment was accomplished at night with a maximum of enthusiasm and a minimum of efficiency. Convoys howled off, with trucks at thirty-yard intervals and no headlights. The regiment was split up into numerous small units and sent out to protect and provide firepower for various aerodromes. The beautiful new twenty-five-pounders we left behind at Tampin to be guarded by a small rear guard along with our store, which bulged with the six months' accumulation of everything the quartermaster sergeant had managed in that time not to issue.

Badly briefed and hurriedly assembled, these various convoys roared out of the area they knew so well and, armed with bully beef and mortars, swiftly proceeded to lose themselves all over districts they had never seen in central Malaya. Before morning, however, each convoy had found itself at least one aerodrome to guard and was assiduously staring into the gloom lest enemy paratroopers descend unobserved.

Nerves (which had not been improved by a rocketing trip of anything up to a hundred miles in complete darkness on one of the most dangerous road systems in the world) grew tauter as, for the third night in succession, there was no sleep. In the darkness, many a sentry blazed away at a signalling fifth columnist only to realize, almost at once, that it was nothing more harmful than a glowworm.

The stand-to period from dawn onwards (by which time everyone had equipped himself with a six-foot-deep slit trench and a firing step) was made even more miserable than that dreary hour normally is by the millions of sand flies which—suddenly awakened—swarmed out of the undergrowth and flew into one's tin hat. Having got in under the headband, they were too stupid to find their way out again and retaliated by burrowing into the hair and biting badtemperedly. Everywhere the watery dawn air was rent by howls of bad language and the clanging of tin hats thrown to the ground as their owners clawed wildly at their scalps.

The situation was in no way improved by the realization on the part of at least one group that they were guarding the wrong aerodrome. They were at Kluang and should apparently have been at Kahang. So they loaded all their mortars again, and all the bombs, and all the stores and went to Kahang—where they were greeted with the encouraging news that Pearl Harbour had that day been devastated by the Japanese and that Kahang Aerodrome had been mined for destruction by the engineers.

Accordingly all the mortars were placed in pits—which had to be dug—round the circumference of the field; all the gunners took up their positions in new slit trenches—which had to be dug—round the mortars: and the gunners then waited for the Japanese paratroopers to land—when every mortar was at once to fire, whereupon the defenders would very successfully wipe one another out.

This point of view had been put—rather forcibly—by several N.C.O.'s to the officers in command, but had not made any considerable impression, as the aforesaid officers were very busy arguing bitterly over the respective merits, in destroying an airfield, of mines and aerial bombing. Since we had no aeroplanes at all in the vicinity —and few indeed in the whole of Malaya—it was purely an academic argument but seemed, nevertheless, engrossing. Reluctant, therefore, but resigned, the men awaited the dawn. They were saved from mutual obliteration by the failure of the wicked Japanese to send paratroopers. It turned out to be typical of the war our staff planned that its initial stages were devoted entirely to the destruction of an airborne invasion—which invasion, in fact, never came and was never even intended.

It was also typical of the war our staff planned against the enemy that when, on its outbreak on December 8, 1941, the troops on the Siam frontier asked permission to cross the border, seek the enemy out, and destroy him, the permission was refused until it was too late anyway. Moreover, it might quite profitably be pointed out, the Allied Conference of 1940 on the defence needs of Malaya had decided upon a minimum of 40 battalions with full support (including armour and tanks) *for the Thailand frontier alone,* plus 566 first-line planes. In actual fact, there were only 32 battalions in all of Malaya; there were only 141 planes (none of them up to international standard); and there were no tanks—none at all. Last-ditch orders assume a somewhat different aspect when these facts are appended to them.

The rumoured "million Sikh troops" on the frontier being in actual fact only a few thousand, the enemy was able to mass his forces at his leisure. When the attack came, the Argylls and the Leicesters and 11th Indian Division were quickly chopped to pieces by incessant tank-supported attacks. And so—within the first days of the campaign—the initiative was handed to the enemy.

When, in the course of the next two months, no really constructive effort was ever made by our command to regain the initiative, the battle was lost. No amount of heroism, nor silly orders talking about the "yielding of our boasted fortress to an inferior enemy" being "disgraceful" to our "whole fighting reputation," could save Singapore. The fierce courage of the British and Indian troops on the northern frontier of Malaya was bloodily pulped by the Japanese tanks on the Slim River—pulped and scattered in a thousand different directions into the neighbouring fever-stricken jungles. The disastrous retreat to destruction had begun.

Of this, however, on the night of December 8, the troop of which I was a member was blissfully unaware. Having recovered from our irritation at leaving behind our treasured twenty-five-pounders, we had careered on all night to the east coast—for we had to reach Mersing before dawn or (the intelligence officer said) be wiped out by aerial attacks on the road.

With the loss of only two trucks overturned on Malaya's narrow winding roads, we passed through the Australian-held position at Mersing. Here, indeed, were encouraging signs of preparedness. The gunners of our sister regiment—the 2/10th—had registered every inch of it and had complete confidence in their eighteen-pounders. They gazed at our mortars with open contempt. The Queensland infantry whom they supported knew every track and inlet in the area, had cleared fire lanes everywhere, had sent the native population packing and were (as their swift challenges out of the blackness indicated) briskly ready for war. To have uprooted this determined body of men would have taken the Japanese many months. As it happened, the operation was achieved far more simply not many weeks later by an order from our own Fort Canning—British Headquarters on the island of Singapore.

This, too, though, was still to come. For the moment we were rushed to the riverbank and there met by the Navy. The Navy had barges and light river craft. Into these we were to load about ten thousand mortar bombs, our food and equipment and—with one company of infantry—proceed up the river to what had been a Japanese-owned mine called Bukit Langkap.

Undeterred by the prodigious nature of this task, we accomplished it in six hours of concerted effort and so found ourselves being towed on close-packed barges up the river. We arrived at Bukit Langkap about two hours later.

Bukit Langkap was a mountain (made partly by man, partly by God) of red clay, cut into open-cast mining terraces and ravines. Access to its summit had been by a railway which the Japanese had, before they departed, thoughtlessly destroyed. The only alternative route was a narrow goat track which ran up alongside the railway. It was raining.

Up this track, therefore, from the barges on the river to the summit of the mountain, we manhandled our ten thousand mortar bombs and our mortars. After the first mile-long trip made by each of the troop's hundred-odd men, the track turned from wet clay to an orange ribbon of grease. The ensuing twenty trips were an agony of aching muscles and calamitous falls which resulted in a most diverting glissade of both the carrier and his very susceptible cargo of six bombs. These abrupt descents proved highly amusing to all except the participant and those other carriers whom he collected on his swift return down the grease shoot to the foot of the mountain.

Nevertheless, we eventually got all the bombs up to the top of the mountain. Even then there was no rest. We dug slit trenches and mortar pits: cleared lanes of fire: laid signal wires and took the bearings of all likely targets—an operation made none the easier by the fact that (because of the ore in all the rocks) no two compasses ever gave the same reading and no one compass ever produced even similar results twice running.

In the midst of these exertions we heard over our wireless set that the battleships *Prince of Wales* and *Repulse* had been sunk off the east Malayan coast. Sunk because they had inadequate aerial and light craft support for capital ships. When we asked what they were doing sailing round with inadequate protection a rumour was whispered that they came to Malayan waters because the Australian Government had (using the possible withdrawal of its troops in the Middle East as a weapon) blackmailed the British Government into sending two capital ships out to Singapore. Sick with the realization that the British Navy had suffered its first real defeat in history and that we on Malaya were now obviously without any substantial naval protection against the landing of enemy convoys, we turned with relief to our burrowings into the side of the mountain of clay.

The next day I wrote to Hugh Moore—still in hospital at Malacca—and asked him what were his chances of rejoining us before "the blue" started. As I took the letter down to our troop officer to be censored (even if there were no chance of its being posted), the three Dutch Wildebeestes which passed our way daily and seemed to be our only air force in Malaya lumbered slowly overhead—bound for Kota Bahru where the Japs had landed. We had come to have an affection for these three antiquated aircraft with their triangular identification mark and their pedestrian gait. It was sad that within a matter of days they should all have been blasted out of the skies by the swarms of Japanese Zeros which protected the convoy they had been sent to attack.

Then, before we had even had time to look at all the dirty pictures our Japanese predecessors had left behind them: before we could properly appreciate that here we were, one hundred gunners and one hundred infantrymen, on a mountain island from which a wall of impenetrable jungle and a moat of crocodile-infested river made all retreat impossible once we had exhausted our ten thousand bombs: but not before we realized that Bukit Langkap was only a derelict mine which had no military value whatsoever—we were ordered to abandon the mine and return to Mersing.

Down came all the mortars, down came all the bombs, up came all the signal wires, and all our computations as to line, range and angle of sight of all possible targets within the scope of a three-inch mortar were flung into the river. The preparations of the last seven days had been as futile as they had been strenuous.

The same barges collected us, escorted by the same naval river craft. The same equipment was loaded onto them and, at Mersing, taken off them. Then, in great haste, we rushed to Kluang Aerodrome—it was about to be attacked, we were told, by paratroops.

At Kluang we made a dump for all our bombs: dug slit trenches for ourselves and pits for our mortars; made a new road through the rubber for our vehicles and all the time waited for the enemy troops to come floating down. We celebrated Christmas Day with a large dinner and the following day with a heavy air raid by twenty-seven Japanese bombers, in the course of which many bombs but never a parachute landed on the aerodrome.

On the same day as our new road through the rubber was completed, the regiment—which had gradually been converging from all sides on Kluang—received fresh orders. We were to be reconstituted as a three-battery regiment instead of a two-battery one. The new battery was to be called the 65th. All batteries were to be equipped with field guns and take up fresh battle stations.

So, abandoning our mortars and the nice new road, we moved off, we of the new 65th, in swift convoy and armed with twenty-five-pounders. We moved one hundred miles across to the west coast of

Malaya to a rendezvous outside a town we had never even heard of called Muar. Eventually we were to know it quite well.

The position as it was at that time was then put to us, in his own inimitably inadequate style, by our intelligence officer—who assured us that he wanted to "put us in the picture." Even as painted by the intelligence officer, the "picture" was no rosy landscape.

It appeared that at least half of Malaya—following the slaughter of the British troops and the 11th Indian Division on the Slim River by Japanese tanks—had been systematically abandoned. A scorched-earth policy had been, however, conscientiously employed. All the dredges in the tin mines had been destroyed: all the rubber in storehouses had been burnt: all the acid used to coagulate latex had been removed: all bridges had been blown. The loss of Kuala Lumpur, administrative centre of the Malay States, was glossed over by the sudden announcement that it had been declared an Open City. Any landings other than the initial one at Kota Bahru on the northeast coast were discreetly not mentioned at all. And now, it was asserted, Australian fighting troops were, for the first time, to take the brunt of the Japanese onslaught on a line which extended across Malaya from Muar on the west, to Segamat in the centre, to Mersing on the east. The calamitous loss of the millions of pounds' worth of machinery, rubber, tin and installations which the retreat to this line inevitably involved were dismissed, without any reference to it at all, by the Intelligence Report.

Nor did the report see fit to inform us that the Argylls and Leicesters and Gurkhas (who fought so gallantly downwards from the Siam frontier) had been withdrawn every day, day after day, to fresh positions. They were never allowed to contact the enemy seriously, but always—just as he advanced—withdrawn ten or fifteen miles by forced marches to yet another line. So that, for day after day and week after week, they marched, dug in, waited sleeplessly at the alert, and then marched again. For two hundred-odd miles they had retreated, without rest, down the peninsula. They were utterly exhausted in this war which—contrary to all classic principles—seemed to aim at neither seeking out the enemy nor destroying him.

Nor did the report see fit to tell us that this method of waging war against the Japanese would be maintained to the bitter end and only circumvented when the enemy moved more swiftly than could the orders to withdraw.

Least of all did the report see fit to inform us that in the precipitate evacuation of Penang, high up on the west coast, hundreds of small craft (launches, junks, fishing boats—vessels of every description) had been left intact for the use of the swarming troops of the enemy. Not having this interesting fact before us, we decided calmly, though wrongly enough, that we would hold the Jap when he arrived. Obviously, he must come down the mainland: then we would clash: then he would stop. He must come down the mainland, we thought, because he had no boats in which to come down the shallow waters of the west coast.

So we received orders to dig in on the southern bank of the Muar River. A brigade of Indian troops were to dig in with us: we were to await the frontal attack by land. The Imperial Japanese Army meantime sent a force three or four times stronger than ours to march against us. This we awaited confidently. Of the other force which the Japanese sent by sea—in the hundreds of small craft so happily presented to them at Penang, we remained in blissful ignorance—that force was to make sure that our lines of communication were severed and that the initial successes we gained against the enemy at both Muar and Gemas should be brought to nothing.

But since the Intelligence Report had made no mention of these hilarious circumstances, we were naturally unaware of what was about to befall us. We simply sat in the rubber plantation near Muar and listened to the young officer's pleasant tones and wondered just how much of it all one could believe this time. Then the battery commander, Major Julius—a dark, stocky, bad-tempered man respectfully known (for he was a brilliant soldier) as the Black Bastard—read out an order from Australian Command, which stated that the Japanese had been fortunate enough so far in their campaign not to have encountered Australian troops. Now they were to encounter a solid line of Australians right across the peninsula. This, the order unmistakably implied, was very sad indeed for the Japanese. They would be halted in their advance. Then they would be driven back. Then they would be flung clean out of Malaya—and all this, the order made it quite clear, by us! It was most encouraging.

Julius finished reading the order, his voice flat and his eyebrow raised cynically, then asked were there any questions. No one had any questions. The battery were then ordered to move out of the rendezvous and take up their various positions along the riverbank.

As if to mark the occasion, the heavens wept copiously and all the trucks got bogged and there was a great deal of bad language. Into the midst of this confusion came a deputation from the fierce Indian infantry brigade who, with our battery of two hundred gunners, were to halt the enemy's west coast advance. They had encountered their first ghastly loss of the war—they had run out of *ghi* (their vegetable cooking oil) and consequently could not prepare their beloved chapatties. What, they asked, could they do?

At first we told them—rudely—at which they were frankly shocked. Then we realized the truth—until they got *ghi* there would be no war for the Indians of this 45th Brigade. If it hadn't been raining so hard, and if there hadn't been so many trucks bogged down, we might even then have stopped to consider this rather unwarlike aspect of the behaviour of our colleagues in arms. But it *was* raining, so we didn't—which, as it happened, was a pity.

From somewhere or other *ghi* was scrounged; the Indians happily set to work cooking; and we managed at last to get out of the bogs of our rendezvous in the rubber onto the firm surface of the road. Late that afternoon the entire force had begun to dig in along the river and the stage was set for the battle which General Percival was to describe as ". . . one of the most sanguinary of the Malayan Campaign."

This "sanguinary battle" had a dress rehearsal of a very mixed quality. Two things quickly became evident in the few days before the enemy arrived on the far side of the river. The first was that our guns, under the inspired direction of Major Julius, were going to wreak a great deal of havoc: the second was that the majority of brand-new rifles issued to the 45th Indian Brigade were going to wreak no havoc at all. The reason for this was simple—the greater part of the brigade was composed of young natives who had been in the Army only a few months (most of that spent travelling from India to Malaya) and none of them had even the smallest idea about how to aim and fire anything.

Very little could be accomplished with them in the few days

before the battle commenced. The more amenable to instruction learnt how to discharge a rifle—which they did without any discrimination at all, in no particular direction, so long as it was *away*—but most of them remained in a state of profound ignorance and growing disquiet.

When the first air raid hit the town and they saw the murderous effects of the anti-personnel bombs dropped by the Japanese—"daisy-cutters" which carved the prostrate Malays into horizontal slices—they decided once and for all that wars were bloody affairs not at all to their liking. Immediately a trickle of these youngsters seeped off into the undergrowth. When the enemy appeared in force on the opposite banks of the river, the trickle turned into a full-blooded torrent, as thousands of Gwahlis shed boots, uniforms and rifles and padded off, barefooted, into the dark silence of the jungle.

On the far side of the river Shearer, the officer in the observation post—he who had played such determined football only a few weeks earlier—announced calmly over his field telephone that the Japs were coming through the rubber on all sides. He ordered his assistant to attempt an escape to the river and then himself covered the latter's long run, at the same time directing fire from our guns. A few seconds later his steady voice stopped in mid-sentence and the new-formed 65th Battery had suffered its first loss.

Our impressive brigade having dwindled abruptly to one battery of gunners with no bayonet training, plus the handful of Jaht troops who had been mixed with the other Indians as a bolstering influence, plus the 45th Brigade's British officers—there were also a few Gwahlis who, though they had no stomach for fighting, had not had the courage to depart with their fellow tribesmen—the Japanese soon found an easy landing place and Muar suddenly swarmed with enemy troops.

Every gun, every truck, every platoon was cut off and overrun. Dive bombers howled down hour after hour, always unopposed. In a series of furious engagements, almost all of the guns and crews fought their way out of the town and took up a new position on its outskirts. There the remaining Gwahlis—now unanimously termed "The Galloping Gwahlis"—decided finally that this business of war was not good enough. They abandoned trucks so that they blocked entire convoys: they ran backwards and forwards in the utmost panic: they lit fires to cook chapatties and shed clothes everywhere.

Never slow to take advantage of any situation, the Australians hurriedly re-equipped themselves with new rifles—our own being all of 1918 vintage. It was quite simple. You just said, "Look out, Joe—AEROPLANE," and, at that magic word, the terrified Gwahli (who had long since learnt what we had all learnt—that aeroplanes were pieces of machinery produced only in Japan) flung himself flat on his face and waited frantically for the All Clear. They waited quite some time, some of them. Anyhow, by the time they plucked up courage to look for themselves, their nice new rifles had invariably gone and beside them they found a battered old Australian one—which seemed just as good to them because they only used rifles as walking sticks anyway.

After waiting a day for the attack, which could not have failed to be our *coup de grâce,* and which did not come, Julius decided to send to Rear Headquarters for the twenty reinforcements who were to arrive that evening. Hugh Moore and myself were sent back with the message.

Next morning, just before we left Rear Headquarters with these reinforcements to rejoin the battery, two battalions of Australian infantry arrived to replace the evanescent Gwhalis, to save what was left of the original Muar force and to halt the Japanese.

All of these things they did in a savage battle that same day. They swept the Japanese back from the heights and our entire force—rescued and rescuers—then formed a hollow square round a crossroads called Barkri. This formation the Japanese attacked that night, and penetrated. Each side of the perimeter turned inwards and fired furiously at the intruders whilst in the centre of the holocaust men fought bitter hand-to-hand battles in the blackness. When dawn came, it was found that friend had bayoneted friend, foe foe, and that the .303 bullets poured so furiously inwards had gone, equally furiously, outwards to the other side of the perimeter and there settled in many an Australian limb. From that time onwards the order was that the enemy were to be engaged at night only with bayonets—and we gunners, who had previously used bayonets solely for the purpose of opening condensed milk and bully beef tins, now had to view these beastly weapons in a new and more serious light, which filled us with dismay.

Attacks and counterattacks continued furiously next day, with the Australian 19th and 29th Battalions more than holding their own against a division of Imperial Japanese Guards. Irritated by this unexpected delay, the Japs sent dive bombers to scour the rubber and heavy tanks to clear the road. But the bombs achieved little and the tanks were awaited by a troop of coldly determined anti-tank gunners who allowed them to approach within twenty yards and then swiftly destroyed five of them. The enemy then lost his taste for mechanized warfare and returned to his policy of infiltration and attacks from the rear—leaving the blazing tanks on the crossroads as a sign of our willingness to "mix it."

In full daylight the battery withdrew from Barkri crossroads about half a mile further back. From there we were to provide our infantry with fire support. All day long small-arms fire smacked around us as, once again, we started the inevitable ritual of digging in. Hugh Moore was with me and was not pleased.

"Dug thousands of these in the last few days," he complained. "What's the use of it?"—and then a dive bomber roared down and plastered the area with noise and metal and, as we crouched in our half-finished slit trench, we both knew what the use was. The task was completed in silence. I dug without a break for an hour. My clothes were soaking in a petrol tin of water, so I worked naked. All around our heads there were fierce detonations which the experts said were the crackers we had been told about by the intelligence officer. Most of the men were taking no risks: but I had watched for some time, observed no marks of any bullets on the sappy rubber trees and decided that crackers they were. Although terrified of bullets, I was not particularly worried by mere fireworks. I therefore ignored them and finished my job—thereby earning myself much undeserved praise as a "brave bastard" from those who, lacking my intelligence, had not identified the sharp explosion for the harmless crackers that they were.

Just as I finished the trench and dropped into it to snatch an hour's sleep, a gun sergeant stood up out of his shelter. Instantly he spun round clutching his neck with a hand that, even as the fingers twitched back from raw meat, quickly became scarlet. One of the "crackers" had struck him in the throat and blown most of it away. Once and for all the myth of harmless fireworks was exploded—they were bullets, and that was that. Shaking with retrospective terror, I crouched at the bottom of my slit trench and wondered whether I would ever regain sufficient courage to leave it.

From that moment onwards we were continuously dive-bombed. Our infantry, just a few hundred yards up the road, were badly mauled and their numbers reduced by half. Our communications with them—even over that short distance—were constantly disrupted by roving groups of enemy troops who cut field-telephone wires and machine-gunned despatch riders. The gunner who had been in the observation post with Shearer on the far side of the river, and who had miraculously escaped at that time, now met his death trying to get word through to the crossroads.

Having dug ourselves securely in, in a position that favoured us, and with our wounded tucked away in trucks in the centre of our position, we waited for the inevitable attack. That was the moment some half-wit with more seniority than sense chose to uproot us and move us back yet another few hundred yards to the edge of a padang. There we had no shelter, man-made or otherwise; our trucks were clearly visible from the skies and numerous tracks led like pointers to our lines. Since attack was imminent, we had no time to dig in and accordingly lay waiting behind whatever offered the most cover.

Hugh and I found a large ants' nest with a wide stump on its top. To the fury of the ants, we lay on the lee side of this—carefully spreading our ground sheets first, so that we would trick the death-dealing hookworm. We cocked rifles and waited.

Julius came up, brows black and bad-tempered as ever, and surveyed us—scowling.

"Good position," he said. "Move your water bottle into the shade, though—you'll need every drop before we're finished." Then he stumped off, halted and turned around again. "By the way," he added, "there's a message just come up from Base that tomorrow we'll get full aerial support. They say the sky'll be black with our planes. Pass it on. I've got to go to a brigade conference." For a second he stood staring through us with that same cynical lift of the eyebrow as when he had read the Australian "Drive them out of Malaya" order—as well he might. We had been given this same message every day for a week. So far we had seen no Allied planes at all. Abruptly he turned away and made off down to a bungalow on the edge of the padang, where the brigade officers were to meet.

"What'd he say?" the men farther down demanded.

"Sky'll be black with our planes tomorrow," I told them.

"What, again?" demanded Johnny Iceton: and someone else burst into "Tell me the old, old story": and all along the line the word was passed that some silly cow at Base had promised that next morning we would get full aerial support.

To give added weight to an already ponderous and palpable piece of official stupidity, a dive bomber lifted angrily over the crest of the hill, roared across the padang, wheeled sharply and (following the long line of staff cars which so sensibly led right up to the doorway of the bungalow wherein all our senior officers conferred) dropped a large aerial torpedo straight through its roof. Thenceforward we had no senior officers.

Ignoring the dive bomber and its spattering machine guns, men rushed down the hill from all sides to give what help they could. In the murderous scene of the wrecked and smouldering bungalow, Julius was one of the few who still lived—and he obviously would not live for long if he did not swiftly reach a casualty clearing station of some kind. We had no casualty clearing station. Dozens of men volunteered to try to get him back. After an ominous day's silence from our Rear Headquarters and B Echelon, it was obvious that the road back was no longer in our hands, but there were still those who were only too ready to attempt the run to get this one extraordinary man back where his life might be saved.

Eventually, with Julius protesting in his customary violent language, his driver, his Ack and an armoured car set out to run the gauntlet. Half an hour later a bloodied figure staggered into our perimeter. It appeared that eight hundred yards down the road their path had been blocked by fallen trees and their vehicles shot to ribbons by machine guns placed on both banks. This was the only survivor. Wearily he sat down and men dug bullets out of his broad back and patched him up whilst he held his head in his hands.

Quickly the report spread that the Black Bastard was dead: and everywhere—the atmosphere tautened by the knowledge that our best soldier had not survived and that we were now surrounded—expressions became grimmer.

Using their enormous superiority of numbers and their undisputed command of the air to advantage, the Japanese now exerted more pressure. One gun, detected from the air, had already been put out of action by a shower of mortar bombs which hit it and its crew squarely. The Japs were proving themselves most adept at this liaison between their aircraft and mobile land groups carrying mortars. The gun had been destroyed, its crew badly injured. Bluey Iceton came back with his arm torn almost off. He and the other injured men had been bundled into a truck and sent off down the road. We wondered now, in the light of Julius' fate, how far they had got.

But now more guns were being spotted and more violent attacks were being made on the hard-pressed infantry. The Jap attacked incessantly, sending in waves of fresh troops all through the days and nights, so that the Australians got no respite and no sleep.

We drew what was left of our guns back a quarter of a mile, so that they would clear the crest of the hill in front: chopped down hundreds of rubber trees—"to hell with the five-dollar fine," the gunners said, and laid about them with their axes—and sent over a heavy barrage, under cover of which, we hoped, the infantry would be able to fight their way back to us.

Eventually they did—whereupon we learnt that the situation at the crossroads had so fluctuated between the time when the infantry had given us their position and the time when we had laid down our barrage that most of our shells had fallen among Australians. They bore it with incredible equanimity.

"Ah," they shouted, as they beat in a steady line through the rubber towards us, "the bloody drop-short boys!" And when we realized what had happened and tried to tell them what we felt, they just grinned and said: "Don't matter, mate, gave us some encouragement to get back quicker. Would have been up there yet if youse hadn't hunted us out," and then they slouched off again in their long line, rifles outstretched, bayonets pointing slightly downwards, tousled hair springing from under tin hats and sticking damply to their foreheads. Only the weary eyes told you what they really felt about this last unkind blow that had added to the already fearful toll of their numbers.

Having thus united into the one small force, we set off at once to fight our way down the road until we established contact once more with our own command and supplies. From Julius' fate, and the fact that for days no ammunition or food had reached us, we knew that this was not going to be easy.

Consequently, all the vehicles—the artillery's tractors and few guns: the infantry's trucks: the commandeered cars and lorries (about fifty in all)—ran nose to tail down the road. In the vehicles were packed all our wounded—seven or eight, it seemed, to each truck. Onto tailboards, running boards, cabin roofs and mudguards clutched gunners and walking wounded. Along each side of the convoy, through the rubber, in a plodding, purposeful and determined fan, strode the infantry—always with that outstretched rifle and slightly down-pointed bayonet. Every bush and shrub was prodded and cleared. Every sniper in every tree was shot down. Every small, carefully concealed machine-gun nest was silenced. They made no fuss about it. They just plodded alongside, clearing our path, so that our whole unwieldy mass of men and machines ground forward in low gear, mile after mile, towards our goal.

We passed Julius' truck, its flank riddled up and down and from side to side with bullets: its inside ransacked. Julius, and his driver, and his escort had been torn to pieces. A few yards farther on the armoured car lay on its side. At a forced-march pace, the entire column passed the spot and headed south—towards no one quite knew what.

And every inch of the way the dive bombers roared up and down —leaving us only to refuel, when they would return, flying lower, slower and more searchingly than ever. But for some obscure reason, they refrained now from bombing our vehicles and were content only to spray the sides of the road with their machine guns. This lent an air of unreality to their presence, which was even more threatening and disturbing than being bombed.

"What the hell . . . ?" men queried, as they thundered overhead. And the wounded, lying in the trucks in bloodied heaps, would follow the course of the planes with their eyes—eyes that moved helplessly as they lay there unable to move an inch if the planes should suddenly decide to shoot up the convoy. We crawled on.

A cutting, long and deep, loomed ahead. In gnawing suspense we moved into it—perfect conditions for an ambush—and a mile later emerged, unscathed. We gunners heaved sighs of glorious relief, but the infantry plodded on like machines—nothing made any difference to them!

The wounded were asking for water, which was given freely—but with some anxiety because when our bottles were empty there would be no more purified water, and no means of purifying it other than boiling it. With their immense numerical superiority, the enemy gave no indication of allowing us the time to sit down and boil water.

An hour later we cleared the crest of a hill which sloped steadily downwards—and there, halfway down, was the explanation of our lack of supplies for the last two days. B Echelon, the source of all our food and ammunition, lay there stark, dead, shattered. The group had been caught unawares and wiped out.

Cooks were dead at the ashes of their fires. Accompanying infantry lay scattered all around, their skins blackening in the sun: trucks—even as they had attempted to escape with their ammunition—had been shot up. In silence, we crawled past what had been B Echelon. A series of violent, desolate scenes—starred windscreens: the dead crews: the clenched fist that protruded through the glass of a driver's window: the sweet stench.

In silence we collected the few tins of food that the attacking Japanese had not carried off. I moved a leg off a case of bully beef and tried not to notice that it belonged to the most cheerful driver in the regiment. We broke the case open and carted the contents out to our faithful infantry. Ten minutes later the whole of our convoy had passed the scene, rolling quietly downhill so that even the harsh grinding of Marmon Herringtons in low gear was for once subdued. And as the first truck reached the bottom of the long slope, the fierce yammering of a machine gun broke the silence. It came from ahead, round a slight bend.

Automatically we moved off at the double to silence that yammering, which could hold us up indefinitely, and give the enemy time once again to start mauling us from the rear. Quickly the infantrymen opened up with their mortars onto the road block which lay ahead. The gunners persuaded reluctant officers to permit a twenty-five-pounder to be fired off the macadamized road—a procedure which the textbook says is not good because the spade on the trail might be damaged by the recoil against such an unyielding surface.

Once again we witnessed a pleasant scene of aggression on our part. The mortar bombs—clearly discernible in the hard hot air—flew up in a graceful arc like so many cricket balls. The twenty-five-pounder cracked and flashed viciously, raising an instant shower of torn timber and dust and smoke where its shells exploded against the road block.

For a few seconds the yammering stopped and those of us who were closest to it seized axes from trucks and ran, crouching low, up to the fallen trees which formed the barrier across the road. While some chopped the tree trunks, others chopped the Japanese who lay behind them: others still lashed out at the machine-gun crew, now once again viciously firing. Beside me a youngster toppled backwards, his chest torn with bullets, into the arms of his friend. The older man held the youngster protectively until he died a few seconds later and then, his blue eyes glittering, went rushing in again with his axe flailing.

In a matter of minutes it was over. We tossed the chopped-up sections of tree trunks aside and the road was once more clear. With some curiosity we surveyed the dead Japs. Not a pair of spectacles amongst the lot. Every one a magnificent specimen of well-developed bone and muscle. Their equipment sensible, adequate and light. "Whackho for our Intelligence Reports," a voice commented quietly.

One of the infantry officers came up and surveyed our axemanship dispassionately. Rolling a Jap over with his boot, he commented: "Imperial Guards, eh," and hummed reflectively to himself. Since Imperial Guards meant no more to us than Imperial Bandycoots, we looked at him curiously. "Best troops they've got," he elucidated and returned to his men.

"Well, at least we know at last," Hugh remarked. "They can see —which we were told they couldn't. They can fight—which we were told they couldn't. And they're behind us for miles—which we were told they weren't." With that, we returned our axes to the trucks from which they came and the convoy, with renewed urgency, started off again.

Night fell abruptly, as nights do in tropical countries, and still the retreat to some place where there would be food and supplies continued. By now there was very little water left and the only canned food was unsweetened condensed milk. The wounded were in an appalling state. On our flanks, barely visible, we could hear the infantry pushing on firmly, hear the odd humming of a tune and, as a man tripped, the odd swearing of words which had come to be even more soothing to our strained nerves than music. For two hours the trucks ground on in low gear at the same walking pace, whilst we peered every second, with aching eyes, into the darkness, only too well aware that here lay excellent country for an attack. Steadily the hills around us flattened out.

"Getting near the Parit Sulong Causeway," Hugh muttered and I nodded agreement. There was something peculiarly ominous about the thought of that long straight stretch of road called the causeway. Slightly raised, it was flanked on either side by padi fields, so that, once on it, our convoy—and its escort—were irretrievably committed to fighting their way right across. The same fear crept into every heart. Were the Japs, as well as being hard on our heels, also at the other end of that causeway? Eyes peered more anxiously than ever into the blackness—and for their pains saw nothing but the forebodings of their own minds.

And then, at the same moment as the front truck swung into the flat country of the causeway, there came a faint shout from the invisible infantrymen just ahead. "Road blown and flooded." The causeway—either bombed or mined by the enemy—had, at its very start, become inundated by the water from the padi fields on either side and, to trucks driving under a complete blackout, seemed impossible even to find, let alone traverse. Instead of a roadway ahead, there lay only muddy water. Fifty trucks ground to a halt.

"It's on!" Hugh muttered.

"For young and old," agreed Johnny Iceton.

Standing on the tailboard of our truck, we leant over the canopy, and, shoving a round up the spout, laid our rifles flat on the canvas and clicked off the safety catches. All down the line of trucks, the carefully muffled metallic snap of rifles being cocked and the click of safety catches coming off broke the strained silence that hung over the approach to the causeway.

"What's doing, mate?" one of the wounded men whispered from under the canopy.

"Nothing. Bloody nothing," Johnny told him. "That's the trouble."

"Got any water to spare?" the same voice whispered. I shook my bottle—empty. Johnny shook his—empty. Hugh's splashed hollowly so he passed it inside over the body of the man nearest us, who was dead.

"Help yourself," he said.

"Can you spare it all?" came the whisper. "There's nine of us in here."

"Sure," Johnny told him, looking sourly out over the rippling surface of what had been the causeway, "we got plenty out here."

Far down the line of trucks a dying man groaned. Fireflies glowed momentarily in the black void around us. Some crickets with a warped sense of humour chirped cheerfully.

The whole convoy crouched still and waited in the darkness.

An elbow nudged me and an arm pointed. I followed the line of the arm, and, in my turn, nudged Johnny. Ahead a red glow—a mere pinpoint which was too still to be a firefly—shone in the dark. Beyond it another. Beyond that a third.

"Japs signalling," I thought and raised my rifle to take aim at the nearest red glow—which at once went out. All the occupants of the leading trucks were doing the same. When next those little lights came on quite a few of the sons of Nippon were going to join their forefathers. It was rather a satisfying thought.

A figure hove alongside our truck and whispered urgently, "See those lights?" I said, "Yes," and Johnny said, "My bloody oath." "Drive between 'em," the figure ordered. "It's our blokes on each side of the roadway drawing on fags. It'll be rough as guts but it's the best we can do"—and with that he scuttled off to the next vehicle.

Having extricated us from Muar and fought all the way from Barkri to Parit Sulong, our infantry friends were not to be frustrated now by a few flooded breaches in a causeway. They had waded out, found the edges of the road by feeling for them with their feet, and now stood on either side stolidly drawing on cigarettes held in their cupped palms.

The leading truck needed no encouragement. There was a splash; for a moment it seemed to flounder, and then it could be heard wading steadily through the water. Another followed, and a third. And the next instant we, too, were slopping our way down that dimly indicated lane. As the truck sogged into each crater and the engine protested violently at its watery reception, we manhandled it out again, always led on by the friendly warmth of a fag that glowed for one quick draw in a closely cupped hand.

For several miles this miracle of spontaneous organization was maintained. Somehow the path ahead—apparently just a featureless expanse of water—was always indicated by those silent infantrymen with their cigarettes. And as we passed each had a word of praise to offer as if we—and not they—were doing all the hard work.

"Good on you, Dig," they would whisper—and if you went over to where they stood up to their knees in water, they would at once say, "Here, have a drag," and thrust their cigarette firmly into your hand.

Hour after hour went by. Splashing, floundering, shoving—a few feet of dry road, and then it all started again. And just before dawn the first truck plodded up out of the padi water and onto the dry road that turned right and led straight into Parit Sulong village. Like a dog shaking itself after a bath, the truck bounded wetly off and rounded the bend. Behind it, vanishing in two long files across the padi, it left the infantry. Between these files the bodies of about fifty trucks could be faintly discerned plodding on. It was an exhilarating moment. In spite of every obstacle, we had escaped the trap. After ten days and nights of ceaseless fighting, and after sixty miles of weary slogging, we were out. Though few words were spoken (and those only in whispers), every face was filled with elation.

"Thank Christ for that," Johnny murmured. "Be able to have a feed, a bath and a sleep."

I leant under the truck's canopy to tell our wounded passengers the good news.

"How are you doing?" I asked.

"Fine . . ." "Couldn't be better . . ." came the answer. Men black with dried blood, their faces and lips looking like bits of boiled liver. I felt sick.

"Have you in hospital soon," I said, and hurriedly pulled my head out again so that I could throw up on the roadside. Hugh looked sympathetic, knowing my squeamishness about blood. Johnny grinned derisively. "Bloody hero you turned out to be," he remarked in affable undertones, "you great bronzed Anzac." I crawled back onto the tailboard.

"Off my back," I told him, "you're lucky I didn't faint!"

At the far end of the road, which turned right and ran into Parit Sulong village, there was an arched bridge. We had crossed it on our way up to Muar. It was perhaps a mile from the corner to that bridge. A mile of perfectly straight road flanked on each side by rubber. Two minutes later the leading truck roared back. It was badly shot up. The bridge, it reported, was strongly held by the Japanese.

So we hadn't escaped at all. After three or four furious bayonet charges against the bridge, it also became clear that we were not going to. It might be possible to swim that narrow river which the bridge spanned and escape as individuals; but the bridge itself was heavily defended with machine guns and mortars and there was no question of our capturing it and driving our trucks across.

This, then, was a death warrant for all the wounded men who lay in those trucks. It was decided that the only thing to do, rather than watch them slowly die as we fought it out, was to send the worst cases in trucks up to the bridge and ask the Japanese commander's permission to drive through his lines back to our own main force.

The Jap examined the passengers of each truck—making sure that they were all men who urgently required treatment. Then he gave his answer. Certainly they could pass through his lines—if the entire remainder of our force surrendered! Since the Japanese notoriously took no prisoners, this was not an altogether attractive proposition. The wounded men themselves answered it. "We'll go back to the rest and let them fight it out," they said. But neither is the Jap one to allow valuable bargaining weapons out of his hand simply because they arrive under a flag of truce.

"No," he said, "you will stay *here* while they fight"—and with that the machine guns and mortars opened up: the battle was on again. Now we all knew why our vehicles hadn't been bombed the previous day. The Jap had hoped to capture them intact for himself.

By this time all these vehicles were out of the padi and standing nose to tail in that straight mile of road that led to the bridge. Of our original Australian force of fifteen hundred at Muar, some five hundred were left. They faced a known ten thousand (possibly more) who had food, water, ammunition, automatic arms, strong aerial support and tanks—none of which things we had.

At the behest of Colonel Anderson of the infantry—a gentleman who was awarded one V.C. (which seemed to us quite inadequate) for his heroism—every man who could crawl and carry a rifle crept out of the trucks and into the rubber. There they formed a deep, single-rank hollow square round the core of vehicles and their cargo of wounded men.

Our side of the square, thinly manned with one soldier every few yards, faced back the way we had come. Whilst we scraped shallow holes with our bayonets in the glutinous black soil of the rubber plantation, the enemy troops pressed in. Fire from mortars was constant: snipers up trees made any position but the horizontal most uncomfortable: a splather of richocets off the road whined into the rubber whenever the dive bombers appeared. These we disliked even more than the bombs.

A few hundred yards back in the centre of the square some signallers attempted to establish contact with our own forces on the only field radio which still worked. Eventually they got through our urgent request for small-arms ammunition and drugs and received the encouraging message that the Loyals were trying to fight their way through to us from the other side of the bridge. Night fell with everyone cheerfully determined to hold on—if necessary—forever.

With the arrival of darkness, however, our anxieties increased. Early bayonet charges by the enemy having failed, they began systematically to mortar the long line of trucks as well as our own positions. The ammunition limber of our only working twenty-five-pounder was hit and burst into a most spectacular blaze. Its explosion and the evil glare it cast behind us (silhouetting us quite clearly) caused the Japanese to shout triumphantly from out of their circle of gloom. Fire poured in at us from all sides, so that the small scraped-up mounds of earth, and the rubber trees, behind which we lay, spurted dirt and latex all over us.

The only cheerful event up to that time was that a young subaltern had released the hand brake of each of the trucks of wounded kept as hostages at the bridge and these had slid gently backwards, unnoticed in the darkness, down the approach to the bridge, and were now once again within our perimeter.

I lay between Hugh and Johnny. A few feet away Piddington was attempting to contract his six feet two inches into a depression no more than four feet in length. He wasn't very successful, but it was giving him something to do and he always liked being kept occupied.

Another bayonet attack was repelled. After it we decided to take it in shifts to sleep. The enemy paused for thought.

We had been asleep for perhaps ten seconds—it couldn't possibly have been more than ten seconds—when we were pommelled into a terrified wakefulness again. Somewhere, something was wrong. A strange noise—frightening because it was strange—and menacing. One could feel the hairs tingling at the back of one's neck; and, still more, one could feel the electric anticipation that flashed round our whole line. What bastardry were the little monkeys up to now?

The problem quickly resolved itself. From a distant and ominous rumble accompanied by authoritative shouts from the gloom on all sides—one assumed the enemy to be passing orders from one attacking group to another—the noise grew into the fast-approaching clatter of heavy machinery. Tanks! And then abruptly, into the now fading circle of light cast by the burning limber, the first brute nosed its way. Behind it one perceived, vaguely, another; behind that others still.

So that was it. Having failed to break our line by direct frontal attack during the day, and unable to locate it at night, the enemy now proposed to taunt us into fire by examining our position from a few feet off—in which case our whole line would be revealed; or to locate our exact position from the turret of the tank and then enfilade us into oblivion. They seemed to have it all their own way. Not a man moved a muscle. Not a sound broke the silence that fell now as the tank halted and an insolently fearless head appeared from its turret to try to draw our fire and so fix where our line lay. No one rose to the bait of that head; no one fired; no flash told the tank crew where we hid. The tank stood some forty feet away from us down the road, and searched, and waited. So did we. Who would break first?

Darkness and electric silence.

A voice whispering behind me suddenly removed my petrified gaze from the fateful tank.

"Braddon," it said, "go with Moore, take hand grenades and get that tank out of the way."

Seldom had I heard a sillier suggestion. The officer who issued this order so airy-fairily had been at school with Moore and myself. To both of us, however, he seemed to be grossly overrating the significance of this fact. Going to school was not, we both felt, at all adequate or reasonable grounds for ordering a grenade attack on a tank. We were in the Army though, and there, it appeared, what was reasonable no longer applied. Perspiring with terror, we accepted three hand grenades each, with great ill-grace, and began to shorten the forty feet between us and the tank by wriggling forward on our quivering bellies, writhing in the flickering shadows cast by rubber trees.

That forty feet had, when the tanks first appeared, seemed so short a distance as to be quite horrifying. It now, as we left it, assumed the proportions of something safe and respectable. I regret to state that I wriggled with a lack of speed that was only exceeded by my lack of conviction. Sydney's whispered "Good luck" and Moore's mute glance of fellow feeling had in no way increased my strength of purpose. I had no love for this strange consequence of the chance that had settled my place of education. Moore was ahead of me. We were both getting close enough to the menacing machine to have to give some serious thought to the means whereby we were to deposit six hand grenades down the hatch—and then, most important of all, depart with sufficient speed to avoid annihilation.

There was the moment when, from our rear, a lone gunner chose to shout out: "clear line; down in front." Utterly amazed, Moore and I looked round. There, not more than twenty yards away, working at the gun, silhouetted by the glare of the lurid fire, was a solitary figure. With great deliberation, he lined up the barrel of the gun and—in the absence of any sights—looked along it. He was very careful to take true aim. He was not at all careful for himself. Seconds ticked into minutes. He straightened up, apparently satisfied that his aim was good. But, as a precaution, in case he missed, he went to the nearest truck and found another shell.

Then, returning deliberately, he looked to see that his line was still clear, and fired. The blast from the gun joined the blast from the tank as the shell hit it—one long sheet of blinding flame. From within the tank, as it burst into flames, came shrill screams. Without further ado, Moore and I legged it back to our line—still too stupefied even to think.

The second shell, with scant respect for the might of Nippon, was dispatched the way of the first and shattered the next tank down the road (now well lighted up by the flames coming from its predecessor). Those tanks which lay farther down waited no longer, but turned and fled. Very sensible of them. The solitary gunner had now been joined by most of the crew, and they were all raring for action.

For the moment, then, we were safe again. Everywhere the line hummed with whispered words about this miraculous shot from a semi-disabled gun. Everywhere men reminded one another that the only other attempt to fire that gun had resulted in the instant death by machine-gun fire of the men who manned it. There was no doubt in any of our minds that if it hadn't been for that one coldly calculated shot the enemy tanks would eventually have run us to earth and obliterated us all.

Piddington stammered in his excitement. "That was Jack Menzies fired that gun, wasn't it?" he asked. Moore and I both said, "Yes." We felt an overwhelming affection for Jack Menzies, even if he hadn't been at school with us. "Should get half a dozen medals," Sydney said. "Did you see him? Mad, he was. Took hours lining her up. Mad. Should get a medal." Needless to say, he didn't—someone else did, but Jack didn't. Yet without that shot no one would have left Parit Sulong and this story would never have been told.

Two infantrymen, who lay beside us, seemed to have enjoyed the whole incident most thoroughly—except for the firing of the twenty-five-pounder, which they declared was "bloody 'orrible." Hugh and I now suggested that they should sleep for a while—we would keep watch. They at once agreed and immediately fell asleep, lying on their backs with their heads pillowed in their tin helmets. Hugh and I then decided to take it in turns to watch, and Hugh, too, went to sleep. I was to wake him in an hour.

My hour's watch was not peaceful. Three trucks were set alight by mortar fire and the men in them incinerated before anyone could lift them out. A few yards to the right the Japs attacked heavily and were repulsed. Ahead their officers shouted an order which was then relayed right round their positions so that, as one followed the sound of the voices, one realized just how securely we were encompassed. And the harsh bellows had barely died down in that outer gloom when a vague figure flitted towards us, flitted from tree to tree. At first I thought it was merely a product of my imagination (which I knew to be fruitful). When it was only three rubber trees away I realized uneasily that it was, in fact, a Japanese soldier. Terrified because of my inefficiency with the bayonet (not to mention a natural tendency to terror anyway), I shook the two infantrymen and Hugh. But I might as well have shaken the tree behind me—one does not awaken, after four days and nights without sleep, at the mere shake of a hand. So, in desperation, I moved alone to the tree in front of me and, as the Jap ran crouching towards it, stepped out from behind it and presented him with a firmly held rifle and bayonet. Upon this he promptly impaled himself. At the moment of impact, as I tucked my right elbow securely against my hip and moved my left foot slightly forward, I found myself thinking, "Just like a stop volley at tennis"—and spent the next hour musing, rather confusedly, over the unpleasantness of a situation which compelled one to apply the principles of a clean sport to the altogether dirty business of killing.

Daylight came. The victim of my stop volley lay with his mouth wide open showing good teeth. I wished that he would shut it. The burnt-out tanks squatted grotesquely on the roadside ahead. And even as I surveyed them, with a resentful stare, Johnny Iceton let out a howl of dismay as a sniper whanged a bullet onto the right-hand side of his tin hat. Ten minutes later the same sniper whanged another bullet onto the left-hand side of his tin hat, and, to emphasize the point, shot the woodwork off the barrel of my rifle, which I found extremely unnerving. Half an hour later two mortar bombs warbled their way evilly over towards our group. One killed the infantryman on my right; the second landed, with great violence but without exploding, between Johnny's legs. Gazing with unashamed horror at his doubly dented helmet and the bomb that stood vertically on its nose between his knees, Johnny emitted a wail of anguish and demanded of the world in general: "Jesus Christ, what are they trying to do to me?"—which provided the only laugh of the day.

That was too much for Johnny. Standing up, he eyed us morosely. "Heartless mob of bastards you are," he declared, "you'll be sorry though," he assured us. "I'm tired of the war on this side of the perimeter. It's too dangerous. I'm going to fight the war on the other side now," and with that he walked deliberately off, defying the sniper, as he presented a broad young back and a cockily tilted though bent tin hat, to hit him a third time.

A last message came through on our dying radio. The Loyals had been beaten back in their attempt to fight through to us. We were alone. Australia, it said, was proud of us—which was nice.

I crawled back to our truck determined to salvage a map out of it. The lanky Piddington had a compass. With a map we could make our way through to Mersing on the east coast if our perimeter was broken and we were driven into the jungle. At Mersing we felt the fight would be on more equal terms.

All nine men in the truck were dead and the map roll was badly perforated by bullets that had come down at a steep angle—machine-gunning from the air. I found the right maps and also, inside the roll, two tins of condensed milk.

On the way back to what I now regarded as "my" side of the square, I passed clumps of wounded men lying together—smoking and dressing each other's injuries—casualties of the night's bayonet raids, of the bombing and sniping. Near the last clump I was amazed to see a fellow gunner raise a heavy Boye's anti-tank rifle to his shoulder, aim high and fire. He was at once flung yards backwards, whilst the half-inch shell most certainly passed harmlessly into the stratosphere. When I reached him he was rubbing his shattered right shoulder and swearing softly but with that consummate fluency which is the prerogative of the Australian farmer who is perpetually harassed by the cussedness of things inanimate.

"What the hell are you trying to do, Harry?" I asked.

"Get that bloody sniper up the top of that bloody tree," he replied tersely. It appeared that, fired off the ground, the Boye's rifle had not sufficient elevation to hit a tree high up. However, since the sniper fired from *behind* the top of the tree trunk he could only be shot *through* it—a Boye's rifle was, therefore, essential for the job. We decided to do it together. With the barrel resting on my shoulder, the butt against his own, Harry took a long aim, apparently quite undeterred by the bursts of bullets from all sides which our stance attracted. I was not in the least undeterred. In fact, as we stood there, our feet spread wide apart to take some of the shock, I was very deterred indeed. Then Harry fired and I was crushed to the ground and Harry was flung against a tree and the sniper toppled gracelessly out from behind his trunk, thudding onto the earth below, and the job was done. I left Harry, still swearing volubly and rubbing his shoulder, and crept back to the line of men I now knew so well. We opened one tin of milk with a bayonet and passed it along, from outstretched hand to outstretched hand, as each lay flat behind his little mound of earth, one mouthful a man. It was very refreshing—our first meal since the previous midday when we had passed B Echelon. On that occasion we had had the same thing. It looked like becoming our staple diet.

The youthful infantryman who had spent the night on my left was hit in the right thigh soon after I got back. An angry blue line deep into the flesh indicated the path of the bullet. He said nothing and kept on firing as the leg oozed blackish blood.

In response to our last urgently radioed request for drugs and small arms, and aerial support, the Air Force proved the quality of both its heroism and its equipment by lumbering up the road at treetop level in what must have been the oldest biplane in the world still capable of becoming airborne. Unfortunately (probably owing to the faulty functioning of our radio), the small arms and drugs were dropped very deliberately among the Japanese, whilst, to provide aerial support, one very large bomb was deposited with loving care into the middle of our own perimeter. It fell on a group of men at the edge of the road—signallers who were trying to rig up another field radio. When the smoke cleared and the rubber leaves stopped showering off blasted trees, we gunners precipitately left the protection of the line to our most competent infantrymen and doubled back to where the bomb had fallen. Three rubber trees lay uprooted: a huge crater gaped like a burst boil; and, of the group of men who had stood there, all that could be discovered was one boot, one shoulder blade and one tin hat—a tin hat with a dent on the right-hand side and another dent on the left-hand side. Without a second's hesitation, as I saw that doubly dented helmet, I lent over a bough of one of the uprooted trees and—for the second time in Johnny's presence—threw up.

Stopping only long enough to collect a field dressing out of one of the trucks, Hugh and I returned to the line. We tied up the infantryman's bluish thigh, which by this time seemed to have locked itself and refused to move at all. This done, we devoted our energies and attention to the enemy in front of us.

Mortars fired on us with increasing fury—many of the bombs, we noted with pleasure, failing to explode. "Can't have had their temperatures taken or their bottoms wiped," Hugh explained.

The day wore on. Beards were noticeably longer, faces noticeably leaner and eyes more sunken. Every man's back and legs were splattered with black spots of congealed latex which had spurted from the bullet-torn rubber trees under which we lay. I looked all along the line. Every man the same. A detonation jolted me. Just across the road a bakelite grenade had exploded under the chin of one of the reinforcements with whom Hugh and I had returned to Barkri days before. As blood gushed out of a torn throat, he said to his companion: "I'm done for, Reg," and prepared stoically to die—whereupon Reg said, "Like hell you are," and, binding up the throat so tightly that it could no longer bleed and its owner scarcely breathe, he presented the patient with his rifle and said: "Now get cracking." Looking chalk-coloured but determined, the wounded man did what he was told. The next second he brandished his smoking rifle in the direction of the now defunct grenade thrower and announced, in a most unchristian croak of triumph: "Got the little bastard"—which he indubitably had.

With the arrival of midday, it became obvious that very few men had more than a handful of ammunition left and that we could not hope to survive another night of tank-supported attack. Our position had ceased to be of any value in the over-all defence of the west coast. Using the small boats left to them so thoughtfully by the evacuees of Penang, the Japanese had landed at every port and inlet down the peninsula, including one of the southernmost towns—Batu Pahat. We were now a hundred miles behind the main Japanese point of attack on the west coast. Militarily we were valueless until and unless we rejoined the forces in central Malaya at Yong Peng or those on the east coast at Mersing, there to fight again.

As against this point of view was an almost insuperable aversion to deserting those of the wounded—who now almost outnumbered the fit—whom we could not take with us if we attempted to fight our way out of our encirclement.

A military decision was made. To fight on meant annihilation for all. To attempt a break-through probably meant the same thing, but doubtless came under the heading of "justifiable war risk." We were, therefore, to endeavour to escape from Parit Sulong: the wounded would, after our departure, officially surrender. We were ordered to take all that we could in the way of equipment and our wounded companions: to leave the line one at a time, alternate men moving: to find our own way out through the Japanese lines and thence proceed independently to *any* British position *anywhere.* The route and strategy of every man was left to the decision of the individual himself. Having for a year or more industriously trained us to "do what we were told: *not* to think," the military machine now cheerfully announced: "The order is—Every man for himself."

With men leaving at about ten-second intervals, bearing rifles, hand grenades and companions as they went, the line rapidly thinned. Most men headed towards the thickly timbered right flank and vanished into it. After an hour the entire perimeter was manned only by a small handful of soldiers, two machine guns and one tommy gun—and still the Japanese failed to realize that their prize was slipping through their fingers. The lanky Piddington, the man on the nearest machine gun, Hugh and myself had decided to leave together. We would head for Yong Peng—fifty miles away in a straight line. Carrying the infantryman with the bluish thigh, two rifles each and the machine gun—with shirts which bulged with hand grenades—we ran, in short bursts and crouched low, to the right flank. We took a last horrified glance back at the area that had been our battle ground and at the clumps of wounded lying huddled round trees, smoking calmly, unafraid. Then we crawled into the heavily wooded fringe of the plantation and left the fight behind. We wriggled half a mile on our stomachs under dense vines and low foliage (dragging the rifles, the machine gun and the infantryman behind us), and at last—after an hour's fearful progress—considered ourselves outside the Japanese circle. As Hugh cleared a small patch of ground under the vine below while we crouched, I started unrolling the map. Meantime the machine gunner gazed contemptuously backwards towards the enemy: "Well, how's their rotten form?" he asked. "Millions of 'em and they let us all get out. Yer wouldn't read about it, would yer?" Nodding our heads solemnly, we all agreed that you wouldn't read about it and returned to the more serious business of the map and our route to Yong Peng.

It appeared that between Parit Sulong, where we crouched in the undergrowth, and Yong Peng, where we hoped to find a British force, lay a fairly high mountain, an extensive swamp and a great deal of jungle. It was about fifty miles.

By midnight, having kept at it solidly, we had covered about ten miles. By that time we had met many odd men and groups of men all heading steadily eastwards; and then, taking advantage of our map and compass, had joined us. We were then about forty strong.

We lay down to sleep when pouring rain made it impossible either to take a bearing or to read the compass. Three hours later we woke and started off again in an agony of cramped muscless. So painful was this period that most men refused to rest again and remained standing whenever a halt was called to consult the map or the compass.

An officer suggested blandly that the map would be of more value in his hands. Though we did not for one second believe it, we handed the map over—having first made a copy of all the data we needed. Distances, bearings, prominent features; the mountain, the swamp and river were all jotted down in Piddington's notebook.

"I'll lead," announced the officer.

We reached the mountain. At its summit a track appeared. We followed it until, over the crest, it forked.

"Right," said the officer.

"Left," said Piddington, as we checked the compass. We went left.

We entered the swamp. It was impossible there to carry both weapons and our wounded, so the weapons were dumped in the brown water. Leeches battened onto limbs, swelled large and black and then dropped off with a plump plop into the swamp—leaving a steady flow of blood where they had bitten. Walking one moment on floating logs, the next in water up to the waist, we covered another five or six miles.

As we emerged, enemy planes appeared low overhead, angrily searching for the prey they had allowed to escape at Parit Sulong. When they roared across our path, every man sank beneath the sluggish brown water and stayed there till he had either to surface or make his submersion permanent. We were not seen. The hookworms, one could not help feeling, were having a field day.

There was a patch of easygoing country for a few miles out of the swamp where rice had been sown. We marched across the raised track in the middle of the padi field. Every few minutes the whole long file, now about a hundred strong, had to sink into the water as more planes wheeled overhead.

We passed out of the padi into more jungle. Another three hours of most unpleasant travelling. Some men were so exhausted that even their hand grenades had to be jettisoned. Feeling that they might still be needed, I kept four down the front of my shirt: but we dumped the machine gun and our rifles and our .303 ammunition.

The jungle thinned and our party, now about one hundred and forty strong as men seeped into it from all sides, halted to discuss the next move. A hundred of the infantry decided against carrying on on our bearing to Yong Peng—which they maintained would already have fallen to the Japanese—and announced their intention of resting for twelve hours, then detouring north of Yong Peng and heading for the east coast. The rest of us carried on. Hunger, thirst and exhaustion had become obsessions.

The jungle vanished and, worse still, the swamps reappeared. At this the officer with the map announced a halt. Hugh, Piddington, the machine gunner and myself, however, carried straight on. We were not stopping till we got to Yong Peng. In a few moments, having been joined by two others (one a gunner officer), the remainder of the party were lost to sight behind us and we were up to our necks in water. Hugh and I, preferring anything to this wading, began to swim. Piddington, with his superior height, still waded. The other three ploughed along behind.

A few minutes after leaving the remainder of the party behind us, we noticed sampans hidden in the mangroves. Heading with a leisurely crawl towards them, we found them to be occupied by Malays, who gazed at us very curiously indeed. We were in no mood to be gazed at curiously. We had walked thirty miles in thirty hours: we had not eaten anything for three days and very little for seven days: fate, we felt, had not been kind to us—and now Malay boatmen looked at us curiously. Ignoring their inhospitable gestures, we all clambered aboard.

"Hullo, Joe," I said, *"ada Japoon?"* Joe waggled his head disinterestedly from side to side. There were no Japanese about, it appeared. "Thank Christ for that," commented the machine gunner; and Piddington, who spoke no Malay at all, then leant over to the boatman and, dripping courteously all over him, asked amiably: *"Apa changkol dua malam?"*—which means literally, "What hoe two night" and was the Australian's idea of the greeting, "Whatho tonight?" The Malay stared at him coldly and replied, *"Tidak tau."* He didn't understand. We laughed and I told him what we wanted.

"Pigi Yong Peng," I said, and when the boatman looked a little mutinous about going to Yong Peng, I took a hand grenade from the front of my shirt, and Hugh examined his rifle, and the boatman at once ceased looking mutinous.

We collected two other sampans and sent them back to the head of the swamp to collect the remainder of the party. Then we made our way steadily and silently down narrow oily waterways, under leprous mangrove boughs and jungle vines, until eventually we emerged from these slimy tunnels into a broad river.

There the planes searched again. But we hugged the high eroded bank and, with clumps of lalang grass attached picturesquely to our tin hats, our clothing and our boatman, endeavoured to look as much like a bit of Malaya as possible. We were scared frequently, but we were not bombed.

We drank many gallons of the river—which grew steadily less brackish as we proceeded. By dusk—the fiery red sort of dusk one would expect on the conclusion of a nasty episode in a nasty war—we had all lulled our appetites with river water and our tired bodies grew relaxed with the peaceful motion of a sampan which is paddled by someone else. We eventually drew into a canal off the river and the boatman pointed left. "Yong Peng," he announced. We clambered out and started walking.

A mile later we met a native. "Japoon," he hissed at us in terror and sped off into the rubber. Another half mile and we met an officer. "Yong Peng?" he said, in reply to our questions. "About six miles. It'll be held for a couple of days. How many of you coming? You're the first." So our officer, whilst we congratulated ourselves on being first out and, therefore, first due for baths, clothes and food, told him, "A couple of hundred"—and was then struck by a thought.

"Someone should go back for that infantry party," he said. This proposition undoubtedly would have had merit if it had been addressed to men who were not in the last stages of exhaustion; *and* if what the other officer said about Yong Peng being held for another two days were true (which was not really probable since no such official forecast had stood the test of time for at least six weeks now); *and* if the infantry party concerned had been the kind of gentlemen likely to be dissuaded from a carefully considered decision by any message which, when it reached them, would be at least twelve hours old. Since none of these conditions existed, I looked at the speaker with complete lack of enthusiasm. I belonged to the school of "If you get a bright idea, do it yourself." He returned my look unmoved. He gave no indication of doing anything himself, but instead stared at Hugh. There was an unpleasant silence. I also belonged to the school of "If there's an unpleasant silence, for God's sake say something, even if it's silly." So did Hugh. We said something very silly indeed. "We'll go," we said, and next instant—the officer having promised us guides who would be left to await our return at that position where we then stood: and having been bid an almost sentimental *au revoir* by the three other men—"See you in Singapore," they said—Hugh and I were heading back down the track again. Heading west, into the angry sunset, away from Yong Peng.

"Wars," said Hugh, "are bloody stupid." I could not have agreed more.

The boatman was reluctant to return up the river. I produced my hand grenade again. We started up the river. As we slipped through the quiet, oily water, Hugh and I discussed, with some rancour, the last words we'd heard: "See you in Singapore."

"Think we will, Hugh? I asked him. He looked tired and, for the moment, didn't seem to care whether we did or not. "What do you think?" he asked.

I said optimistically that I was sure we would, and then added, more honestly: "But I think we'll be hoofing it all the way. I don't see us getting to Yong Peng before the Nips."

Hugh looked greatly depressed at the prospect of walking all the way to Singapore. "If we do have to," he finally summed it up, "we've got to have a ruddy great sleep and a dirty big feed first," and with that he proceeded to put the first part of his programme into immediate effect.

We reached the head of the swamp, passing again through the dank tunnels of mangrove, finding them just as bewildering as before. Then, after crawling through the mud, we marched for some hours up the same track we had so recently descended until halted by a voice out of the gloom, which challenged us in tones that were not to be disputed. We gave our names.

"Never heard of you," the voice answered disagreeably, and—still more disagreeably—clicked back an invisible, though clearly audible, safety catch. We hurriedly quoted the names of every footslogger we had ever known in an urgent attempt to endear ourselves to this unseen and obviously unfriendly sentry. Finally, he said: "All right, come on." So we went forward again.

We asked for the officer in charge. We told our story. We told him the report that Yong Peng would be held for another eighteen hours. We told him the way there.

He called us bloody fools to come back; pointed out that his party had made it clear that their decision had been final *not* to go to Yong Peng, and reaffirmed that decision. Then, a little more sympathetically, he asked why we had come back. One could hardly say, "Because there was an unpleasant silence," so we just said, "For the walk—it's a nice evening," and left.

No one ever saw that party again and the presumption is that they met the enemy in force somewhere on their wide detour of Yong Peng and were wiped out.

We staggered back to the swamp. Hugh, still weak from his long illness in hospital just before the events of Muar, was now completely exhausted. He needed sleep and food—but most of all sleep—and he needed them at once. I felt heartless as I kept dragging him along, refusing to allow him to lie down. Intuitively, though, I felt that only a terrific effort could get us to Yong Peng before the Japanese. We pressed on.

We got back to the sampans—and this time I arrived flaunting two hand grenades, which must have made their impression, because we set sail at once. Down through the evil tunnels, now misty and dank: out into the moonlit river: down to the canal. I woke Hugh and we started walking.

Twice he fell to the ground sound asleep. Each time I woke him, dragging him up, almost hysterical myself. "We've got to get to those guides," I told him, "before it's too late." "Blast the guides," he replied, "I want to sleep."

The third time he fell I couldn't wake him. No amount of shaking stirred him. We still had about half a mile to go to the point whence we had started back. I lost my head and my temper and kicked him. He groaned and stood up. With his arm round my neck and mine under his armpit, we staggered up the path. "Sorry, Hugh," I said.

"Doesn't matter, Russ," he replied, "how much farther?"

"Not far," I said, "you'll be right."

Thus we reached our departure point. The moon had gone. It was very dark. The track was completely deserted. There were no guides there—no one. Only mosquitoes and the croaking of frogs.

We sagged to the ground without a word and instantly Hugh was dosing. As he was drowsing off, Hugh, in tones of utter indifference, asked what would happen if the Nips came.

"Maybe they'll think we're dead," I said, hopefully.

"Close enough to it, anyhow," Hugh muttered, and I put his head in his tin hat, pillow-wise; adjusted my own tin hat in the same way; placed a grenade ready by his side and three by my own and, in another second, joined him in the bliss of unconsciousness.

We were awakened, it seemed, almost immediately. A glare fell into my eyes and, filled with wild terror, I grabbed at the grenades by my side. I could see nothing beyond that glare. I remembered the native who had said "Japoon" and scuttled off into the jungle. I remembered that the guides promised us so faithfully by the officer had vanished. Now this glare: and I was very frightened indeed because it came from a powerful torch held inches from my face, while I lay helpless on my back and beside me, still sound asleep, lay Hugh.

And then a surprised voice said, "It's Braddon and Moore," and the moment of terror passed. There were seven of them—Australians—and we joined them, now sufficiently rested to attempt the last six miles to Yong Peng, using the torch to find the faint track.

It was only when we had covered about three miles and the sky was beginning to lighten with the false dawn that I remembered that my four grenades still lay on the track at the canal where we had slept. Carefully I put the thought away from me that they would ever be needed. No one else in our small band had any arms.

We reached the road which led down into the town at dawn. What we saw was not pretty. Many dead in the foreground and, at the bottom of the hill, a shattered bridge and thousands of milling men in a uniform that was not familiar.

"Japs!" announced one of our party. I looked at him and nodded. He should know, I thought, recognizing him as Harry—the gentleman who shot snipers out of trees, using anti-tank rifles from the standing position.

From the bottom of the hill the Japs shouted at us rudely. We did not stop to argue but quickly crossed the road and ran into the rubber. There was not much time to make plans.

Our party now consisted of three gunners, one officer, one sergeant, two signalmen and two infantrymen—nine in all.

"Where to now?" demanded one of the infantrymen.

"Singapore," three of us answered simultaneously.

"How far's that?" demanded the same infantryman.

"About a hundred miles," said the officer.

"Jesus," said the second infantryman, a gentleman who for some obscure reason sported not boots but sandshoes, "I couldn't walk that far."

"Then you bloody better crawl," Hugh told him curtly (Hugh did not suffer fools gladly), with which we started off on the second leg of our trip from Parit Sulong.

We passed an open, mass Japanese grave which made us feel a little better. Then, as the sun rose higher, we passed heaps of British bodies and the air swam with humidity and the stench of death. Next we came to an abandoned native hut. I broke in and found a tin of condensed milk crawling with ants and half empty. We scooped out a finger-tipful of milk and ants each. As we started off again, two Tamils—rubber tappers—appeared a few hundred yards ahead. They halted, startled, for a second as they saw us, then padded swiftly off over the hill, their sarong-clad hips swaying and their bare feet splayed wide.

We worked on a "two-man-ahead patrol" system—on the All Clear from them the remaining seven moved up, whereupon the next two took over. Thus we leapfrogged for about two hours. Hugh and I patrolled together: Harry and the first infantryman, called (we now learnt) Herc: the two young sigs: and the sergeant and Sandshoes.

The latter pair were now ahead. We waited for their "All Clear."

"Pair of no-hopers, they are," declared Harry acidly, as he lay with his feet resting high up against a rubber tree, "done nothing but bellyache ever since we started."

There was a moment's silence whilst everyone thought of the undoubted degree of the no-hopers' capacity for bellyaching.

"O.K.," said one of the sigs, "she's clear up ahead." We looked up and saw the sergeant waving us forward.

Harry got to his feet and Herc with him. Roy and Rene, the sigs, followed with the officer. Hugh and I brought up the rear. As fast as possible we walked forward to where the two bellyachers waited and then on along their patrolled beat. We had covered perhaps fifty yards of it when we cleared the first small rise in the rubber. The jungle lay cosily by our left hand. We trotted down the far side of the rise. And instantly the air was full of bullets, whilst ahead of us and to our right about fifty yards away, with automatic weapons blazing, were Japanese soldiers. We had walked straight into an ambush. The bellyachers had funked their patrol.

I didn't wait to see what happened. I was off at once, sprinting wildly, towards that jungle on the left. Beside me, I was aware without seeing him, ran Hugh. Cursing myself for every fool in the world, I thought yearningly of those four beautiful hand grenades now lying uselessly beside a canal the other side of Yong Peng.

"Stop there," I heard the officer's clear voice directed at us, "stop and surrender or we'll all be shot"—and my absurd Army training made me falter for a second and look back. I saw Herc already bleeding from a wound in the arm; and Sandshoes and the sergeant lying on the ground; and the officer standing quite still, the sigs looking at him questioningly and Harry in outrage. Just for a second we faltered. As in any race, when one falters, it was then too late. The path to the jungle was cut by a Jap soldier with a tommy gun. We stood still, our only chance lost. Then, very slowly, very foolishly and with a sense of utter unreality, I put up my hands.

At that moment all that occurred to me was that this procedure was completely disgraceful. I have not—since then—changed my mind. I have no doubt at all that I should have continued running. One does not win battles by standing still and extending the arms upwards in the hope that one's foes have read the Hague Convention concerning the treatment of Prisoners of War. It was unfortunate that the Army had trained me sufficiently neither to disobey instantly and without hesitation, nor to obey implicitly and without compunction. Accordingly, I had done neither: and I now stood in the recognized pose of one who optimistically seeks mercy from a conqueror whose reputation is for being wholly merciless.

The enemy patrol closed in on us. Black-whiskered men, with smutty eyes and the squat pudding faces of bullies. They snatched off our watches first of all—and then belted us with rifle butts because these did not point to the north as they swung them around under the ludicrous impression that they were compasses. They made dirty gestures at the photographs of the womenfolk they took from our wallets. They threw the money in the wallets away, saying, "Dammé, dammé, Englishu dollars": and, pointing at the King's head on the notes, they commented: "Georgey Six number ten. Tojo number one!" And all the time two Tamils stood in the background, murmuring quietly to one another, their hips tight-swathed in dirty check sarongs and their wide-splayed feet drawing restless patterns in the bare soil of the rubber plantation.

"Done a good job, haven't you, Joe?" demanded Harry savagely—but they wouldn't meet his eye. Just kept on drawing in the dirt with their toes.

Hugh picked up a ten-dollar bill and stuffed it defiantly back in his pockets. Then they tied us up with wire, lashing it round our wrists, which were crossed behind our backs and looped to our throats. They prodded us onto the edge of a drain in the rubber. We sat with our legs in it, while they set their machine guns up facing us and about ten yards away.

"That bloody intelligence officer would have to be right this time of all times, wouldn't he?" demanded Harry—we all knew that he referred to the "Japanese take no prisoners" report, and Herc, bleeding badly, nodded rather wanly.

"We must die bravely," said the officer desperately—at which the sergeant howled for mercy. Howled and pleaded, incredibly craven. Neither he nor Sandshoes had been hit at all when I had seen them prostrate on the ground, merely frightened. The sergeant continued to bawl lustily. We sat, the nine of us, side by side, on the edge of our ready-dug grave.

The Japanese machine gunner lay down and peered along his barrel. It was my twenty-first birthday and I was not happy.

At the first long volley of shots I jerked rigid, dragging my right wrist out of its wire binding, but experiencing no emotion other than a faint surprise that I was still alive. A second volley rang out, and still the anticipated tearing of bullets into flesh was absent. Then I looked up and realized that the machine gun was firing not at us in the trench but up the slight rise at a solitary figure who dashed across the sky line. Japanese soldiers were fanning quickly out through the rubber and his flight was obviously hopeless. In a few moments he was dragged down the hill to where we sat. He was an officer of our regiment, fair-haired, tall and lean. They tied him up with his own puttees, at which he protested indignantly. He wore that most useless of all weapons, a .45 revolver. His captors quickly took it from him.

Under cover of all this, I had untied Hugh, and he the sigs, and they were about to unloose Sandshoes, when the sergeant noticed what was happening and let out a wail of terror which got us all lashed up again, this time with a narrow, cutting rope. I was beginning not to love the sergeant.

The Japanese, of whom there were about fifteen, held a conference. They were squat, compact figures with coarse puttees, canvas, rubber-soled, web-toed boots, smooth brown hands, heavy black eyebrows across broad unintelligent foreheads, and ugly battle helmets. Each man wore two belts—one to keep his pants up and one to hold his grenades, his identity disc and his religious charm—and when they removed their helmets, they wore caps, and when they took off their caps, their heads had been shaved until only a harsh black stubble remained. They handled their weapons as if they had been born with them. They were the complete fighting animal.

Mopping his forehead with the silk scarf which they all carried—some painted with Rising Suns, others with dirty pictures—their leader surveyed us morosely and idly waved the revolver he had taken from our latest recruit. They conferred in low voices of a pleasant tone, which contrasted strikingly with the screams and bellows they invariably used when speaking to us.

The leader addressed us, his left hand resting proudly on the hilt of a cheap-looking sword, his right clutching the revolver. He spoke little English.

"You," he said, pointing to Roy, "age-u?" Roy looked blank, so I told him that the little ape wanted to know how old he was.

"Twenty," said Roy.

"Twenty-ka?" queried the leader and looked most surprised.

"You?" he said, pointing to Hugh.

"Twenty," said Hugh.

"You?" continued the Jap to Rene.

"Twenty," said Rene.

"You?" he demanded of me.

"Twenty-one," I told him. He muttered to himself, then turned to his men and informed them, with a contemptuous gesture at us, "*Ni-ju.*" They all registered astonishment.

"Baby," he said. "Twenty no good. Nippon soldier twenty-four. Nippon soldier Number One, Englishu soldier Number Ten."

"Balls," replied Hugh, whereupon the Jap—who did not understand the word but could not mistake the inflection—hit him with the butt of the revolver.

"You," he pointed at me, "wife-u-ka?"

"No wife," I told him.

"Baby-ka?" he persisted.

"Not even any babies," I assured him. He hit me with the revolver butt. He asked Rene and Roy the same questions; they gave the same answers—and received the same treatment. Harry, short, confident, and thirtyish, watched all this with his shrewd farmer's eye.

"You," the Jap asked him, "wife-u-ka?"

Harry, the bachelor, smiled his crooked smile. "Yeah," he said boldly.

"Yes?" questioned the Jap, delighted.

"Sure," said Harry: and then, driving home his advantage, added: "Three wives and eight babies."

This information was received with open admiration by all the Japs, who at once made many lewd gestures in Harry's direction and gave him a cigarette, placing it carefully in his mouth. Harry continued to smile—we had learnt our first lesson in Japanese psychology.

Our execution, apparently, was for the moment forgotten. Taking a long swig at his round water bottle, the leader suddenly declared: "All men come," and, putting his cap and helmet back onto his bristly skull, prepared to move off. Emboldened by the cigarette gift, Harry asked could we have some water. The Jap did not understand. "Water," repeated Harry, and nudged with the elbow of his lashed-up arm at his own empty water bottle.

"*Misuwa nei,*" bellowed the Jap, and—all admiration for Harry's matrimonial prowess vanished—hit him with the revolver butt, at which Harry smiled more crookedly than ever and we all grinned at Harry. "Come," said the Jap, "all men come"; so we were prodded upright with bayonets and then set out on what was to be a long and rather unpleasant march.

We were used as pathfinders through a minefield: we passed ambushed British ambulances packed with men who had been only slightly wounded and had been slaughtered as they lay there, their drivers still clutching the wheel. we marched briskly all day—a day of harsh heat during which we were allowed no water and no rests.

Japanese bombers roared low overhead and our captors took their scarves, the flag ones and the dirty ones, and waved them at the planes—which then roared off again, satisfied. At about four in the afternoon our captors sat down under a banana tree to eat. We were kept standing in the sun on a hard-baked track which ran through the small clearing. We were not guarded with much attention. On the other hand, we were too securely shackled, hand and foot, for all of us to unloose ourselves and escape. Since we had agreed that only a joint escape attempt would be made that subject had, for the moment, to my fury, to be dropped. I seized the opportunity, though, whilst the Japs were preoccupied with refreshments, to pull my wrists free and untie my ankles. Then, when the Malay who had brought the Japs their cooked food reappeared, I walked down the track to meet him and, giving him my empty water bottle, demanded that he fill it. He refused. Water by this time, though, had become essential. I was sufficiently lightheaded to make murderous advances at the old man rather than let him pass me on that hard-baked track and reach the security of the banana tree where the Japanese sat.

"*Ayer,*" I snapped at him, "*Ayer! Ayer lacas* [Water . . . and quickly!"] As I raised my voice, the other men looked anxiously at me, and the Japs themselves raised their eyes from their oval mess tins and watched intently.

"They're on to you, Russ," Hugh warned, "better skip it!" The sergeant, heroic to the last, shouted: "Come back here, you silly little bastard. You're drawing the crabs for the rest of us. Come back here." But water was now my main interest in life and nothing would have given me more pleasure than to draw all the crabs in the world on my friend the sergeant. "*Ayer,* Joe," I demanded again, "*Ayer,*" and thrust the water bottle at him. He reached out, took the bottle and returned a few moments later with it filled.

I walked back to the rest and fed them two mouthfuls apiece, taking care to attend to the sergeant last each time. When the Japs had tossed us a coconut at noon, the sergeant, whom I had just untied, had grabbed it. He had drunk all its juice at a draught. We were not going to be caught like that again. So I now went from man to man holding the bottle to his mouth—a procedure necessary with the others only because their hands were still lashed behind their backs—until all the water was gone.

The whole operation was watched, in venomous silence, by the Japs. Now that it was completed and I had nothing to do, I felt terror-stricken by the fact that I was so obviously unshackled. I could feel my right eyelid twitching and I had a frantic desire to drop my eyes from the long gaze of the leading Jap. On the other hand, I felt certain that if I did my number would be up. So apparently did Hugh. "Stick to him, Russ," he muttered. Desperately I stuck—and after another interminable ten seconds the little Jap turned away, apparently, of a sudden, quite disinterested.

He spoke, once again in that pleasant undertone they used among themselves, to one of his men. That individual rose to his feet, did up his fly buttons, put on both his belts, mopped his skull and placed on it first his cap, then his helmet, and then walked slowly towards me. Quite dispassionately he tied my wrists behind my back again, looped the rope around my throat and down to the wrists once more. Then he ordered the sergeant over and joined the loose end of my rope to the knot which secured his wrists. Then he dragged the two of us to Hugh and tied Hugh to the other side of the sergeant. The other seven men were tied up in a three and a four. Then he returned slowly to the banana tree, took off his helmet and his cap, removed his two belts, undid his fly, sat down again in the shade. For twenty minutes they murmured quietly among themselves and examined the paintings on their scarves. Then they rose—we were on the march again.

After a few miles the sergeant found progress easier if, every now and then, he took both his feet off terra firma and we carried him. By now I hated him as I had never hated in my life before. Not only was he heavy to carry, but the sudden jolt of his weight on the thin rope when he lifted his feet cut our wrists and sawed at our throats. Undoubtedly, from his point of view, his theory was a good one. I, however, found it disagreeable and Hugh was pale with pain.

"Drop the bastard," advised Harry from behind. We warned him, Hugh and I, that if he persisted we would free ourselves and wring his bloody neck. He laughed, a little madly, and said we would never ditch a fellow Australian—and then swung more lustily than ever. Hugh warned him again. Then, when next he lifted both feet off the earth, I tore my wrist free. The loosed rope snaked round my throat and the sergeant thudded to the ground.

The march stopped abruptly. As the Japs crowded round the sergeant, who lay kicking childishly on the track, I stepped over to Hugh and separated his bonds from those of the fallen man. Hugh straightened up.

The sergeant refused to get up off his back, so the Jap leader asked would Hugh and I carry him. I made the first adult decision of my life. I said, "No." The sergeant screamed that we wouldn't dare let him lie there and the Jap indicated his intention of shooting him if he did not either get up or find someone to carry him at once. Since Hugh and I were the only two untied, we were obviously the only two who could carry him. The Jap glanced at me. I said, "No."

The Jap unholstered the revolver he had taken from our second officer. He glanced at me again, enquiringly. Again I moved my head negatively. Holding the pistol within a foot of the sergeant's stomach, he fired. The sergeant twitched—the Jap fired four more times. Hugh was suddenly very white and shivered, although there were little beads of sweat on his upper lip. "He's dead," he said. The others said nothing. "Good!" I told him. As the ropes were tied round my wrists again, I reflected grimly that for once in the presence of death I did not feel sick. I supposed that I was growing up. I decided that I had been nicer when I was young.

We marched the rest of that day and much of the night in grim silence. Marched with a speed and sureness that were astounding. We did not once see a road: we were usually in jungle: when we did hit a clearing, it came as no surprise to the Japs, who were instantly greeted by a Malay who had hot food ready. This clockwork organization of fifth-column sympathizers and the timetable marching was almost incredible when one realized that the Japs who guarded us had been in Malaya only six weeks and that they had spent the previous seven years fighting in China. It was explained only when one saw their cheap wrist compasses (strapped on like watches) and the map by which they marched—a map which ignored all main routes and gave only creeks, padi tracks, jungle pads, native huts. Every minute detail was there. Where our British maps would have marked nothing but jungle and a few contour lines, these Japs marched according to a plan that looked like a route through London. Every yard of their progress had been charted by twenty years or so of Japanese tailors, photographers, launderers, planters, miners and brothelkeepers in the period before the war. Now those years of work bore the fruits that were desired of them in the sure passage through the Malayan wilderness of this, and a thousand other, roving Japanese patrols.

At midnight we halted and the patrol slept—leaving us always heavily guarded. It was unnecessary. We slept, too. Nothing could have kept us awake—not even being trussed together, all nine of us, into an immovable and inflexible lump of humanity. At dawn we were off again. The Japs had washed, eaten and drunk—but we received nothing.

At midday we passed a large formation of bicycle troops. They carried small mortars, civilian clothes, mortar ammunition and rifles. We were severely manhandled and each of us was punched and kicked a hundred times. In addition, some of us had our boots taken from us and marched, thenceforward, barefooted. The jungle is not kind to those who walk in bare feet.

Five times we managed to untie every man but one—when we could have attempted escape. And five times we were observed, thrashed and tied up again. Sandshoes suddenly declared that he would have no part in any future attempt: he would, he said, stay captured. I was all in favour of abandoning him: the officers with us, however, were more humane and urged us to wait for better opportunities.

We passed another group of bicycle troops. They had just been shot up by our artillery. The sound of our own gunfire rejoiced our hearts and we prepared to make our run for it. Six of us were already marching with our hands held behind our backs but quite free. Rene was just untying Roy's bonds. The stage seemed set—though not even I felt that we had much chance. And at that moment we were herded into the very midst of the bicycle troops and chaos ensued. We were kicked, punched, slugged and slashed. Boots, rifle butts, bayonets and swords came at us from every angle. We were all bloody when we emerged at last from the gauntlet. Hugh's arms gaped widely where he had warded off a sword blow.

As we stood there, licking our wounds, there came another onslaught and we were kicked into the padi water. We seized this opportunity to take a drink. Then we were all tied up afresh and kicked into the padi again. When nine men are bound together hand and foot and thrust face downwards into three feet of water, it requires considerable mutual confidence and co-operation not to drown. With the exception of Sandshoes, the men who were with me in that predicament behaved like heroes—we emerged a trifle waterlogged but alive. Another three hundred yards of screaming hatred and the ordeal was over. We marched out of the padi, leaving the bicycle troops behind us, and came to a road—our first since we had seen the ambulances at Yong Peng. The Japs halted to study their map and we took advantage of the delay to try and stop the wound in Hugh's forearm from bleeding.

This first aid was barely completed when we were kicked to our feet again and we then marched till midnight, when we came to another road. There the nine of us were incarcerated in the chicken coop designed for as many chickens. On either side of the road were vast numbers of enemy troops. Our chicken coop adjoined a small copra drying shed of galvanized iron and a bungalow of weather board. The road lay twenty yards away.

Sandshoes complained that he had an uncomfortable position. To shut him up and to be nearer Hugh, I changed places with him. We slept till morning, a guard facing into our coop, his bayonet inches only from our faces.

A few hours after we wakened, all hell broke loose outside and we realized that a battle was raging on the road. Bullets tore through the chicken coop. One hit Sandshoes in the thigh—Sandshoes, who sat in my place! He moaned and screamed, so the Japs took him outside and bayoneted him.

The battle died down. Thirty prisoners—the only survivors of an entire convoy, and most of them wounded—were brought in. We were joined with them and flung into the small red iron copra shed, which was about ten feet square. There we stayed for two days.

During those two days the more serious wounds went gangrenous and the packed shed stank with the stench of living death. The man on my right had his jaw shot away from just below his ear down to his chin. He was hideous to look at and the flesh, like greenish lace at the raw edges, stank sweetly.

"Am I very badly disfigured?" he asked anxiously—he had become engaged just before leaving England and his looks were important to him. Hugh looked him full in what remained of his fearful face and declared: "You're as beautiful as ever." Hugh was fair-haired and young. He could look extraordinarily angelic at times. He did so now, his eyes gentle and his smile reassuring. The horror leant back content.

During those forty-eight hours we received one lot of water—about three mouthfuls each—and four coconuts. I managed also to scrape in, through a hole in the wall, a double handful of flyblown rice off the Japs' garbage heap. This worked out at a spoonful each. We ate some of the drying copra but, though it makes good oil, it can hardly be described as appetizing. Dysentery broke out, which was awkward.

The new prisoners were all either English troops or Malay volunteers and were magnificent in their courage. During the night quite a few men were chosen by torchlight for questioning—mainly on the use of gas, about which none of us knew anything. They were taken outside and then, in the semi-gloom, just visible through the hole in the wall, stabbed and bashed to death. They died shouting defiance. At the end of the forty-eight hours those of us who were left were herded into a truck—one of ours captured in the ambushed convoy—and driven off. We stood in sticky blood and the road on both sides for ten miles bore witness to the fury with which British troops had fought the enemy. No Japanese bodies remained—they were always swiftly removed—but the corpses of our own men lay everywhere, blackening and bloating in the sun like cattle in a drought.

The truck stopped suddenly. The driver had noticed an old Chinaman standing on the edge of the road. He was very old indeed and senile. The driver leapt out and with two other Japs battered him viciously. His cries brought more Nipponese troops to the scene. Soon there were hundreds. They decided to make a day of it and their preparations were soon complete. They set fire to the old man's head. As his hair blazed and he screamed the sort of screams that only burning men can scream they offered him water with which to extinguish the flames. When he seized the can of water it was boiling. He flung it over his head. The flames hissed out and he screamed even more piercingly. Petrol was poured onto the roasted scalp: a match applied: more boiling water offered. It was quite some time after he expired that the Japanese laughter and excitement died down. Rather like an English crowd at the conclusion of a closely fought football match.

"Api," they shouted in Malay to one another. *"Api: ayer panas. Api: ayer panas* [Fire: hot water. Fire: hot water]."

Chattering gaily, our driver got back into the truck. With a grind of gears and a jolt as the clutch was let carelessly up, we were on our way again.

We reached Ayer Hitham, where the superficially wounded were given some inadequate treatment by the Japanese and the seriously wounded—including The Face—were, we presumed (for no one ever saw them again), killed off. We slept the night in a school which reeked of death. In the morning one of the English soldiers produced a safety razor and a blade. About thirty of us shaved with it. There was a well in the schoolyard which provided water for shaving and bathing and (in spite of rumours of a corpse in it) drinking. We were questioned, beaten up and moved to Batu Pahat.

At Batu Pahat we were questioned, beaten up and moved to Gemas. At Gemas we were questioned, beaten up (with especial fury because there the Australian 2/30th Battalion had staged a particularly successful ambush) and put into a cattle truck on a train. In all that time we had eaten only a few spoonfuls of rice. We had now been ten days with virtually no food at all and eight of us had marched about a hundred and eighty miles in that time. It had become physically impossible any longer to attempt escape.

The train stopped thirty-six hours later at a bomb-wrecked station which the Malay Volunteers told us was Kuala Lumpur. We were marched from the station through the city; and the march was made unforgettable by the stoning and spitting meted out by a native population which had only a fortnight before been hysterically pro-British. Also, there were the crops of Chinese heads that were stuck up obscenely on stakes at every intersection—symbol of the new order of Co-Prosperity.

A mile from the station high dun-coloured walls looked down at us. We turned a corner and marched beside them. Huge doors opened and we passed through them. The doors closed. We were prodded into a small courtyard and that, too, was closed. Inside the courtyard we found seven hundred men. It had been designed to provide exercise for thirty female convicts. In it, and the cells for those thirty female convicts, we seven hundred were now to live, sleep, cook, excrete, wash and die.

Which is how I came to be on the fourteenth of the twenty-two steps that led up from the courtyard to the women's cells in Pudu Gaol, with an Argyll at my feet who was dead. I looked at him again, sad because of his youth, frightened because of his death. Tears came to my eyes, almost equally for the Argyll and for myself. And ahead lay four years of it. I struggled hard to convince myself that it didn't matter.

A figure loomed up at the stairhead behind me. "What's the matter with you?" it demanded in a broad Scots accent that would have been more in place in Sauchiehall Street.

"Tired," I replied.

"And what's the matter with him?" demanded the Scot, pointing at the Argyll.

"Dead," I replied. The Scot moved quickly down past me and touched the Argyll's face.

"Aye," he agreed softly, "he's dead." He thought for a moment and then asked: "Can you help me carry him up the stairs?" I suggested that first we clean the youngster up. So we carried him down to the tong at the bottom of the stairs, undressed him and washed him—watched throughout in stolid silence by the sentry, who sat with his knees wide apart and his rifle across them. Then we carried the Argyll to the head of the stairs, where we laid him down. I put his forage cap on his head and set it at the right angle. The Scot took off his own shorts—"I'll wear the wee lad's in the morning when they're dry," he explained—and we put them on the Argyll. After hesitating in awkward silence for a few moments, the Scot muttered: "Good night, Aussie," and I muttered: "Good night, Jock," and we went to our respective places on the floor and lay down to think—whilst all around, close packed, helpless-looking as children, hundreds of men slept the restless sleep of captivity.

2

1 OUR FIRST GAOL

Pudu Gaol was a place of fascinating stories. Every man in it had been captured in extraordinary circumstances miles behind the Japanese lines. Some had been betrayed by the native population—in return for a reward from the Japs: some, having succumbed to exhaustion, had woken to find themselves surrounded by curious Nipponese soldiers: some had given themselves up rather than allow the enemy to take reprisals (because their presence in the area was known) upon the local population. A few, like myself, had been dazed by the swiftness of events and, unable to act decisively to avoid capture, had been forced to surrender.

Thus, once more I met Arthur Farmer, whom I had last seen protectively holding his mortally wounded friend at the road block before Parit Sulong. And Jack Menzies, the man who stopped the tanks at Parit Sulong by firing our last gun singlehanded. He had hidden in the jungle's edge and lived for weeks on green pineapples until his mouth was raw and bleeding. Then Malays brought the Japs to where he hid.

There was Jack Mullins, the man whose throat had been blasted with a hand grenade: and with him Reg Dudley and Dan Winters, the two who had refused to allow him to die. And Frank Van Rennan and Bill Harvey, whose exploits were sketchily described in *The Jungle Is Neutral* and who were betrayed—after an exhilarating career blowing up Japanese troop trains—by natives. Also there were numerous survivors of those mass executions of the wounded which the Japanese had carried out during their advance—like the Indian

Army officer whom a Japanese officer had carefully shot through the heart, only he got his sides mixed and shot through the right breast instead of the left.

There was young Jimmy, then just eighteen years old, who had been collected with one hundred and thirty-four others of the wounded we abandoned at Parit Sulong and—having been tied up and made to kneel in the centre of the road—machine-gunned. Jimmy's mate, also eighteen, and Jimmy himself (though both shot through the chest) still lived. Jimmy's mate writhed in pain and Jimmy lay across him, whispering frantically: "Keep still, keep still." But he could not keep still, so the Japanese noticed that he still lived and, tossing Jimmy off him and into the storm-water channel at the side of the road, lifted the slight figure to its feet and riddled it with tommy-gun bullets. Clinging to the weeds at the edge of the storm-water channel, Jimmy spent the next three hours in the black water. He saw the hundred and thirty-four machine-gunned men bayoneted and then set on fire with petrol and—after their incineration—systematically run over, backwards and forwards, by Japanese-driven trucks.

Then the enemy marched out of Parit Sulong, stamping their feet and singing their Victory Song: but Jimmy found that he was too weak from his wounds and shock to clamber out of the canal. Too weak until wild pigs came out of the jungle onto the carnage of the moonlit road, and along with a few dogs, started eating the burnt flesh. Then, in horror, he leapt out of the channel and ran, mile after mile, through the night, until he collapsed in the jungle. For a week he wandered round, the bullet wound—which ran clean through his chest—full of swamp mud. Then he was captured: and although his chest seemed to be healing, in spite of the mud and the complete absence of treatment in our gaol, his eyes were constantly full of what he had seen. He and dozens of others had the same story to tell.

There was even Dusty Rhodes. Dusty was about five feet two inches tall, dark of complexion, strongly built in a squat kind of way, and not fearfully intelligent. He was in the middle thirties and tended not to understand things unless they were said slowly.

Dusty had escaped from Parit Sulong and had then swiftly become lost. Eventually, he saw a British tank, so he knocked upon its side with his stick and, before it had occurred to him that the occupants who emerged from the tank looked strangely unlike Australians, had been captured by the Japanese. Here, however, native shrewdness intervened where intelligence could never shine. He, too, carried Mills bombs down his shirt front (a fact which the Japanese did not suspect in one who looked so harmless), so he shoved his stubby-fingered hand into his bosom, plucked out a grenade, deposited it carefully among his captors and then stepped smartly behind a rubber tree. When, after a shattering explosion, he deemed it safe to emerge, he was most gratified to observe that all the Japanese gentlemen were dead. He accordingly departed with great speed into the jungle and there, once more, lost himself.

Unfortunately, Dusty learnt only slowly. Two days later he came to another road and on it he observed another tank. "Surely," thought Dusty, "these are British tanks"—with which he again rapped firmly on the side with his stick. To his astonishment he was instantly overwhelmed by what he declared roundly to be "bloody battalions" of Japanese who first relieved him of all his remaining Mills bombs, then treated him very roughly indeed and finally flung him into Pudu Gaol. By that time, it is regrettable to relate, Dusty had become firmly and irrevocably convinced that in Malay *all* tanks were Japanese—and in this, of course, he was quite right.

Dusty's story for comic value was only equalled by that of the amateur astronomer who, being lost, decided to march by night, guiding himself by the stars. He therefore headed south, night after night, religiously following the pointer on Orion's belt. The only flaw in this impeccable plan was that the pointer on Orion's belt points north. He was most astonished when, after three weeks' marching, he was roughly seized by hostile natives and handed over to the Japanese. Instead of reaching Singapore, he had landed in Thailand!

Our quarters were on the first floor. On the ground floor beneath us were the peacetime administrative offices, now occupied by the Japanese guards. There was also one small room in which dwelt two British brigadiers who seemed to hate all men of rank lower than brigadier and who asserted their now non-existent authority by urinating anywhere except in urinals (which is both anti-social and malodorous) and by demanding larger rations than anyone else because of their seniority. It became customary to regard them as mad and to ignore them.

A second ground-floor office was the gaol's hospital. It was, perhaps, ten feet by eight feet, with a tiny alcove off it about six feet by six feet. Into this "hospital" we carried those of our dysentery cases who were so ill as to be helpless. They lay on the floor side by side in filth and squalor and under a cloud of blue-nosed flies. The stench and helplessness of it all was abominable and they died quickly, those unfortunates who entered it. The Japanese occasionally visited it, wearing heavy white gauze masks. Far from granting us the drugs that one would imagine such sights would invite, the little Nip only made gestures of disgust and looked as if it were all our fault.

The block in which all these cells, offices, makeshift hospitals and evil-tempered senior officers were housed constituted the base of a triangle. The other two legs of the triangle were wholly devoted to cells. They were separated from the base by a triangle of grass round which ran a path and that triangle of grass was itself neatly dissected by another path which ran from the centre of the administration office (or base) to the apex made by the junction of the two main cell blocks. Such was the architecture of our new life.

The transition to gaol life—even from the career of constant retreat and anxious refuge which all of us had followed for many weeks—was violent. As each man entered the gaol he was stripped of everything which could possibly be used as a weapon. This included, as well as the obvious items, all nail files, knives, razors and blades. Beards consequently became unavoidable and for many days we itched maddeningly. Not only that, but we had no eating utensils—no plates, knives, forks or spoons. We ate out of the lids of gaol bedpans, old hub caps, battered kidney dishes. We ate with our fingers and bits of wood. And what we ate was no less violent a transition than anything else—rice, with no salt or flavouring or vegetable matter of any kind, and cooked as only Army cooks who do not know the habits of rice can cook it. We consumed a couple of pints of this glue a day.

Finally, there was the inevitable emotional adjustment which had to be made in men who only yesterday had been fighting the enemy and were now incarcerated in his hands and at his mercy—this the more so since he had hastened to assure us that we were not deemed official prisoners of war but only slave labour to be used at will and disposed of just so soon as the demand for our talents had vanished. This lent a certain doubtful quality to the average man's expectation of life and resulted eventually—in most cases—in a rather delightful air of detachment. The philosophy of "It doesn't matter" had its birth in those days.

So, during the day, we huddled, all seven hundred of us, in our small exercise yard designed for thirty. We dug in shifts to try and keep latrines available and found it difficult—even though constipation of a truly spectacular degree was almost universal. (Except for those who had dysentery, most men found, to their horror, that the diet change-over brought, on an average, nineteen days at least during which the bowels remained as unmoved and immovable as the Albert Memorial. By way, perhaps, of compensation, however, one's bladder functioned with all the irrepressible propensities of an Elysian spring.) We huddled against the wall, as far from the latrines as possible in that tiny space, and told our respective tales.

Beards grew, stubble first, then scruffy fur. We had no soap, no towels, no clothes other than those we wore—usually only shorts. We huddled in the sun against the hot wall and threshed it out. Threshed out how we'd had no air support but that, provided we'd held the little bastards up for as long as possible, then we'd done all we could ask, either of ourselves or of officialdom. It was agreed that when one volunteered for Empire service, one volunteered for whatever came—not for a war of complete safety fought under an umbrella of Spitfires. This conclusion having been reached after four days of fierce and continuous wrangling, we accepted our lot philosophically. The odds had been difficult. That was one of the things we had volunteered for—if it were necessary. There was no more to be said. No more would have been said had it not been for subsequent orders sent to Singapore.

Singapore, however, had not yet fallen. We did not think it would fall. We thought that our forces would withdraw to the island and there fight a war of bitter attrition until aerial support and armour eventually arrived. We did not know that a halfhearted civilian administration would complain of civilian casualties and demand capitulation—shades of 1940 London! We did not know that the big fifteen-inch guns on Singapore could not fire north, whence the attack came—only along the southern 180° of the compass, where there were no enemy objectives at all. We did not know that the architects of Singapore, the impregnable fortress, had omitted to provide an adequate water supply on the island itself—most of its water coming from Johore *across* the causeway. We knew none of these things. And remembering the stubborn retreat of the British down to Slim River, the victory at Gemas, the delaying action fought from Muar to Parit Sulong, we had no fears for Singapore's ultimate safety. We had no doubts—nor ever at any time thenceforward did have—that eventual victory would be ours.

Meantime, we squatted in the courtyard; tanks rumbled endlessly down the road outside; bombers barely lifted off the nearby Kuala Lumpur airfield and over the gaol walls; the guards surveyed us ceaselessly with sullen venom; and every afternoon, towards evening, it rained. We ate our two pints of glue, drank our one pint of boiled water, grew steadily weaker and more hirsute, and then—at dusk—went to bed.

Bed meant the floor of the verandah round the cell block and the few cells themselves. It meant every inch of floor being covered in a sprawling mass of mixed Scotch, English and Australian humanity. They lay on bare boards with no covering. Wounded men: men with fever: men who dreamed and men who couldn't sleep and had no cigarettes. And all the time, over this carpet of sprawled bodies, a constant pilgrimage picked its urgent way towards the stairs—paying homage to the irresistible power of the Great God Bladder. As if nine or ten such interruptions by Mother Nature a night were not enough, millions of lice joined enthusiastic issue with us over our respective rights as tenants in possession of Pudu Gaol and did their best to make sleep impossible. Morning always came as a relief.

The first thing that happened each morning was the check parade —*tenko,* the Japanese called it; but Japanese was not a language for which we cared, so, as far as we were concerned, it remained a check parade. There we Australians fell in on one side of the courtyard midst much chatter and horseplay (after all, this was only a performance for the "bloody Nips"). On the other side, to the accompaniment of numerous unintelligible bellows from regular Army warrant officers complete with waxed moustaches, the British troops formed an immaculate squad which fairly quivered to attention. The two squads stood about ten feet apart, the Australians openly amused at the antics of the British; the British frankly astounded at our disorderliness; the Japanese stamping up and down between us counting, in their customary infantile and inaccurate manner, on their fingers. After an hour or so, it was usually over—whereupon we of the disorderly element broke off by mutual consent, whilst the Regulars opposite us carried on for minutes longer with the ritual of the Dismiss.

There followed the morning meal—a few dollops of greyish clag—and after that the parade to the so-called "hospital" of those who were optimistic enough to think that by parading they might get medical attention. Admittedly, for this purpose, there was an M.O. But he had at his disposal no drugs, no dressings, only a few pairs of forceps and an old stethoscope. He had to cure gangrenous wounds, amoebic and bacillary dysentery, incipient avitaminosis, malaria, dengue and soon scabies. In those early days there seemed to be nothing that he could do—but one still paraded, if only for the cold comfort of hearing him say so.

As a result of my jungle march in bare feet and of the frequent rough treatment those extremities had received from any loving Japanese who had happened to notice that they were unprotected, I was a regular attendant on these parades. My feet had deep holes in them, mainly on the top where they had been stamped on, and these holes joined in evil-looking tunnels under the sinews and tendons that led to the toes. The doctor declared that these burrows must be kept clean. Since they were at the time full of black mud and rotten flesh, this proposition did not appeal to me in the least. I lacked the moral courage, however, to say so and consequently was attacked each morning by one of the handful of medical orderlies who had come to the gaol. Brandishing one of the pairs of forceps and a swab of gaol canvas (canvas that had been used by the peacetime convicts to make mailbags), he would pursue me round and round the small concrete cell—much to the agitation of the dysentery patients over whom we skipped, and to the fury of the blue-nosed flies whose vile feeding we interrupted—until I was cornered. Then he would thrust his beastly instrument in and out of the tortuous tunnels in my feet. The holes gave no indication of healing; but, on the other hand, they became no deeper—and with this the doctor and the orderly seemed well pleased. Hugh enjoyed similar medical frolics with the sword wound in his arm. Hundreds of other men went through agonies a thousand times worse in silence as their more serious wounds were dealt with.

One instance of the latter will do no harm. Jackie Marr had been a jockey. In the recent battles his brother had, it was reported, been killed, and his own leg had been smashed by a mortar bomb just below the knee. It was now a very odd shape. There were no splints, so he lay on the verandah for weeks having the mortar wound in his leg picked clean of maggots and bone splinters each day and waiting for the shattered bone to knit. This it did after about a month, leaving his leg bent badly backwards and shortened. At the earliest possible instant, he started walking on it: then running: then bending it. The smallest movement still sent him grey with pain; but every day he walked and ran round and round the courtyard and bent the leg little by little. On that same leg in 1943 he marched two hundred miles into the heart of Thailand and in the whole time I knew him I never heard him complain or ask for help. His only concession to the havoc of war was to enquire frantically of every newcomer to the gaol had they seen or heard anything of his brother.

Against this background, we came down to check parade one morning and there, on the wall of the gaol, hung a large banner on which was printed in large letters and shocking English a statement to the effect that Singapore had unconditionally surrendered to the Imperial Japanese Army. This we did not for one second believe. Even the British squad dissolved into laughter at such nonsense. But when, two days later, all the tanks we had heard rolling down past the gaol and all the planes that had lumbered overhead, and all the soldiers who had sung their victory song as they marched through the city—when all these were heard heading past us again, but this time north towards Burma, then we knew that it was true.

The appalling fact was accepted in the usual British fashion—there were a few moments of sick silence, then everyone began assessing where the British would counterattack and when the eventual victory would be won. It is encouraging to recollect that from that day forwards life was divided into six-monthly periods in the course of each of which all one's companions cheerfully disregarded the facts and looked forward confidently to Allied landings, a German collapse, the destruction of Tokyo and the end of the war. Though the world resounded to the thunder of the Japanese race through the Pacific islands, and Rommel's march on Suez, and the Nazi destruction of Russia, the British prisoners of the Japanese—like their folk at home—remained so obdurately optimistic and so temperamentally resilient that they could blandly disregard all this gloom and at any given moment announce: "Well, I reckon the war will have had it in six months!" And at the conclusion of that period they experienced no difficulty at all in forgetting that they had ever said anything so silly and in stating—quite categorically—that before the next six months were up, it would all be over! Intellectual irresponsibility of the first water, of course—but heartening. They're nice people to be in gaol with, the British.

2 "SHANGRI-LA"

Almost concurrent with the fall of Singapore four other factors entered our lives—and these factors were to colour our entire *modus vivendi* for the next four years. They were, to employ the vernacular of those days, Bastardry about Drugs (which the Japs refused at all times to provide): the Imperial Decree that workingmen only got food: Happy Feet, and Rice Balls.

Rice Balls is not an elegant term. It was not, however, an elegant complaint, and no picture of the life we led from 1942 to 1945 is complete without its inclusion. It was the most apparent symbol of our greatest need—vitamins—and, at the same time, of the common man's indomitable humour under even the most humiliating of afflictions. For Rice Balls, to us, meant not one of the favourite dishes of the Japanese, but the ripping raw (by the denial of even a tiny quantity of Vitamin B_2) of a man's scrotum and genitals. One felt first a faint discomfort, as of chafing. Then the skin split and peeled off an area which might spread from the genitals right down the inner thighs. This entire surface then became raw and sticky and painful. As one disconsolately surveyed the damage one could not help being reminded of our redheaded sergeant major and his tinea that crept. By refusing us a spoonful each day of the worthless polishings taken off rice (and they could easily have given us a sackful), the Japanese wilfully condemned their prisoners to years of living with a scrotum that was red weeping flesh. It was a constant factor in one's life that varied between acute discomfort and acute pain. But it was always there—and it thereby had its effect upon everything one thought, everything one ate, everything one stole and upon every risk one was prepared to run to alleviate the avitaminosis of which it was the most degrading symptom. It was the outward and visible sign of a physical need which was to kill thousands and send hundreds of others blind, or near blind. And because the men who suffered this affliction ironically—and aptly—applied to it the name more commonly given to a food very close to the heart of every son of Nippon, it is fitting enough, however indelicate, to use it here. We ate rice. We ate rice only. Consequently we had Rice Balls.

Happy Feet were another symptom of the same thing—lack of vitamins. This scourge struck about half the men in gaol only, but made up the balance by striking them with a pain twice as severe as anything any of us had ever seen before. It inflicted them with a persistent series of searing stabs in the soles of their feet. The pain was like fire. But when they put their feet in water, the coolness immediately tore at them like ice, so that once again they moaned for warmth. As you looked at them, the flesh dropped off their bones: the light of youth from their eyes: the life from their faces. Boys of twenty became suddenly, in physique and expression, old men—shrunken and desperate. As one looked at them, and from them to the Japanese who had so blandly brought about this needless condition, one was filled with a pity for them and a hatred for the enemy that nothing can remove.

Japanese Bastardry, as we Australians called it, applied to almost everything in our lives, but most of all—because of the far-reaching effects it had—to our requests for drugs. Of these they had captured vast quantities and also had vast quantities of their own. Yet, despite the ready availability of emetin to cure dysentery, of quinine (the Dutch East Indies are the source of all quinine and the Japanese now owned all the Dutch East Indies) to quell our malaria, and of Vitamin B tablets (of which they had billions, for they are easy of manufacture), to counter the deficiencies of a rice diet, the little Nip constantly refused all requests for any of them. His best answer was: "*Ashita* [Tomorrow]"—which, in the Jap mouth, means "Never": his more common reply was a savage bashing for him who was courageous enough to ask.

And, finally, with the introduction at this time of working parties, came that other Japanese refinement—food only for those who work. Needless to say, this did not mean that those men who lay ill and dying in the gaols and prison camps of Malaya starved, because whatever food the Japanese sent in as rations for the workers was at once distributed to all. The point was that the ration was wholly inadequate, even for the coolie standards to which we had been reduced: but when that ration had to stretch over an extra twenty per cent at least of our working population, then gradual starvation became a very real prospect.

The Japanese reasons for this policy were at times specious, at times brutal, but never convincing. They varied between the proposition that noble Nippon had much reconstruction work to do in wickedly exploited Malaya—wherefore we must be *encouraged* to work—and the ruthless statement that warlike Nippon did not greatly admire men who surrendered and that they had more than enough of us anyway. Anyhow, until the end of the war, rations were issued to us on the basis of workingmen only. Within a few weeks of the introduction of this generous catering system our M.O. pronounced that at the present rate of supply, with everything else in our favour—which he did not think a probable eventuality—we could only survive for a year. For some obscure reason, the verdict that in twelve months we would all be dead seemed to provide everyone with a perverse sense of hilarity and we felt happier than we had for days.

Only one other factor remains to complete the scene in which we were for the next nine months to live. That is the imprisonment, as well as ourselves, in our gaol, of political prisoners—mainly Chinese—seized by the Japanese for alleged British sympathies or rebel activities.

The right-hand leg of the two which, with our quarters, formed a triangle of buildings, was the one into which the Japanese herded these unfortunate natives. There they questioned, tortured and murdered them. The process was noisy since the last thing any Oriental ever does is to endure physical pain or mental anguish in silence of the impassive nature invariably ascribed to them by writers who have never been to the East. When an Indian, Chinaman, Jap, Korean or Indonesian is in pain he screams and moans with an abandon which, to the European, is downright embarrassing. They are all of them admirably impassive about inflicting pain on others—

being apparently immune to the European's ability to suffer vicariously—but when stung themselves, they become most vociferous.

Thus, in the course of their questioning, when they were whipped on the gaol whipping triangle, or filled with water and jumped on, or made to stand for hours with a heavy stone held above their heads, or suspended by their ankles while urine was poured down their nostrils—Japanese refinements which I had seen British soldiers endure in stolid silence—the air was rent with their shrill screams. And when at last an entire cell of six natives was informed that at dawn *one* of the six, any one, would be taken out and executed, then the impassive Orientals really went to town. All six of them would maintain an uninterrupted vocal lament throughout the night. Then in the morning another head would appear on a pole in the streets and the surviving five would relapse into ecstatic silence, for they were still alive; whilst the native population outside would remain totally unmoved, for the head was not theirs; and we, who had so despised their screaming, would notice the head with shocked pity because a young man who had lived was now dead. All a matter of outlook—but, of the two, I preferred ours.

In spite of the horror of these heads as we marched out of the gaol each day, and in spite of the humiliation of natives watching us work for the Japanese, the working parties were—in those first weeks of captivity—a glorious release. It was delightful, even though the work was heavy and the Jap engineers in charge of us vicious to the point of insanity, to get out of those high walls with their layers of loose bricks on top so that escape over them was impossible. It was bliss to walk ten yards without, in that interval, having to cross twenty legs and smell the all-pervading smell of latrines. It was restoring to snatch a piece of frangipani off a tree as one passed—to smell its clean scent and carry it till the white petals went brown.

We worked for several weeks before this novelty wore off—worked, repairing Kuala Lumpur's demolished bridges, with that hysterical speed and to the accompaniment of those incessant hysterical screams and bellows that seem to be the main equipment of the Japanese engineer. Then one day we returned to the gaol and were told some good news—we were to move, all of us, out of the women's quarters designed for thirty, into the left wing of the two legs of the triangle. There we would live in supreme comfort, with only three men in each cell meant for one.

On the move being made, it was discovered that the V of the two cell blocks which, with our old quarters, made a triangle, was, in fact, an inverted Y and into the stem of the Y moved all the British troops. Thus in the Y we had Asiatic political prisoners screaming their heads off on one side, Australians on the other, the British in the stem.

I moved, with Hugh Moore and Arthur Farmer, into the cell nearest the junction of all three blocks and started at once drawing a full-scale map of the world over the whole of the left-hand wall so that we might the better follow the destruction of Nazidom in Europe and of Nippon in Southeast Asia and the Pacific. Our life had begun to assume the shape and pattern which was to dominate the next four years—turning gaols and jungle into our home: living close to death by disease: working for the Japanese, and stealing from them.

After we had done an initial reconnaissance and killed all the bugs we could see in our cell, I walked out into the wide passage on either side of which the cells ran. Next door Roy and Rene had chalked up over their door "Shangri-la": across the way, three infantrymen had printed cheerfully: "Abandon hope all ye who enter here": through the grill which separated our cell block from the British, I could see five Englishmen who sat on the floor and, in close harmony, assured the world that "There's No—o Place Like Home"; whilst across to the right six Chinese wailed incessantly because tomorrow one of them must die. Harry came up, smiling his crooked smile, and slapped me on the back: "Never mind, Russ," he said, "it's a great life—if you don't weaken." A meaningless cliché—it could well have been our motto.

3 "PUDU'S GROWING PAINS"

The most outstanding personality in Pudu Gaol—more outstanding than any of the soldiers with their hair-raising tales of the last few months: more outstanding than any of our own leaders or than any of our Japanese guards: more outstanding even than the two evil-tempered brigadiers—was a rosy-cheeked little man who a few years before had been small enough to cox the Cambridge VIII all over Europe, and who at the battle of Batu Pahat had been big enough, though a non-combatant and ordered not to, to stay behind with the wounded who could not be evacuated. He stayed there and, when the Japanese swept down the road and would have slaughtered the wounded, this little man flayed them with such a virulent tongue that they were sufficiently disconcerted to refrain. They beat him up very cruelly for days, because they did not care for being verbally flayed, even in a language they did not understand, but they did not kill the wounded men he had stayed behind to protect. In the end, they allowed the little man, and the handful of R.A.M.C. orderlies who—with equal heroism—had faced certain capture, possibly murder, to look after their charges, to collect what food they could and provide for the helpless men. This little man with the rosy cheeks and the cheerful grin and his mop of hair like a small boy's eventually brought all his orderlies and his wounded to the comparative security of the gaol. His name is Padre Noel Duckworth. It is a name which tens of thousands of Australians, Englishmen and Scots will always remember till the day they die.

He was without any doubt at all the mainspring of the orderly way of life we managed to carve for ourselves out of the rather improbable material of Pudu. He was fearlessly outspoken, and yet could be very kind. He was the easiest man to talk to most of us had ever met. He organized lectures and delivered his own inimitable version of the European tour of the Cambridge VIII to initiate the series. He created out of a cell a chapel to which even such heathen as I were glad to go and sit and think about Home, or God, or whatever it is people do sit and contemplate when they're lonely. He founded the gaol's black market with the Japanese—selling them anything from gold fillings to fountain pens. He discovered a non-existent "well-dressed Eurasian" whilst on his numerous visits to the cemetery to bury our dead and, from him, obtained a daily news bulletin which made our hearts glow.

Duckworth's news was no mealymouthed, fainthearted news. Having determined to give us good cheer by lying, the noble padre lied most blackly. Russian tanks swarmed through Poland towards

Germany: Britain planned a huge invasion of Italy: millions of Japanese were being annihilated in Burma—all this in early 1942, at the time when the advance on Stalingrad was about to start, India seemed about to fall and Italy was still only being vaguely referred to as the "soft underbelly" of Europe!

But to men who were ill and starving and dying off at a quite alarming rate, the padre's "well-dressed Eurasian" was exactly what was required. By the time his resounding triumphs had begun to attract scepticism, we had all become sufficiently toughened to the sordidness of our surroundings to be of good heart without the artificial boost of "Duckworth's news," as it was called. We even acquired a wireless set and with that received regular B.B.C. bulletins which, though they contained no resounding triumphs—at least, not on our side—nevertheless gave us what we needed, which was contact with the outside world.

The padre's black market—though it might not in theory have secured the blessing of the various archbishops of the Anglican Church—was, nevertheless, conducted with considerable *élan*. The padre was a realist as well as a Christian—not for nothing had he worked in the slums of English cities. We needed food: the Malays would sell us food: the Japs coveted any Western trinkets such as watches and fountain pens. Though there were few of these that they had not already looted from the men in Pudu Gaol, the padre fully intended to sell them those few, so that the proceeds could be used to buy from the Malays.

"Nippon," he would shout peremptorily at the weakest-willed-looking guard available. The gentleman addressed would leap uneasily. "Come here, you little sewer rat," the padre would continue in honeyed tones, "Come here, you charming little lump of garbage, and buy this perfectly worthless pen."

"Ah so-ka!" the Jap would murmur delightedly as his eye caught sight of the pen in the padre's hand.

"Pen-ka?" he would ask.

"Yes," the red-cheeked, boyish little man would agree, "it's a pen. Only a half-wit like you would ask anything so silly."

"Parker-ka?" the Jap would ask. The padre would look instantly at the inscription on the side of the pen and, though the inscription very rarely said Parker, he invariably replied, "Yes, Parker. Parker Number One, eh? you walking example of the horrors of V.D. They should hang you up in all public lavatories instead of those rather dull little notices. Now tell me, Tojo, how much of your ill-gotten pay are you going to give me for this very inferior pen?"

And in the end he would bleed the Nip white, give him the pen and send him packing with a fresh blast of insults which were delivered with so sweet a smile that the guard would bow low and gratefully, convinced that he had both made a good deal and been flattered. Thus did all the pens, watches, grubbed-out gold fillings from teeth, signet rings, cigarette cases and other valuables—or alleged valuables—go the way of Nippon: and the money we gained in return for these possessions went the way of the Malays: and the food we gained in return for the money—well, as the proverb says, all roads lead to Rome!

The padre did not, however, limit his anti-Japanese operation to pleasantly delivered vituperation in the course of his business transactions. On Sundays he blasted them in his sermons—lumping them together as "The incarnation of evil" and pointing an accusing and fearless finger at them as they stood nearby, self-consciously guarding us. And at nights, during the week, he frequently played the gaol game of wrecking Nippon's rifles.

This consisted of getting any Nip guard into conversation—by showing him photographs or teaching him games—till he leant his rifle against the wall and devoted the whole of his miserable mind to trying to master the white man's skill. Then, while he was absorbed, the bolt would be taken from his rifle and removed to a nearby cell where it was ensured, by bending the firing pin, that that particular rifle would never be much use again. By the middle of the year it was estimated that, with the padre's enthusiastic support, there wasn't a rifle in the guardhouse that would fire. There were, however, unfortunately, plenty of machine guns and grenades; and there were still those layers of loose bricks on top of the prison wall. Nevertheless, one felt, it was a start.

The middle of the year, however, had not yet come. It was still early in the piece and it was a March day when the Japanese suddenly presented us with a form which we were to sign. It declared that we promised not to escape. Since this was contrary to both military law and our own inclinations we at once refused. All our officers were locked up—a procedure which they endured with remarkable equanimity since there were seventeen or eighteen of them to a cell—but we still refused. The Japanese uttered nasty threats. We refused. Then they rang Singapore and Singapore, who had been having similar trouble with seventeen thousand prisoners at Changi, changed the request to an order and accompanied the order with the permission of the senior British officer in Singapore to sign. The signatures having been obtained under duress, it was unanimously accepted that the forms meant nothing anyway and we signed.

Our officers were released—grubby after three days' and nights' close confinement without benefit of water or latrines, and hoarse from seventy-two hours' practically non-stop defiant singing. They were a good lot, those men, and we felt a closeness to and affection for them, which no amount of subsequent regimentation in other camps could destroy. They ate our food: lived our lives: worked with us—and in our few leisure moments—talked and played with us. They were, or became, men anyone would have been happy to follow—which was not always, in those difficult days, to be the case.

My map was now complete and I was very proud of it. I had drawn it in the most minute detail that school atlases and the pooled knowledge of all the gaol's intelligentsia made possible. I had coloured all Axis-held territory black, all Allied-held territory red. This started a running battle with the Japanese.

A little gentleman, who wore a white short-sleeved shirt, Bombay bloomers which reached well below his knees, brown socks of the type usually referred to as "hosiery, natty gent's," suspenders and two-tone shoes, arrived in the gaol one day and announced to a truly astonished Australian audience that he was a colonel.

"Looks more like the Queen of the May to me," commented Harry —which comment the colonel ignored. He began his tour of inspection, his long Samurai sword clanking along on the concrete floors behind him, his short legs the subject of open admiration.

Lest anyone should miss this exhilarating spectacle, men were summoned by their friends from all sides.

"Hey, Reg! Reg! Get on to him, will yer?"

"Rocky, c'mere, take a gander at Nippon."

"How's his rotten form." And, from just behind him, a lecherously inflected, "Ooh, you gorgeous creature." Nippon looked most gratified—then he spotted my map and moved over to it.

With even more gratification, he moved his finger through black Japan, down black China, into black Indo-China, thence through Thailand, Burma, Malaya, the East Indies, Borneo and Timor, all of which were dark as night. There, however, the gratification ceased. New Guinea, India and Australia were *all* bright red.

"You have done this?" he asked me. I nodded.

"These-u," he asserted, pointing to the red countries concerned, "these-u *all* Nippon. Tomorrow changey changey"—with which he swept off, a truly impressive example of Japanese sartorial splendour.

Next day, accordingly, a guard arrived and painted New Guinea, India and Australia (and, for good luck, New Zealand) black. That night I painted them red again. A few days later this hideous crime was discovered and, after emphasizing their point with prolonged smacks and thumpings, the red spots were again blackened, South Africa being added to the list as a reprisal. I retaliated by reddening them all again and by removing Burma from the list of countries I had originally been willing temporarily to grant the Axis.

That, when it was discovered, produced a real crisis. Most of the guard trooped down to my cell and there examined the offending map. With much jabbering among themselves and an occasional bellow of "*Currah*" at any sympathizer who tried to look in and encourage me, they discussed my crime. Brown fingers were pointed one after another at the countries and islands in question. Brown eyes flashed darkly when Burma was seen to be incarnadined. There seemed little doubt that the Imperial Japanese Army was highly displeased and that very soon an execution would follow. I could see from the expressions on my comrades' faces that they were under no illusions as to who would be the subject of this execution. I was extremely frightened and wondered why on earth when, at school, my highest mark for geography had been twenty-eight per cent, I should at this lamentable stage suddenly have gone mad on maps. Then the decision as to my fate was made. With a falsetto giggle, the senior Japanese N.C.O. decided that it was all too much for him, muttered, "*Dammé, dammé*" at me reprovingly, and, tapping me lightly on top of the head with his bayonet, gave me a cigarette. "Tojo presento," he said as he handed it to me. "*Aringato*," I thanked him. The whole guard trooped out of the cell:

the incident was closed: the map remained red. Not being a smoker, I gave the cigarette to Hugh, who lay on his back on the cell slab. He inhaled deeply and then blew out a sharp cloud of smoke.

"Not bad," he said, looking at the cigarette appreciatively, "Virginia."

"Tojo presento," I told him.

"Balls," he replied.

In any community where near starvation prevails, the first thing to get settled to the satisfaction of all is the distribution and cooking of what rations there are. To this problem the thousand-odd men of Pudu devoted themselves with earnest application in the time-honoured way of all Britons—they formed a committee.

As a result, the existing cooks, who for weeks had produced only glue, were summarily sacked and men of initiative put in their place. The gaol cookhouse had already been wangled for us by protracted negotiations with the Nips. The cooked rice was now collected in tubs from that cookhouse and carried—in sight of all—to the distribution points where so many men fell in per tub of rice. The contents of each tub were then issued, a scoop at a time, to the men in the queues, the whole operation being supervised by an officer. The officers themselves collected their food last and only ate when they were sure that every one of the men had received his ration—a point of military etiquette which I saw in no other camp and which speaks volumes for the calibre of the officers we had with us at Kuala Lumpur.

There remained, however, one extremely difficult problem—what to do with the few crumbs of rice which, inevitably, were left over after each man had received his ration. (The few crumbs *were* always left because the men who dished the rice out received their ration last—and when you are starving you never leave yourself in the position where your own food has gone to someone else.)

Early on these crumbs, perhaps three or four pints of rice in all, were left in the tub and anyone could take them who got there first. It was found, however, that good manners survived, even in gaol; and that every day, every meal, the same two or three pigs swiped the lot, whilst the same hundred sat, exerting every ounce of self-control, and in anguished silence watched them. Then one day the three pigs fought. And one of them, in his desperation, hurled himself head foremost into the tub, where he snuffled the rice up, his legs twitching with greed in the air above. Thus to acknowledge, so unashamedly, that we had been reduced to the status of animals was too much. There was a roar from all sides and a decision was made, there and then, whereby to deal with all future surpluses.

We would all, it was decided, have numbers. We would take it in turn to receive an extra ration. The extra ration was known as a *leggi* ("leggi" being Malay for "more"): the number you had was your "leggi number." Thus does any society develop the rules by which its communal life is made both possible and tolerable. "Leggis" were an institution that remained with us through all the days that were to follow until the war ended in 1945. They are a striking example of civilized man's ability to resist even the animal gnawings of starvation in the interests of the communal effort. It cannot be too strongly stressed how, in those days, the individual had to subordinate his desires to society rules if that society were to survive. The three things that could, at any time, kill us all off were work, disease and starvation.

To overcome the murderous effects of the almost impossible tasks set us by the Japanese, teamwork was required to the nth degree. Only split-second timing and simultaneous effort by a squad of sick men could enable them to lift huge dredge cups onto railway trucks—and, having lifted them, to deposit them so gently that fingers and limbs were not severed. Only rigid self-discipline could keep latrines unfouled so that the maggots did not breed round them and the disease-carrying fly increase its numbers. Only a faithful adherence to the rules could ensure that the tiny quantity of food which came into the camps would keep everyone alive: and that the limited water available would slake one's thirst, keep one clean and wash one's eating-irons. All those things were managed. The prisoner-of-war life of those four years was an object lesson in living together.

One of the many advantages of our new accommodation was that there was not only more room in which to sleep at night, but also extra space during the day. The triangle of lawn enclosed by the cell blocks and administrative building became common ground for all troops. On the left of the Australian wing—as one faced it from those administrative buildings—was another area of lawn which stretched thirty yards or so to the gaol wall and contained what had been a prison workroom in its centre. In the area bounded by the stem of the inverted Y, the Asiatic wing and the back wall of the gaol was another exercise yard which contained a rather ornate fountain and a small cloister.

The lawn to the left of our quarters was given to us Australians: the exercise yard between the British quarters and the Asiatic cells was given to the British: the workroom in our area became the gaol hospital: the cloister in the Pommies' exercise yard became the gaol church: the fountain our communal bath—it was white and ornate and strangely out of place in the grimness of Pudu. Around it thenceforth hundreds of naked men were to be observed splashing water over themselves in the nightly bath—hundreds of deeply tanned bodies among whom the Pommies were quickly distinguishable because of their passion for tattoos. Arms blazed with pink and blue females of most lecherous allure. The complete crucifixion scene across a broad Highland back was just as common as hair on an Australian chest.

The existence of bare concrete walls and floors (already becoming infested with bugs), of a makeshift hospital, an impromptu church, a communal bath and that common triangle of lawn—this skeleton life we clothed with a sack upon which to lie at night, a work roster to keep the gaol free of all dirt, flies and blocked drains, and whatever miracles of improvisation the Anglo-Saxon mind could evolve. Our new civilization had begun.

Hugh developed happy feet: Arthur developed chronic wind: my ankles swelled ominously and we all passed beyond the itchy stage of beard-growing. The gaol population was now becoming most interesting to look at with its assorted beards which ranged from magnificent black growths with sworls and curls, like the one Dan Winters sported, right down to the three mandarin-like hairs that sprouted desperately from Hugh's stubborn but youthful chin. I myself looked like a rather melancholy airedale.

These beards were nevertheless intensely uncomfortable. With our long hair, they overheated our skins, and were also difficult either to keep clean without soap or to dry without towels. Moreover, one lived in terror of their being infested by the ubiquitous louse. One did, however, derive much comfort from suspending oneself from the end of one's own beard whilst one talked at night.

Night talks turned out to be one of the never-failing charms of a life that was remarkable for its lack of charming aspects. Among our numbers, as happened in every camp for all the ensuing years, were men who had done everything. There was no part of the world, no job in the world, no profession, no hobby that someone in Pudu had not himself done or seen. Whilst one retained any zest for life at all, there was always good conversation to be had in prison camps. If one wanted information on any of the professions, the trades or the arts; on exploration, big-game hunting, skiing or any other sport; on professional soldiering or professional crime; on great men or the common man, one had only to search within the few hundred cells of Pudu to find someone who was an authority. To a youth like myself—just twenty-one and, except for the last few months, nurtured solely in the groove of a public school, a university and as many games as daylight would allow—the experience was invaluable. I could have wished, though, that it had been acquired in a slightly less rugged environment.

In consequence of all this, however, it came as no surprise to anyone that when the Japanese discovered that all the frozen meat in the Kuala Lumpur Cold Storage Company was bad and therefore graciously presented it to us, we had in our midst both butchers and health inspectors. The former cut up the few carcasses of Australian beef allotted to us each day and the latter expertly sought out glands and cavities in the flesh and declared whether or not—though rotten—it was beyond consumption. Usually it was, whereupon the carcasses were burnt, watched with fierce longing by hundreds of pairs of meat-hungry eyes. But occasionally it was not—and then the cookhouse would prepare a stew of surpassingly vile savour and we would be issued with two cubes each of greenish meat, a shred of nauseating fat and a scoopful of juice which looked like sewage.

The taste of this stew was quite remarkably foul. In spite both of that, however, and of a boyhood aversion to all fat and any food that smelt even faintly "off," I consumed it unhesitatingly. But upon the occasion of the arrival of the first of these stews, Hugh and Arthur, I noticed, both left theirs.

"Belt it into you," I advised them. Arthur did so and at once vomited, bringing up not only the stew but the morning's rice and a tapeworm about eighteen inches long as well, which was interesting. Hugh looked stubborn and left his stew untouched.

"Belt it into you, Hugh," I repeated, "good for your happy feet."

"Rather have the happy feet," Hugh asserted grimly, to which, unsympathetically, I replied: "Come off it."

"Whose feet and whose food is it?" demanded Hugh. I agreed that all three were his.

"Well then?" he queried.

"Well then," I concluded, "belt it into you."

There were a few seconds' smouldering silence, then Hugh spoke again: "You know bloody well that I hate fat," he said.

"Look, Hugh," I told him, "I don't care whether you hate fat *and* meat *and* rice . . ."

"I do," he assured me.

"I reckon," I went on aggressively, "you should still eat the lot."

"What you reckon," pointed out my fair-haired friend, rather despondently, "is that no one is entitled to disagree with what you reckon." I was astonished at the possible justice of this remark, but he was continuing his home truths so I said nothing.

"You've changed, Russ," he said, "you used to be the easiest bloke to get on with I ever knew. Now you're just an argumentative bastard." So that was that. Hugh got up and, slinging his dish of stew irritably across the concrete path at me, hobbled off to cool his aching feet in the water of the fountain. I sat for some time thereafter chewing over the undoubted change in the Braddon outlook of late and interrupting myself every now and then with a burp that was redolent with very dead, very bad meat.

A lad called Pete—until recently a fat boy—sidled up and asked me what the leggi number was up to. It was his only interest in life. He never discussed or asked about anything else. I said I didn't know (which wasn't true) and he ambled disconsolately off to ask someone else. I carried on thinking about me.

An hour later things were fairly clear in my mind. I had changed, I knew. I remembered that before becoming involved in a war I had been pleasant-mannered and agreeable enough. If I felt upon any occasion either unpleasant or disagreeable the veneer of politeness impressed upon me by a strict father and a mother who (though capable of both extreme frivolity and delightful vulgarity) stood no nonsense, had always managed to conceal the fact quite adequately. The nearest I ever came in those days to open disagreement in discussion was to say: "Oh, I see. I must have got it wrong."

And, for those halcyon days of family life, tennis tournaments, football matches, week ends of surfing and sporadic attendance at lectures which were on the whole neither inspiring nor well delivered, that had been enough. Since then, however, I had rather abruptly been required to kill other men and to avoid being killed myself: to decide whether or not, regardless of their rank, men's orders were worth obeying: to see a fellow Australian murdered on my own verdict: and to adjust the limited Braddon material available so that it would best and longest stand up to the strain of life as a guest of the Japanese.

I acknowledged at once, not for the first time, that the old Braddon was the nicer one. I even admitted that the present Braddon was probably not nice at all. I nevertheless faced up finally to the fact that what I had become was, if I were to survive, what I would stay. In the absence of all clothes except a beard and a G string, it seemed definitely the case now that "circumstances maketh the man." If they hadn't done a good job, it was sad—but too late. Thus resigned to myself, I got up and made my way to my cell—where Arthur told me that the M.O. reckoned we all had worms like the one he'd just sicked up, whilst I went systematically round the walls killing bugs. One stopped on my map, right in the middle of Berlin. Viciously I jabbed him with my thumb. Smelling the musty stink of crushed vermin, Arthur looked up from his biological dissertation and grinned at my still twisting thumb. "Got the little bastard," he pronounced. I grinned back. "You know," he continued, "the M.O. says that's the longest worm he ever saw. Says you pick up the eggs from eating rice." "Go on," I answered him. Then his wind got the better of him: so I left and went looking for Hugh to see if I could help by rubbing his feet.

Each day a party of most of the men in the gaol who could walk went out to work—mainly ant labour on bridge reconstruction, carrying sandbags in an endless chain of half-naked, barefooted misery under the mocking eye of local natives (especially the Indians).

Bridge work, however, was infinitely preferable to the collection and loading onto lorries and trains of the wrecked dredges that lay all round Kuala Lumpur. These had been blown up and destroyed as part of the scorched-earth policy of our own administration and now lay in huge unwieldy lumps of reluctant metal in every tin mine. The Nip engineers were collecting every bit of it and shipping it off to Japan, there to be converted into armour. By generous applications of pick handle to any exposed portion of the body, and by piratical slashings with their bayonets (usually the flat of the bayonet, but every now and then—just to make it interesting—with the edge, which they always kept sharp), our captors urged us on to lift almost superhuman weights. The days were a bedlam of their incessant, maniacal screaming—maintaining a steady crescendo until the glaring tropical sun began to set. "Speedo," they screamed —which explains itself.

"*Bugero!*" they screamed—which means "Fool!"

"*Yazumé nei,*" they screamed—which means, in answer to the request "*Yazumé-ka?*" "No. No rest."

"*Dammé, dammé,*" they screamed, which means "Wrong, lousy, bloody awful." For a language which contains no swear words, Japanese can sound more hideous than any other I know. The pink dusk would see us marching, bedraggled and blood-smeared, back to the gaol: the evening was spent licking our wounds, dreaming of home and food, and wondering whether tomorrow could possibly be quite as bad.

But whatever the job and wherever it was, we still, at all times, had one means of asserting ourselves—we stole! We stole with all the cunning of professional burglars and with all the incorrigible enthusiasm of the kleptomaniac. Although it was universally accepted that in this pastime the Australians were without peers (probably, the Pommies maintained, because of our dubious background of convict settlements and bushrangers), the British troops were nevertheless just as diligent and frequently achieved spectacular successes. Thus, though it was the Australians who stole the most food, it was the Pommies who first stole drugs: though it was the Australians who smuggled into Pudu a wireless set, it was the Pommies who brought home some emetin: though it was the Australians who brought in the first weapons—broken bayonets—it was the Pommies who, with typical British abandon, went the whole hog and blithely lined up for the usual search at the gaol gates with hand grenades resting comfortably in the curly hair under their various hats.

One of the earliest successes in this direction was the party who, working near a hospital, managed to "send off" (as the language of those days was for the verb "to steal") a large number of lumps of sulphur and several packages of something labeled Mg SO_4. Anything labelled Mg SO_4 must—the gentleman who sent it off thought—be extremely precious. He accordingly deposited one large package down his G string, gave another to his comrade, who did the same, and they then waddled off with every outward and visible sign of being afflicted either by acute elephantiasis or chafe. They were both of them extremely displeased, upon successfully passing all searchers and re-entering the gaol, to be told by the M.O., to whom they presented their treasure, that it was no more nor less than Epsom salts. The M.O., however, was delighted both with the Mag. Sulph.—as he insisted upon calling the salts—and with the lumps of sulphur. He asked only that we acquire for him a grease which he could use as a base for the sulphur, whereby an ointment might be produced. Next day accordingly three ten-pound tins of British Army mosquito repellent—which had been singularly useless as a repellent of mosquitoes and was now to be given another chance as a base for ointments—were sent off and brought home to the noble doctor. Thus equipped, the doctor, his hospital in our courtyard now littered with dysentery patients and his medical parades attended daily by a long queue of those who suffered from rice balls, set to work.

All internal complaints were treated with Epsom salts: all external complaints—work-party injuries, battle wounds or skin diseases that ranged from tinea to scabies—were smeared with sulphur set in a base of mosquito cream. This latter, when applied to a raw scrotum, produced the most lively results and proved highly diverting for those who still awaited their treatment. The sulphur-and-mosquito-cream mixture was known, unlovingly, to the inhabitants of Pudu as Hell-Fire Ointment and produced no cures whatsoever. Perhaps, however, the psychological effect of queuing up to see a doctor, even though it meant the partial and public incineration of what one had once regarded as the most private and inviolate portions of one's anatomy, was good. In retrospect, I'm not sure—there must, however, have been some reason, I feel, why I queued so persistently.

The problem of dysentery the M.O., a young New Zealander, attacked with decision and courage. The death rate was now so high this his violent methods seemed justifiable. He put all dysentery sufferers onto a liquid diet—rice gruel and the juice of a few boiled sweet potato leaves which grew outside the gaol—and flushed them out violently with repeated doses of salts. It must have taken great strength of mind to deny starving men any solid food and then to shatter their weakened frames with the explosive qualities of concentrated Mg SO_4. He did it, however, and quite a few of those who had seemed to be dying survived.

Quite a few, however, did not. The hospital in those early days was a shambles—in spite of the tireless efforts of the few orderlies. Every inch of floor space was occupied by the sick—some lying on the bare concrete: some on sacks: some on stretchers. Everywhere orderlies ran with improvised bedpans, or with pails of water, to clean up men who in their helplessness had fouled themselves. In between the patients squatted their friends, murmuring words of encouragement and brushing off the flies. And every now and then a low moan would presage that pool of black blood which meant that a man's bowels had burst and his life gone.

It was weeks before the liquid-diet-cum-salts campaign slowed this flood of death down to the steady trickle that endured right through the last six months in Pudu Gaol. Distressingly the toll of death in those days fell almost entirely on the British troops. This, perhaps, was not surprising. Hundreds of Argylls and Leicesters had been almost dead from starvation and fever when, after weeks of refuge (from the time of the battle at Slim River), they had eventually been captured. Nor is anyone from the United Kingdom as hardened to heat as the Australian. Finally, we Australians had all had the benefit of a lifetime of rich food and sunshine and exercise, which the average Pommy most decidedly had not.

So the unequal slaughter continued and we Australians looked on appalled as, day after day, little Padre Duckworth held funeral services for two or three. As the body was borne out through the communal triangle, loosely crated in a crude coffin, everyone who was not out at work stood silently to attention. The fear that had first gripped me when I saw the young Argyll dead at my feet on the staircase used to hit hard at those moments. And on every frowning forehead of every silent man one could, as the bodies were borne out to be buried, read the same thought—who next and how to stop it?

Then one day the impossible happened—an Australian died! Died of dysentery like anyone else. It was most unnerving to our recently acquired sense of national immunity. To overcome our spiritual malaise at this outrageous blow, and to reassert our national pride, we resolved to face it out with as elaborate a funeral as we could contrive.

By borrowing almost every stitch of clothing in the entire gaol and by conducting the ceremony in the early morning before the working parties were due to leave, we managed to line both sides of the path which passed up the centre of the communal triangle of lawn with men who wore shirts, shorts, socks and boots. All hundred and thirty-odd Australians stood there at attention: behind them the English and Scottish troops whose clothes we wore. Four friends bore the coffin up the path. The moment should have had dignity. Unfortunately, however, it was impossible not to observe that the coffin was only a crude plank crate with three-inch gaps all round; that the shrunken little body inside rocked grotesquely from side to side in this ill-fitting couch: and that the stench of decomposition—so swift in that climate—was most pronounced. All dignity was entirely gone—this was just a corpse that stank. As I resolved that never in my life would I go to another funeral, the Japanese guard at the main gate stood up off his chair, saluted and bowed to the passing cortège.

"It's the only time those little apes care a hoot for us," Hugh muttered. I replied that, as far as I was concerned, it was much too late. We went inside; took off our borrowed clothes and redonned our G strings; returned the shirts and shorts to the Pommies from whom we had borrowed them and then fell in, ready to be marched out by Nippon for a day's work.

4 HOW TO BE A P.O.W.

4 HOW TO BE A P.O.W.

It would be as well, perhaps, at this stage, if I made clear my views on "How to Live as a Prisoner of War." With world events now so faithfully following the time-honoured build-up to a war, these views may be of value—and it will do me personally no harm at all to repeat them as the only thing for which, in time of war, I am now fully trained is capitulation.

The first essential for any would-be P.O.W. is, of course, to find a suitable foe to whom to surrender. Such a foe should most definitely be a signatory of the Hague Convention and—if possible—a fully affiliated member of the International Red Cross as well. He should *not* be Japanese. On second thoughts, he shouldn't even be an Asiatic—which includes, of course, the Russians and, therefore, limits the field of potential captors most sadly.

Next, having selected one's future host and surrendered to him—a procedure which should be carried out well away from the heat of battle where even the purest of intentions tend to be misunderstood—we come to equipment which the prisoner-of-war-to-be should bear with him into captivity.

First and foremost he should carry no military documents which are likely to involve him in any foolish questioning by his captors. The safest status is that of stretcher-bearer; failing that, cook. The prospective prisoner is, therefore, advised to hand himself over to the enemy fully documented as either one or the other of these. This will ensure his safe and immediate accommodation without the dubious benefit of interrogation.

Thereafter life becomes the usual story of buying and selling. The prisoner must be able to buy what he needs and, for this purpose, he must have goods to sell. From my own experience, and all the distilled wisdom of four years' such unscrupulous dealing, I would advise him to equip himself before surrendering with a headful of gold-filled teeth, as many signet rings as he feels he can decently wear, at least one Parker pen, possibly two Rolex waterproof watches (two watches can quite legitimately be worn so long as they are not both on the same wrist), and finally a Bengal razor. All these commodities have international value and should, therefore, be readily salable anywhere. Bulkier objects, such as typewriters and motor-car parts, though they command a good price, are not advisable since they are not so easily recognizable as personal effects and may, therefore, be confiscated by an unsympathetic foe. This, however, depends entirely upon the discretion with which one has selected one's foe.

The prisoner by this time is securely installed in some gaol, or concentration camp, or other penal institution and his physical condition has now passed beyond his control. His well-being henceforth depends upon the supply of medicines, food and clothing which can be ensured for him by the Red Cross (in our case, in Malaya, virtually NIL) and the skill with which he can exchange his various assets for those things of which he finds he is in need. So much for material aspects of the art of being a prisoner of war.

But in the mental sphere it is left to the prisoner to make himself or break himself. He may even kill himself. There is no one, other than himself, to whom he can turn for spiritual help.

So, even in those early days, I adopted the inflexible philosophy which all who would survive such incarcerations as the Japanese offer must adopt.

First I determined that I would eat *everything*—thus, cats, dogs, frogs, snakes, bad fish, bad meat, blown tinned food, snails, grubs, fungus, crude vegetable oil, green leaves from almost anything that grew, roots and rubber nuts all went the same remorseless route.

In addition I determined that I would never complain about any food we did receive because that might unnerve someone who had just steeled himself to swallow it: similarly, that I would not tolerate the company of anyone, however much I liked him, who himself complained. One could have no time for the man who pointed out to you that your rice was full of weevils—one pretended that the weevils were not there and ate them, being grateful for the calorific content they might yield.

I determined that, so long as trees grew leaves, or the earth grass, I would eat of these products in an effort to stave off the vitamin-deficiency diseases which were already rampaging through me. It was significant in those days that the ornamental bushes which grew round the gaol were quickly stripped of every leaf that grew on their branches.

Finally, I determined that I would seek help from my friends as seldom as possible and expect it never. I would make my own decisions unaided and abide by them. I would steal whenever and wherever possible. I would keep my mind active by reading whatever I could lay hand to and by talking to whomever could endure me.

I started this policy of mental activity to ward off mental atrophy by reading the Bible, which I found in Pudu's execution cell, twice. I enjoyed it the second time infinitely less than I had the first time, and the first time I had not enjoyed it at all. It was with relief that I turned from the high-flown Hebraic imagery of the world's best seller to the cynicism of the complete works of George Bernard Shaw—a volume I found one day whilst a party of us repaired the sadly battered beds of a Japanese brothel, and which was later to be the cause of my being involved in much nastiness with a gentleman called Terai. That, however, was to come later. For the moment, armed with G.B.S. and a thousand men to talk to and a diary in which I entered numerous uncharitable remarks about Nippon and Nipponese civilization, I felt that, from the point of view of remaining articulate and sane, I was adequately equipped.

Life staggered on. Hugh's arm healed up, leaving his fingers badly weakened. I developed a savage purple swelling right up the leg which the doctor prodded, leaving a suety dent for hours afterwards. "Edema," he pronounced—which sounded impressive enough to me. Nevertheless, I asked: "Edema—what's that?" and he replied tersely: "Swelling," which did not please me at all, being no more than the least medical clod in the gaol could have told me. The swelling became acutely painful with electric stabbings—then vanished. Hugh's happy feet drove him to join the sleepless band who every night walked round and round the second-floor balcony which flanked the well of the three tiers of cells. Arthur's wind got worse, his figure gaunter and his blue eyes more glittering. And one day, as our work drew to its bellow-rent close, I turned to Harry and said: "Thank God in another hour we'll all be back at home." So, after only a few months, those high claustrophobic walls, the bare bug-ridden concrete cells, the crowded patches of worn grass and that ornate white fountain which was the communal bath of a thousand men had changed from being a prison to *Home.* Life was indeed assuming a different aspect.

The next day, having arrived at the stage where I could think of a cell in a gaol as "home," Hugh and I determined to make it so. We mentioned the subject to Arthur and he was enthusiastic. We set out on the day's work determined to steal fittings suitable to the embellishment of a room in one of His Majesty's lousiest prisons.

At night, when we returned, we had some promising material. Hugh had sent off an electric light globe and a lamp shade. Arthur had collected a vase, a small mat, some signal wire and four nails. I had acquired a Balinese head in wood and a stool. The stool, during the search, I had sat on and it therefore escaped the guard's attention: but the head (life size), even though I lay it negligently on the ground and rested my foot on it as if it were a rock, the guard spotted. Much bellowing and pushing about. Then, unfortunately, the unhealed wounds in my foot began to bleed furiously and (as usual at the sight of blood) all the Nips became very unpleasant.

It was explained to me, by gestures, that my head was about to be rendered as bodiless as the Balinese one. Though most reluctant, I was forced to kneel. The guard commander took out his sword and swished it. Then, advancing left foot foremost, pace at a time in that graceless fashion which the Japanese swordsman always uses, and swinging the sword, double-handed, sharply downwards at each step, he moved towards me. Finally, with a hoarse "Banzai," he bounded the last few feet and brought his sword down with a resounding thud. The Balinese head lay beside me cleft in two.

As the Nips laughed uproariously at this demonstration of their national humour, an Argyll put a hand under my elbow and helped me to my feet (a service for which I was grateful). We marched inside the gaol. When I sat in my cell a few moments later, a squat, broad-shouldered figure, a coal miner from Newcastle-on-Tyne, appeared in the doorway.

"Here's the head you brought back, Aussie," he said, holding it out, "half of it, anyway," he amended. To bring in that half head after the demonstration the guard had given of their temper at that moment was a gesture which would have taken more courage than I shall ever have. All I could say, though, was: "Thanks, Shorty," whilst Arthur said: "Good on you, mate," and Hugh curiously examined the wooden carving.

"That's all right," said Shorty, rather embarrassed, "I hate those mookers anyway," and strode out, through the grill, back to the British cells.

Pete—the ex-fat boy—appeared in the doorway.

"Any of you blokes know the leggi number?" he asked.

"No," said Arthur and I together.

"Go away," said Hugh rudely. Sadly Pete left. One could see in his every line that no one understood how hungry he felt.

We stood the half head—the face was intact, the back of the skull had been severed—on the stool in the corner of the cell. The signal wire we made into a length of flex and ran it along the top of the wall out through the door. There, using two of Arthur's four nails, we plugged the flex into the main gaol power line which ran along the front of the cells just above door level. Then we fitted Hugh's bulb into the lamp shade, which included a socket, joined the socket to the flex and—to our delight, for none of us was mechanically inclined—we had light. Pale pink light. Next day Arthur brought home frangipani blooms and that night we sat on the cell slab, our feet on a mat, our beards gleaming in soft pink light, my map of the world confronting us from the wall, a delicately carved wooden face gazing at us from the corner, a vase of white, sweet-scented flowers on the floor. We felt most elegant. The doorway was crowded with admiring soldiery. Hugh suddenly spun round from the back wall of the cell against which he had been leaning and jabbed with an indignant thumb: "Blast those bloody bugs," he declaimed, and, as he scratched at his left shoulder and jabbed with his left thumb and the air became full of that familiar musty smell, the illusion of elegance vanished. Nevertheless, it had been worth it.

5 TOJO NUMBER TEN

Our community in Pudu received fairly regular injections of fresh blood, which were stimulating to us old hands even if they involved some personal discomfort to the newcomers. Thus, all throughout the first six weeks of our imprisonment, there was a steady stream prisonwards of these "new boys" (as they were called). But by April the stream had slowed down to a trickle—a trickle which by its very smallness attracted more interest each time it found its way through those big gaol gates.

One of the most interesting of these additions to our number was the case of Mowatt and Elliott. Geoff Mowatt had been a government official near Tampin in the blissful days of the peace. He was cultured, young and played the cello. Softly spoken, short and curly-haired, he seemed the last sort of person to go irritating the Japanese. Nevertheless, he, with Elliott, a dark and rather sombre athlete, had decided after the capitulation of Singapore that they would escape.

Accordingly, they climbed through the wire round Changi Camp and made their way by night to the northern coast of the island. There they appropriated to themselves a small sampan and two shovels. With the shovels they then paddled themselves across the causeway to Johore—paddled in a brilliant moonlight which the poetic cellist found quite beautiful. His more sober companion was not markedly interested in the beauty of a moon which could so easily make their presence known to the Japanese and urged him tersely to concentrate on his paddling.

They crossed the short gleaming stretch of water undetected and headed north through Johore. Before they had gone far, daylight compelled them to lie low. Next night jungle slowed their progress to a few miserable miles. Next night both men found themselves laid low with malaria.

Upon the rock of this wretched disease their whole gallant enterprise seemed to be foundering. Nevertheless, they compelled themselves to struggle on until eventually they collapsed just outside a Malayan kampong—where they were discovered by natives when daylight dawned.

For a few days the kampong debated what to do with these white men. Then, relying on the extreme illness and weakness of both, they decided to hand them over to the Japanese and claim the reward of several hundred dollars per head which Nippon offered. They therefore arrived one morning and announced their intention of so doing.

In spite of their illness, now very grave, both Mowatt and Elliott thought poorly of this plan and at once put up a most spirited opposition. This the Malays quashed by laying them low with parangs—a procedure which left a huge wound gaping in the left side of Mowatt's skull.

Thus they arrived in Pudu—Mowatt half scalped, yellow with fever and loss of blood: Elliott, tall, athletic and, with his classic beard, looking rather like a Christ. Slowly they were nursed back to life. The wound in Mowatt's head healed into a savage cicatrice: Elliott's fever subsided. Mowatt told us their story (Elliott never talked to anyone) and Pudu settled down once again to its routine of working parties, inside-hygiene parties, sleeping in cells, living in G strings, and bare feet.

Having resurrected all the bridges which our own troops had blown in the course of their evacuation, the Imperial Japanese Army—better known to us as the I.J.A.—now required us one morning to remove bombs and heavy shells from a huge underground dump outside Kuala Lumpur—better known as K.L.—and to load them onto trucks, thence onto trains. We refused.

The Japanese brought out all their machine guns and lined them up opposite our mutinous squads. They repeated their request. We agreed.

All that day, and for weeks thereafter, we moved bombs, shells, grenades and explosives out of the dark caverns of the dump. We loaded them onto waiting lorries and then transhipped them onto trains. We were thus making a direct contribution to the Japanese war effort and it was a fact for which we did not greatly admire ourselves. The munitions we manhandled were, we realized, to be used against our own Allied troops in New Guinea and the Solomons.

It was only natural, therefore, that men should attempt to reassert their pride by various and devious means, none of which would greatly have recommended themselves to the Nips had they been discovered.

Mortar bombs are extremely susceptible to moisture. Therefore, in the darkest recess of that cavern, men queued up to urinate in case after case of mortar bombs. It required organization and cunning to dampen the maximum number of bombs with the limited facilities (as it were) available. We nevertheless felt that we had done well.

Anti-tank guns do not fire very accurately if the rifling in their narrow muzzles is blocked. Accordingly, we poured molten pitch down the barrels—a hit-and-run operation which involved the sacrifice of many a mug or dixie as a receptacle for this boiling down and carrying to the gun. But it was done. And for every breechblock which we scrubbed and scoured free of rust there was one barrel which we sabotaged with tar.

Sticks of gelignite and grenades—particularly bakelite grenades—are small and easily secreted when one is practised in the art of secreting. Thus, under the inspired leadership of Frank Van Rennan, who taught us the value of cold-blooded bluffing, all those who had headgear wore a hatful of explosives back to Pudu. When we were searched, though our guards looked in all the usual places and anywhere else that was even remotely anatomically feasible, they did not look on our heads. The gaol became infested with sudden death and as a result the mass execution with which we were so constantly being threatened assumed a less one-sided air.

Finally, as we emerged for the last time one shift after a particularly vile day's work in these subterranean dumps, one of our number announced blithely that he had set two booby traps inside which, in his considered opinion, would start a chain of detonations sufficient to destroy all the ammunition in that hillside and half of K.L. as well. This remarkable feat was greeted with mixed emotions for several excellent reasons. Those reasons were, in this order: (1) The gentleman concerned was a sapper and should, therefore, know his stuff. (2) The gentleman concerned had not made any particular note in which of the branches of the main tunnel he had set his booby traps, and could not remember even approximately where they were because of the Stygian gloom inside: and (3) we were all due to return to the dump for more bomb loading the next day.

The prospect of treading on the sapper's booby trap, however uplifting from the point of view of the Allied war effort, was generally agreed to be depressing as far as the more immediate problem of oneself surviving the war was concerned. The most that we could extract from him in the way of encouragement was that a firm footstep was required to set the booby trap off. We all resolved thenceforth never to tread firmly. In our bare feet the next day, and for a week thereafter, we worked with catlike tread in sixteen-hour shifts of agonizing apprehension that the booby trap, the dump, Kuala Lumpur and ourselves were all, in one glorious detonation, abruptly to ascend heavenwards—a fiery tribute to the ingenuity of the Royal Engineers. But for a week there came no noise more explosive than the shuffling of our own bare soles, and the incessant screaming of our guards and the rather monotonous thuds of blows as they urged us on to more "Speedo." And then the lorries which were used to carry the ammunition we brought out of the bowels of the earth all broke down and the task was abandoned. In spite both of the sapper and of the fearsome risks incurred by the "grenade runners," who so cheerfully followed the example of Van Rennan, we had all survived.

Van Rennan had not so assiduously been acquiring ammunition for nothing. He had come into the gaol (after a month's guerilla warfare against the Japanese, in spite of the fact that Singapore had fallen) only to save the native population from further reprisals against his own energetic demolition activities. Already at that time, one village of two hundred had had all its menfolk killed and all its women mutilated because Van Rennan and his few friends had blown up a Japanese troop train in that area. But though he had surrendered himself voluntarily neither he nor his friends intended staying. They proposed leaving the gaol as soon as their plans were complete, heading for the west coast, where they had arranged—through native contacts, for they had all lived in Malaya as planters before the war—for a boat to be waiting for them: and from there they were going to sail to India.

It was an ambitious plan and yet it was by no means hopeless. Van Rennan, Harvey, Graham and two others had lived in the area and knew it well. They all spoke both Malay and Tamil. They had organized a chain of contacts right across to the coast. Those who were to remain behind had perfected a system whereby the check parades could be faked to conceal their departure for twenty-four hours.

Thus they hoped to evade capture by the local vigilantes and we hoped to delay the hue and cry until they were well out of the way, and then to protect ourselves from reprisals by informing the guard commander of their escape as soon, apparently, as it had been made. Of the two the former was the more difficult operation, for the Japanese had stirred all the natives in Malaya into a fiercely anti-European frame of mind by promising them that if Europeans escaped from a point A and were recaptured, or reported, at a point B, then mass executions would be carried out on all communities between points A and B for having condoned that escape. This meant that travel could only be undertaken by night and that, even then, it must only be undertaken by those who looked like natives and talked like them. For this reason a tentative suggestion that I might join the escapees was abandoned. I had fair hair of a conspicuously un-Malayan hue.

In both these respects the escape party itself, however, was well equipped. They had all acquired sarongs and native shoes and shirts: they were dark: they all spoke the local dialects. Moreover, they had stolen sufficient food to enable them to do the whole journey to the coast without asking for any help from the native population, and they had ample grenades with which to defend themselves if that regrettable contingency should arise.

To make up their numbers to an adequate crew for a trip across the Indian Ocean in an open boat, they accepted two recruits. One an Australian named Bell: the second a young Dutchman called Jan who, as co-pilot of a Wildebeeste, had already survived death when his plane crashed in flames and he found himself without a parachute. He had climbed to the tail of the blazing plane—the only portion not alight—and when it struck the earth, he had been catapulted hundreds of feet through the air into the soft foliage of the top of a high jungle tree. He had climbed down unharmed and wandered round for a few days until eventually he found his pilot, badly burned, at the foot of another tree. The two had been handed over to the Nips by Malays. Jan was generally agreed to be lucky and his acquisition by the escape party was accepted by all as an omen of its success.

The big night came and the party left the gaol silently by the side gate, the locks of which had been receiving their attention for some time past. Early next morning we Australians fell in on the check parade with the task of covering up for the departure of Jan and Bell. Though this was simple enough, it was worrying because it had to succeed the first time. If the little Nip miscounted the four men who asked his permission at the beginning of the parade to go to the latrine (two of whom instead took up blank positions carefully left for them in the rear rank), then he would recount our whole parade and then go over to the latrines and count the men there. Then we would be two short. Then there would be explanations to make, which would be difficult. And it was quite possible, knowing the Nipponese standards of addition, that by adding four alleged absentees to the total of the men who stood before him, the guard—who rejoiced in the name of "Frogface"—would NOT reach the total which was daily required of our particular squad.

It was with considerable relief, therefore, that we heard him say, at the conclusion of his count: *"Okayga—yazumé* [O.K.—stand at ease]." Now all that remained to be seen was whether three similar such bluffs had worked with three of Frogface's equivalents on three other check parades so that all the escapees were covered. It was not until the figures for the entire gaol had been received and checked against the figures of the day before that any one parade was dismissed, so we had to stand there and wait.

Harry stood beside me and laughed. He was one of those to whom the task of asking for permission to go to the latrines and then joining the back rank had been allotted.

"The raw prawn of all time," he commented, "and Frogface fell for it. Get on to him," he urged me, pointing a contemptuous finger, "will you just get on to him?" So we watched him approach us: Harry with open scorn, I with considerable anxiety. Would he dismiss us or would one of the other squads have slipped up, which would involve the whole gaol in a recount?

"Okayga," he grunted, "all men go." We were dismissed and the escape party now had twelve hours' start.

That was the theory of it. Unfortunately, the practice was different. Before they had even cleared the outskirts of K.L. the small band of escapees had been seized by natives and had been forced to fight their way free. Twice more during the night march natives attempted to grapple with them and at dawn a large patrol of Japanese infantry had suddenly surrounded them as they studied their maps. Escape was impossible and to attempt to fight was suicidal. They therefore surrendered with the best grace possible.

At lunchtime they were back in the gaol—their return witnessed by a horrified community of prisoners. They were shackled, looked badly shaken and pale and were not allowed near us. We shouted out to them and they smiled back wanly. They were taken to the cells above the guardhouse—the ones we had all originally inhabited before our move to the main wing of the gaol.

We asked could we give them some food. The request was refused. Instead the guard commander asked some very awkward questions as to just how, with eight men missing, the gaol had nevertheless managed to return its full numbers on the morning check parade. Without any hesitation at all, the blame was cast squarely upon the shoulders of Frogface and his three revolting friends and their combined inability to count. Though this was not very feasible and did not really endear us to Frogface or his three friends it served for the moment to addle the guard commander, who retired to think it over.

In a manner typically Japanese, when he did think it over, he went off at a tangent and arrived at a completely different but most unwelcome conclusion. The recaptured men, he recollected, had had in their possession grenades. There might, he thought, be other grenades in the gaol. Fortunately he said so to one of the guards and the English duty officer, who was a bright lad, heard him.

Consequently when, five minutes later, the guard suddenly swept through cell block after cell block looking for bombs, they swept through just three minutes behind two officers and a rice sack. Into the rice sack went every piece of explosive material we possessed. As the tour continued, the sack grew heavier, but the officers struggled gamely on until they had collected all the incriminating evidence. Then, just about thirty seconds ahead of the guard—who were now very bad-tempered indeed—they lugged the sack out into the British courtyard, dragged it to the fountain which was our communal bath and deposited it and its contents into the top of the tall lily-shaped basin out of which the water spouted into the main fountain below. When the guards appeared in the courtyard, they observed two childish officers playing rather silly games in the water. With curt "Currahs" they ordered them out and sent them packing. Then they themselves went back to the guardhouse and reported that there were no grenades in the gaol. We resumed our breathing.

It became fairly obvious, after two days in which they had been allowed no food, no water and no latrine facilities, that the Japanese were evilly disposed towards our escape party. Van Rennan himself sensed this and managed to throw a note into the main triangular courtyard urging us to ask for clemency towards Bell and Jan, both of whom were only in their very early twenties. This was done and the Japanese seemed agreeably inclined towards the request, nodding their heads and saying, "Baby-ka," many times.

But, in spite of their head-noddings, the next morning we saw the whole party suddenly appear in the gaol's entrance just outside the guardhouse. All their gear had been dumped near them—haversacks and clothing—but they themselves were still fiercely shackled and were filthy dirty. They looked very weak.

The Japanese motioned them towards the gaol gate. Enquiringly, Van Rennan gestured with his foot towards the pile of kit bags. The Japanese nodded negatively, emphatically. It could mean only one thing. They knew it: and we knew it.

They were brave men, those eight. Their heads went up, and while we shouted cheerful remarks at them, trying not to let them know what we sensed, they grinned back at us so that we shouldn't sense what they knew. They went through the big gate. Whenever one of them turned our way, a mass smile would appear on all the strained faces that watched their departure. As soon as their backs were turned, the smile vanished. They were prodded and shoved, clumsy with their arms and legs bound, into a truck. They turned to face us; we smiled. The guard spoke to them: they looked down at him: our smiles vanished. The guard stopped speaking: they looked up: we smiled. Then the truck lurched off and the big gates shut.

They were gone. "There," I thought with a lump in my throat, "but for the grace of a mop of sun-bleached hair, goes Braddon."

The Indian who drove the truck told us later that they were taken to K.L. cemetery, there made to dig their own graves and then shot down into them. So ended the first, most promising and last escape plot of Pudu.

A month later, as if to compensate us for the loss of eight of our best men, two more Argylls were brought in. Theirs was a proud but sad tale. Cut off at Slim River, forty Argylls had fought a private war for weeks in the jungle until their ammunition vanished. Undaunted, they built themselves a palm-frond shelter and settled down to live a life of freedom in occupied Malaya until the British reinvaded.

Malaria attacked them. One after the other died. Carefully each was buried and a cross with his name and number placed on his grave. By July only four remained. One day all four fell ill and two died. The remaining two buried them and then—realizing that they had not long to go and yearning for the company they had heard was to be found in Pudu Gaol—they handed themselves up to the Japanese.

They came to us emaciated and dying. But for their last few days they had plenty of company, comrades who talked their own almost unintelligible dialect, and as much comfort as we could bestow. When they died they seemed happy enough.

The year was now jogging steadily along in this strange life. The Emperor of Japan—to our unanimous regret—survived yet another birthday (the occasion being celebrated by the lavish gift to each man of two half-inch cubes of canned pineapple). Beards were luxuriant and coiffures poetic. We even played fiercely contested games of baseball on the communal triangle of lawn—a practice which ceased abruptly when we defeated a team put up by our guards. Our nightly dreams about food—quaint phantasies of chocolate éclairs mixed with steak and served heavily garnished with egg—became less recurrent and sometimes stayed away for as long as a week on end. Meantime, our own meagre ration of rice was distributed with machinelike smoothness, a faint flavour being added to it by the additicn of the few native vegetables we grew in the gaol garden (mainly a Malayan root most aptly named ubi kayu—which means "wooden potato").

Tokyo time was applied to all towns in Malaya. We were ordered to talk only in terms of Tokyo time. We accordingly stole an old clock and placed it prominently in our cell block. It always read British Malayan time and we ordered our life by it. A foolish gesture, perhaps, but, in a life where little more than gestures was possible, most gratifying!

The Japanese declared generously that they would pay us for our work—ten cents a day. Thus, if one worked every day of the month, one earned the lavish sum of three dollars. This would buy a small handful of dried fish, a little coconut oil in which to fry it, and perhaps a banana or two. (Bananas became almost a "must" on one's shopping list, because they were reported to contain Vitamin E. And Vitamin E, we were told, combated the sterility with which we were all threatened by our M.O. if the rice diet continued—which it gave every indication of doing for years.)

As soon as we received our pay, we seized the opportunity to do something for the men who lay day after day in the hospital in our courtyard. We all gave twenty-five cents from our three dollars and this Padre Duckworth took into town with him and with it bought soap and food and odd titbits. No money was ever better invested. It was sheer delight to see the faces of those near corpses, who for weeks and months had been living a life of the most complete squalor, as the little padre dished out his purchases to each one.

We resolved that we would make the same contribution each month. An officer, with the soul of a born Socialist pleasure wrecker, suggested that the scheme was, in fact, a form of health insurance from which any man who fell ill would benefit. He was howled down with the greatest promptness. In our life, where we mostly had nothing to give, we were not thus lightly to be deprived of our once-monthly opportunity to be human. It remained a direct gift to the sick and after the first payday we were delighted when the Pommies announced their intention of "being in it." For the next six months there was always cash in hand to buy anything within reason for a sick man who needed it—whether it was black market drugs or black market food.

We also, at this time, learnt how to increase our own comfort by laying any pieces of wearing apparel which became louse-infested on ants' nests. The ants then devoured not only the lice but also their eggs, which they laid deep in seams and un-get-at-able corners. Having rid ourselves of the itch of lice, the next step was to rid ourselves of the itch of beards. We drew up a roster and one by one had our beards removed with a razor ground out by Harry from a Japanese bayonet he had stolen. It was not a comfortable operation (Harry himself described his laboriously ground-down blade as "rough as guts"), but thenceforward we were clean-shaven—that is, we each had one shave a week which, by the standards of those days, was clean-shaven. Our barber was none other than Jack Mullins—his bomb-torn throat now healed—who, equipped with scissors and clippers as well (these latter mysteriously acquired by the padre), kept us all fairly tidy.

Strangely enough, our life was almost totally devoid of friction. It is remarkable to record that in the Pudu community of one thousand, and the Changi community, which fluctuated between seven and seventeen thousand, and all the camps in Thailand, over a period of four years, there were no cases of murder, remarkably few of theft (from our own men, that is—the Nips, of course, were fair game) and only three suicides. Very few other such large communities over such a long period could boast similarly. It was a tribute to the Anglo-Saxons' ability to live together—one which was in marked contrast to the Dutch camps and, later, an Italian influx, all of whom brawled incessantly.

It was natural, however, that such an environment should breed extreme philosophies. Every cell had its rabid Communist, or its rabid atheist, or its rabid Roman Catholic. There were only two qualifications to anything one thought or did in those days. The first, that you should tolerate other people being equally as extreme as yourself even though diametrically opposed to yourself. The second, that your opinions and actions should never fall within that category known to Australians as "bludging on your mates"—in other words, that they should never conflict with the common well-being.

There were, of course, cases where the border line was difficult to determine. Thus, in Pudu a small group—very small—became fanatically religious and convinced themselves that *all* ills could be cured solely by faith. Part of their way of life consisted of calling everyone —even the most improbable types—"brother": part in praying vociferously and fervently at all sorts of unexpected times (during the course of which praying they banged their foreheads on the gaol's concrete floors with thuds that were quite distressing): and part in refusing even such little medical treatment as was available.

Since they all had ulcers and dysentery, it was a fine point of gaol ethics whether they should be forcibly treated or allowed to pursue their own path of prayer, which—on specified dates—was to be followed by miraculous cures. When the cult showed no signs of spreading it was generally accepted that they were entitled to their own point of view. And when—a month later—the last of the small group died (the requisite miracle on the appointed day having failed to materialize), religious fanaticism vanished forever from prisoner-of-war life as I saw it.

We were sent to a lime kiln, quite a large group of us, to load lime—that is, to bag it up and put it on lorries. A filthy job, which scorched all the oil out of one's skin, leaving it cracked and leathery. And when you sweated the lime burnt holes in the flesh—small black holes that you couldn't clean out, so they just grew deeper.

An Australian jacked up and was soon afterwards sent back to the gaol unconscious for his pains. But when the whole party returned at night, he had warned our friends at home what was happening and they were ready for us.

As we marched in—our legs and arms covered in those black burning holes—we were seized by the waiting Pudu-ites, stripped and thoroughly anointed with coconut oil. Every ounce of oil in the gaol—bought with those hard-earned three dollars a month—was there waiting for us. We were smeared and rubbed down as lavishly as if it grew by the thousand gallons in our gaol courtyard. It made no difference who you were, what your unit or nationality—you were smeared and rubbed, then smeared again, until at last all those black burns were clean of the lime that burnt into them and all the precious oil had gone.

It was another of those moments when the friendship of one's fellow men and the warmth of their generosity made the life of Pudu well worth while. Forty of us had consumed the oil supply of a thousand. And to the accompaniment of the Australians' "You'll be right, mate," and the Pommies' "Just a minute, choom, while I put some more on your back," we were made to feel that, except as a solvent of lime, coconut oil was utterly unimportant.

A party of Australians went to work one day on the outskirts of K.L. We worked in one of those chaotic dumps in which the Japanese seem to specialize. It contained lengths of railway line, mortar bombs, drums of petrol, three anti-tank guns, coils of barbed wire and signal wire, a few Mills bombs and a wireless set—Army type. We stacked the petrol, re-coiled the wire, wet the mortar bombs in the traditional manner, shovelled sand into the breech mechanism of the guns, loaded the railway lines onto trucks and endured all day the bellows of "Currah" and "Bugero" from an even more than usually repulsive little Nip.

At the end of the day this worthy was laying about him with his naked bayonet—a habit common to most guards, and one of their less endearing traits—and had laid open the flesh on two foreheads already. It seemed only fair then that, while one of the lads set a Mills-bomb booby trap among the petrol drums, the rest of us—at the instigation of a sergeant called Robbie—should steal the wireless set.

The set was bundled into a rice bag and slung swiftly and unceremoniously from one man to another as we were searched. At the gaol we had another search and felt a certain apprehension. It is remarkable how prominent a field radio in a sack can seem on a search parade. In the midst of this search, however, the Almighty weighed in heavily on our side with a sudden violent tropical storm. Shouting, "*Dammé, dammé: taxan amé* [This is no good to me—too much rain]," our searchers lost all interest in their quest for contraband and scuttled back to the guardroom. We strolled casually past them and down to our cells—Robbie bearing a sackful of potential B.B.C. news bulletins slung negligently over his shoulder.

A few weeks later the set—under the loving care of the small group of officers to whom it had been entrusted—was coaxed into contacting London. For the first time, the resounding triumphs of Duckworth's well-dressed Eurasian gave way to official news. We found the switch-over quite effortless—we had now reached the stage where we could instantly adjust ourselves to anything. Thus, it cost us no grief that whereas the padre's mythical Eurasian had encouraged us with reports of tank battles in Rumania between triumphant Russians and routed Germans the B.B.C. now reported that the Germans were racing down on Stalingrad. The fact that for the first time in eight months we had contact with "Home" almost compensated for the lack of letters to or from our families. The completely irrational confidence in ultimate victory which ran through the veins of every man more than countered the momentary shock of the events of late 1942. To the accompaniment of the Nazis' boasts about the imminent destruction of Russia and the capture of Suez, with the shrill demands of the Nips that India should join the Co-Prosperity Sphere and Australia abandon the cause of the British exploiters ringing out all around us, we left the gaol each day to work. But we left more content than ever before in 1942 because we now had what all prisoners of war crave more than anything else—news from Home, better known in those days (for security reasons) as Ice Cream!

A new field of work was opened up for us by the Jap decision to move everything in the Austin works from wherever it was in the building to some other place in the building. The Jap engineers who supervised this task were quite the most evil-tempered gentlemen we ever encountered.

During one of our midday breaks, an N.C.O. approached us to air his knowledge of English and gloat. "War," he announced, "finish-u soon."

"Go on, eh, Nippon?" Harry encouraged him. "How's that?"

"Birrima, you know?" asked the Nip—we said yes, we knew Burma, a word the Japs could never master.

"Indiah, you know?" asked the Nip—we said yes, we knew India.

"Australiah, you know?" asked the Nip—we said yes, we knew Australia (and an Argyll added testily, "Och, mon, cut oot the geography and tell us your news").

"New Zealand, you know?" asked the Nip—wearily we said yes.

"All," said the Nip, with an embracing gesture towards his own bosom, "all Nippon." We laughed heartily and the round yellow face with the shaved eyebrows and the brown eyes glittering went as close to a flush of rage as the Japanese can manage. Exercising all of his limited self-control, the Nip produced the daily newspaper printed in K.L.—printed in English because no one could read Japanese—and pointed to the headlines. We Australians took one look and became convulsed at once with laughter.

"Nippon's Warrior Gods of the Air Destroy Outer Suburbs of Broome," the paper announced grandiosely. We laughed and laughed and—determined to back us up, though not really understanding—the Pommies laughed, too. In between outbursts, we explained to the Pommies that Broome—whose outer suburbs the Nips claimed to have destroyed—contained one makeshift air strip and about four tin sheds. The laughter became louder as this information spread and the Nip flushed deeper. Finally, his hand, as always when in doubt, flew to the bayonet that hung from his second belt.

"Nippon Number One," he screamed. A solid chorus of British voices assured him that Nippon, on the contrary, was Number Ten.

"Tojo Number One," he bellowed, his eyes bloodshot—and slashed the Argyll nearest him, who, looking as indifferent as if he had been stung by a mosquito, replied: "Churchill Number One—Tojo Number Two Hundred." The hysterical Nip looked to the rest of us for confirmation of this astounding statement. We did not fail him.

"Churchill Number One—Tojo Number Two Hundred," we declared with authority. It was on! Our party was at once fallen in in two ranks and the entire guard, armed with lumps of timber, then marched up and down slugging anyone whose face did not appeal to them—which, I must admit, seemed to be most of us. There is something in the British physiognomy which, it would appear, is most disagreeable to all Japanese.

After twenty minutes, the mass bashing still continued and the Nips—far from getting over it by their outburst—seemed only to be whipping themselves up into a state of murder. Half a dozen of them ran, flailing indiscriminately, their faces contorted, up and down our lines. It was ceasing to be amusing. This was another of those occasions when the lighthearted bashing had passed into the realms of possible massacre. Our survival now depended upon our taking everything standing upright and in silence (to fall to the ground or to complain was a stimulant which, under these conditions, always sent the Japs completely out of control).

Typically, the Nips picked on the biggest man on the parade—an Australian. Standing before him, the smallest guard hit him with everything he had. Lumps of wood, his bayonet, his rifle, his fist.

The Australian took it all expressionlessly. Both ranks of men stiffened with revulsion and a muttering broke out. Another few seconds, and, consequences regardless, discretion would be abandoned and the Nips disposed of once and for all. It was an Argyll who saved us.

Leaping out of the front rank, the little Scot, no taller than the Nip, young and furious, sprang on the guard and rocked him to the foundations of his web-toed canvas boots with a clicking left to the chin.

The silence that ensued was startling. The Nip stood dazed with blood trickling from the right-hand corner of the mouth. All the other guards stood with their hands on their bayonets. Two ranks of prisoners waited, tense. The Scot faced the Nip.

"Leave the Aussie alone, you animal," the Argyll said quietly, his left foot still forward and his fists, though only half clenched, at the ready. On his bare forearm two tattooed hands clasped each other firmly. It was the only friendly thing about that forearm just then. "Leave him alone," he repeated. The Nip moved, raising a hand slowly to his mouth to wipe it. Then, as he lowered the hand and noticed the blood on his fingers, the stillness broke. He screamed with rage and flung himself at the Argyll. Simultaneously the other guards hurled themselves forward and, before we could move, the youngster was lying broken on the ground. The episode was over. We Australians carried him back to the gaol. We did what we could. There was nothing he could not have had so long as we ourselves had it. He died a few days later.

Wherever there are two or three gathered together who come from the United Kingdom, there you will have song. Listening to the Pommies singing was quite a favourite pastime with us Australians. Lacking their unself-consciousness about singing (not to mention their skill in harmony, and their voices), we seldom burst into song ourselves: but we enjoyed them. The corridors of gaols make excellent sounding boards for songs well sung, and not many nights passed without a good lump of vocal nostalgia from our neighbours after darkness had fallen. It was pleasant—or sad, I'm not sure which—to go out to the courtyard as they sang so strongly and pick out the stars that form the Southern Cross lying low and sideways over the cookhouse roof. The stars were about the only things in those days at which one could look and feel "well, at home, at this time, they can see that too." In the absence of any letters between us there was some little comfort to be derived from that thought.

It did not do, though, to go too far out into the courtyard because, if one did, the voices faded a little and one heard instead the Nips in their camp further down the road chanting out the fierce triumphant notes of their victory song—a strident marching song to which they added a new verse for each fresh conquest. It now contained altogether too many verses. I wondered whether they would have the decency to lop off a verse each time one of their conquests was retaken. Hugh said he was certain they wouldn't.

But as well as the noise of Nips singing, if you went far out into the courtyard, there was the sight of tropical lightning, which flashed and flared on the horizon and which—a hundred times since our captivity—had had us out there thinking: "This time it's shellfire. This time our people have landed over there on the coast," and we would go back inside (because the guard got cranky if one stayed out more than the few minutes required for the visit to the latrine one was alleged to be making) and inside we would stand with our faces against the bars, our fingers round them, trying to make out if those flares and flashes really were bombs and shells. Then, late in the night, we would give up hope and crawl back to our cells to lie on the concrete, whilst upstairs—indifferent to everything except their own pain—padded round and round, round and round, the haggard band of those who suffered from happy feet.

The happy-feet men were, with those who suddenly succumbed to cardiac beriberi, our main worry now. Two or three times a week—in the midst of our massaging the soles of those whose feet pained them—a man would suddenly fall flat on his face, smacking it on the concrete with the sound of an apple splitting open, and when one turned him over he was dead. Cardiac beriberi—the heart, suddenly seized by lack of vitamins, stopped. There was no warning, no symptoms, just that sudden noise like a splitting apple, and death. A disconcerting disease to have in one's midst.

And the happy-feet cases seemed to be losing interest in life. Though we set aside the best of our rations as supplementary diet for them—rich vegetable stews that made the mouth pour with water—they were not interested. They were too tired even to collect it at mealtimes. Too languid to eat it if you brought it to them. I became alarmed when Hugh at last refused his helping of the delicious stew I made almost daily by scavenging vegetable peelings from the Nips' garbage heaps.

"What shall I do?" I asked the M.O.

"Leave him alone," the M.O. advised. "They must be left so alone that they're *compelled* to do everything for themselves. Then they might feel hungry again. Then they might eat. It's hard, I know, but they must be left alone."

So, feeling like a murderer—particularly when I caught the startled look in Hugh's blue eyes as I deserted him each mealtime—I left him alone. It was a most difficult decision.

Roused at last by the lamentable absence of our own voices from the nightly sessions of song, we Australians laid our plans. First we negotiated with the Japanese for a piano which we had seen in a brothel of theirs. Pianos, we pointed out, were not essential in brothels. Indifferently, they agreed. Could we have it? Since we could not eat it, nor put it on sores, and since they themselves could not play it, they again agreed. Pudu Gaol thus acquired its first musical instrument.

We then started working to put on a show. Whilst all those who had any pretences to a voice practised assiduously at such indigenous products as "Waltzing Matilda" and "The Maoris' Farewell," another group of us frantically rehearsed the well-known lines of "Pansy, the Mill Girl," and a very vulgar ballet. We rehearsed in the cell set aside for coffin making—an essential industry in our life—but enjoyed ourselves nevertheless. The songs, the melodrama of Pansy (especially the lines when the villain sharpens a knife on his boot and his equally villainous daughter enquires: "Father, what are you doing with that knife?"

"Whist," says Papa—still sharpening.

"But, Father . . ."

"Whist," says Papa, emphatically.

"But, Father," persists the girl, who, though villainous, is literal, "you don't play whist with a knife"—to which Papa, most sensibly, retorts: "Shut up!"), all these, and the ballet, went down enormously well.

The concert was staged at one end of the wall between the cell floors in the British lines. It was watched with wild enthusiasm by the gaol's entire population—including the guards—tier upon tier of spectators gazing down into the well. It reached its unparalleled climax when, in the ballet, Jack Menzies decided that it would be more spectacular if, instead of catching his partner as he (or rather "she") sailed through the air, he refrained from catching him (or rather "her")! As Jack Deloas soared into space, aiming himself accurately at the outstretched arms of Menzies, the gunner accordingly folded those arms over his hairy bosom and watched the furious infantryman hurtle past. To ecstatic cries of "Encore, encore," the show concluded and we all sang "God Save the King"—a song in which the Japanese joined with enthusiasm because it, along with "Dinah," seemed to be one of the few Western tunes they knew.

From then onwards, once a week, we had concerts after the day's work The officers gave a concert, the Pommies gave three or four. Wild Gaelic laments, so dear to the hearts of the Highland regiments, became well known to us: the Welsh sang hymns and Army songs with equal facility and enjoyment: the Englishmen roared "Bless 'Em All." They were nights of deep nostalgia, those concert nights when the Pommies sang. It was an enjoyable nostalgia, though. At those moments Pudu Gaol seemed a real home.

And at this stage, quite unexpectedly, the Nips suddenly announced: "All men go to Singapore." We were not to be shot after all. Some said this was because the Australian Government had made a gesture to Nippon by sending home the ashes of all the Japanese sailors who were killed in the suicide midget submarine attack on Sydney Harbour. Some said it was because they wanted to ship us to New Guinea to use as a bargaining weapon in their propaganda campaign urging Australians to withdraw from the war. Some said it was just Japanese bastardry. Whatever it was, in November of 1942 we left—and for the first time experienced that strange prisoner-of-war obsession of being reluctant to abandon what one had made one's home. Only once did I know men to leave a camp without considerable anguish—that was from Kanchinaburi in Thailand to return to Singapore. And that, of course, was rather different.

So we were split up into parties, mainly according to nationalities, and left. The Australians were one of the first parties to go. The entire gaol fell out to say good-bye: presents were exchanged between "Pommies" and "Aussies" (miserable gifts like the small lump of gulah malacca—a brown sugary substance—given to me by Geoff Mowatt, the cellist who had escaped from Singapore: miserable gifts that meant more than most we had ever received before). As those who remained for later parties shouted and waved, led by the little padre, we marched out of Pudu's big gates for the last time. We marched out leaving the hospital in our courtyard and the fountain full of hand grenades and my map on the wall. Carrying our sick, we headed down the long road to the railway station. This time the natives did not spit at us and stone us—they had already had a bellyful of Co-Prosperity. Everywhere we noticed the desolation which Japanese administration had brought. The drains blocked and foul: pools of water dotted round—breeding ground for the anopheles, and malaria already rampant in K.L.: the demented mobs waiting outside the Opium Centre—further refinement of Japanese civilization, whereby they induced the craving and then maintained ruthless control of the addicts by being themselves the sole distributors: the once immaculate padangs now rank with high grass and weeds.

We clambered into cattle trucks, steel and covered in, thirty or more to a truck. We lay the men with happy feet flat on the floor of the truck, then huddled ourselves in what space remained. In the centre of the truck, in between the doors in either wall, sat two guards, back to back, watching over us. There was a dixie of cooked rice for the trip, rice which was already sour with fermentation. Looking at it longingly, Pete said: "What's the leggi number?" at which Hugh snarled something unintelligible from his place on the floor and Harry, smiling his most crooked smile, said quietly: "Pete, the main reason why I'm so glad we're going to Singapore is that there I shouldn't ever have to see or hear you again."

The train started. A day and a half later we reached Singapore. There, eighty or ninety to an Army lorry, we were driven to Changi—the camp of about ten thousand Allied prisoners of war on the northeastern tip of the island. The second phase of our P.O.W. life had begun.

6 THE PHONY CAPTIVITY

If 1940 France was the phony war, 1942 Changi was certainly the phony captivity. To us who came from Pudu, it was unbelievable.

We arrived in our truckloads and were greeted with a certain official aloofness by a duty officer. This latter at once addressed us dispassionately upon our duties as prisoners of war and the need for discipline—subjects on which we were all of us infinitely better informed than he. He then lost interest in us and said: "All right, gentlemen, break off." So we broke off. Howls of rage. "Gentlemen," it appeared, meant only officers, of whom there were two in our midst: the remainder of us were emphatically *not*, he gave us to understand, gentlemen.

Gentlemen and scum alike, we Pudu-ites gazed at him with growing hostility and prepared not to like Changi. The man beside me, who in K.L., by virtue of his ability to lead and the guts which had carried him from Parit Sulong to Yong Peng on a bullet-torn leg, had been one of our leaders, and who now—by virtue of his two pips—was one of the blessed few entitled to break off, stood his ground and said loudly: "Christ Almighty." That made us all laugh and when the duty officer tersely remarked: "All right, Mr. McLeod, fall out," he did so to the accompaniment of amused comments from the rest of us of: "Ta-ta, Rod—see you in Australia," and "Oh, Mr. McLeod, sir, your slip's showing." The duty officer was incensed at such frivolity and asked us what we thought this was. Harry replied, "Bush week," and the duty officer thereupon—having lost the initiative entirely—dismissed us.

Changi was phony not because of the mass of men in it but because of the official attitude behind its administration. The command determined to maintain full military discipline and establishments, regardless of circumstances or psychology, waiting upon the day when Malay would be invaded by a British force. Accordingly, two principles seemed to guide every decision. One, to retain full divisional and regimental staffs pottering round achieving nothing useful at all in divisional and regimental offices: two, to preserve the Officers—Other Rank distinction by as many tactless and unnecessary orders as could be devised.

This latter was equally hard on both parties. It meant that officers could not freely mix with their friends who were O.R.'s, nor O.R.'s with officers. It meant that O.R.'s were compelled to salute officers whom they had seen cowering in terror at the bottom of a slit trench as well as those who had done a good job. It meant that O.R.'s were compulsorily stripped of clothing which (at their own discretion and on their own backs) they had carried from Singapore seventeen miles out of Changi, so that these garments might be distributed to officers who—though they did not work—must, it was deemed, at all times be well dressed. It meant that officers, far from waiting till their men ate and then eating the same food themselves, ate—under orders—in a separate mess and usually before the men. It meant that officers were allowed to keep poultry, O.R.'s were not. It meant that there was fuel for an officers' club to cook light snacks, for the O.R.'s there was not.

All of which casts no reflections upon the officers concerned any more than it did upon the men. They were under orders. Those orders were inspired by a sincere conviction at top level that it was absolutely necessary—in the cause of an imminent invasion, which, in fact, never came—to preserve the class distinction by privileges not based upon responsibility. It is no cause for complaint. But as a most relative factor in the life of those days, and one of the things most difficult then to comprehend, it must be recorded.

In the same way, to the naïve Pudu-ite, Changi had other shocks. The docile acceptance of Tokyo time as the camp standard rather than the old British time to which we in K.L. had clung so tenaciously. The ceremonial parades at which we were handed from N.C.O. to N.C.O. and officer to officer until, hours later, we were dismissed—all so that the Japanese might know how many of us still languished in their custody. The rash of concert parties and theatres —dozens of them playing each night: everything from *Androcles and the Lion* to Army smoke-ohs. The drug-selling ring which shamelessly traded M. and B. tablets from our own British hospital—tablets more priceless than diamonds—for bully beef from the Malays and Chinese. A ring which could not publicly be stamped out because, it was once rumoured, an M.O. was one of its members (he left the keys of the drug store where the stooges could pick them up) and because some senior officers were also involved and to prosecute them would be "bad for morale." For whose? we Pudu-ites wondered.

Then there were the Spivs of Changi—men with courage and no scruples who went outside the wire each night to collect tinned food from old Army dumps in the rubber and then returned to sell their booty at black market prices to their brethren back in camp. Every community has its villains—and Changi's preoccupation with such laudable though impractical conceptions as respect for officers and salutes thereto allowed its villains a scope which to those of us who had lived the fraternal life of K.L. was nauseating.

But if these follies and blacker sides of human nature became obvious to us for the first time in Changi, so did other things which were wholly delightful. For one thing, we hardly ever saw the Japanese (and the ideal life is, of course, one in which one *never* sees *any* Japanese). For another, the common man of Changi greeted us with overwhelming warmth. We had all been posted "Missing, Believed Killed" for nine months and though, upon our return to the fold, we ruined many a model honour roll upon which we had optimistically been inscribed as "dead," we were, nevertheless, made to feel most welcome.

Thus, all of us found ourselves equipped with a shirt and a pair of shorts and boots. And Piddington, whom I had last seen when I left him at Yong Peng at the beginning of the year, gave me a toothbrush and a pack of Gibb's toothpaste—delightful gift after so long using a finger and ground-up charcoal. The men of Changi were solid gold right through, as men, on the whole, always are.

And as well as the men and the lack of Japs, there were the miles of grass and the trees and the hospital. Changi Camp was made up by the Barrack Square of what had been the Selarang Garrison; plus all its outhouses, officers, W.O.'s and sergeants' quarters; plus Roberts Garrison, across the valley, and its attendant quarters. Selarang had been given to the Australians: Roberts—three quarters of a mile away and separated by a quarter mile of no man's land heavily patrolled by Nips and Sikhs—was made the hospital and British and Dutch area.

The hospital, though badly bomb-damaged (like most of the buildings in Changi), was a joy. It had beds and sheets: anaesthetics and drugs: instruments and an operating theatre. Though there was not a hundredth of what was required, at least there was something. To it went all our happy-feet cases and, for the first time since they were stricken, we felt that they had a chance of getting better.

An extra fillip was given to one's sense of well-being in Changi by the sudden arrival at this time of a few Red Cross parcels and some mail. Though most of us did not get letters, we all received a couple of cigarettes and the flavouring of our rice ration with these few newly arrived tins of condensed milk and bully beef made a most welcome change. The main thing, though, was that something from the outside world had got through to us. Unfortunately it was more than a year before a second tiny consignment (one parcel to each forty men) arrived, and the same interval again before the third and final issue was allowed.

I revelled in the Changi life of wide stretches of grass and trees and buildings where taps ran and people who, though on short commons, still retained an outlook that knew nothing of gaols. Even if a gaol outlook was to come and the bliss could not last, it was still delightful to experience it at all. And each night after the day's work, I would wander down to the Australian Concert Party's quarters, where, sitting on the wood heap at its rear, talk would range freely on all subjects until all hours—with no fear of a guard shouting "Currah" because you should be in your cell.

But it was the day's work that caused the trouble. The command maintained, with admirable lack of understanding, that all men must be kept fully occupied all day. Thus, when I was ordered to sweep a concrete path—a job which was obviously desirable since absolute cleanness meant health—I swept it quite happily and very thoroughly. But when, having completed the task just before midday, an officer arrived and asked: "Finished, Gunner?" and I replied, "Yes"; and he said, "All right, sweep it again!" I became very aggressive. Thereupon he explained that this was for the good of my morale—how we hated that phrase—and that if I continued to be aggressive he would put me on a charge, so I at once became placid. But as soon as he turned his back, I vanished down into the scrub in the gulley between the Convalescent Depot and our quarters and went to sleep under a tree. This I did each day as soon as I finished my allotted task and when, after a few weeks, I was posted on to a Singapore working party, due to leave Changi almost immediately, I was not very sorry.

I went down to the Concert Party and said good-bye to Piddington and his friends: then over to the hospital to say good-bye to Hugh—now looking less wan but still very ill: then on to a truck which transported us back to the realities of prisoner-of-war life—to a native hutted camp set in the middle of a mud flat with lots of Japanese guards. This swamp revelled in the euphemistic title of River Valley. It had been built by the British to house native refugees during the war and had, very sensibly, been deserted by them as early as possible and left to the mosquitoes, the frogs and the bugs who now, as we entered, reigned supreme.

7 SINGAPORE INTERLUDE

River Valley Camp lay on either side of an especially foul little stream from which we were in the habit of fishing frogs for the purpose of conducting frog races and gambling thereon. This gambling was quickly forbidden by the authorities—which ban we habitually ignored, our three-dollar monthly pay check having by this time been rendered valueless by inflation.

Apart from the frogs and the foul little stream, there were rows upon rows of dilapidated attap huts with two tiers of bamboo decking running down each side of a mud passageway. On each of these slept hundreds of men, whilst in the bamboo supports and decks and the attap roofing there lurked many billions of bugs—all of them with Anglophobia.

And as well as the huts and the bugs there was masses of mud—which mud the English troops on the far side of the stream declared to be more villainous in their area, whilst we asserted that it was worse in ours. Over the whole joyful scene hung the cloud of depression caused by evilly disposed guards—Japs who bashed and Sikhs who, given the smallest chance, would rape.

Our work lay in the docks of Singapore's Kepple Harbour—in the go-downs. These go-downs had, in the weeks just before Christmas 1941, been stacked with the food and gifts that Singapore was to buy in the festive season. The festive season, regrettably, had deteriorated into a war which we did not win. The food and gifts were now being sorted, packed and reshipped by our conquerors.

Needless to say, a great deal of the material we handled "went off." Food especially went where it did us most good. The sheds were littered with punctured milk cans and disembowelled tins of fish: the ill-fated gifts were sold (to the accompaniment of the usual bitter wrangling) to the native population.

Came the unprecedented day when in Go-down 2 we found a mixed cargo. For eight riotous hours, as we worked under the justifiably suspicious eyes of our guards, we ate chocolates and cough jubes, drank bay rum, cough mixture, cod-liver oil and essence of vanilla—in equal and indiscriminate quantities: applied hair tonic to the hair, face cream to the face and iodex to almost everything; mixed handfuls of sugar with handfuls of herrings in tomato sauce and devoured the resulting mess and sold lipsticks by the dozen to the Chinese outside the back door. It couldn't last, of course, but by the time we were caught we had all of us stored vast quantities of patent medicines, concentrated foods and culinary flavourings where they could never be retrieved. Though severely thrashed, we were happy. We were also—some of us who hid the money more cunningly than others and, therefore, did not lose it in the search—quite rich. I had gorged to the utmost and smeared myself liberally with great quantities of oils and lotions. I reeked like a chemist's shop. But I had twenty dollars strapped with adhesive tape to my armpit and I had found a truck going back to Changi and had placed on it a packet of tinned food for Hugh. I felt well pleased. Next day we found, to no one's surprise, that we were working not in the food stores but in the go-downs that housed 500-pound bombs instead.

To the accompaniment of the usual bellows of "Currah," "Dammé, dammé," "Speedo" and "One man one," we lugged bombs from the go-down up the gangplank and down into the holds of ships bound for the Pacific islands. Though the 500-pound bombs were obviously beyond the powers of one man, the Nips would not compromise over the 250-pounders. One man one it was. And for day after day, anything up to sixteen hours a day, we staggered under the weight of those bombs in their crude deal crates. They tore the skin and flesh on one's shoulders and the bashings were incessant. For the second time in my career, I found myself thinking of a most unsavoury abode as "home," and towards the end of a day's violence I would long for the mud and the bugs of River Valley.

River Valley was only a brief interlude in our prisoner life: it was not, however, a dull one. The I.J.A. demanded "volunteers" to broadcast their propaganda to the Allies. Unanimously we refused. They threatened: we still refused. They cajoled, offering us the dubious privilege of a monthly visit to their Army-issue geisha girls (rather battered-looking prewar models): we refused. The matter was then dropped.

In an effort to soften us up, though, the guard commander came into our hut one night and announced: "Rockhampton, boom, boom, boom." This meant that Japan had bombed Rockhampton.

"Go on, eh, Nippon?" he was queried as a knot of men gathered round. "Rockhampton, eh?"

"Hei," agreed the guard commander.

"And Sydney?" asked someone else. "Sydney, boom, boom, boom?"

"Hei, Sydney, boom, boom, boom," agreed the Nip.

"Melbourne?"

"Hei," said the Nip, "Melbourne, boom, boom, boom."

"Wagga?"

"Hei," confirmed the Nip. "Wagga, boom, boom, boom."

"Garbo?"

"Hei," he stated. "Garbo, boom, boom, boom." It was obvious that there was no place and no person Nippon had not bombed.

"Tokyo?" Harry asked, his smile wicked.

"Tokyo hei," said the guard, "boom, boom . . ." and then realized how he had been caught.

"Tokyo NEI," he denied. "Boom, boom, boom NEI Tokyo," and swept out in high dudgeon.

That same day, in the course of the pursuit of a particularly agile frog (with which he hoped to win hundreds of dollars in our frog races), one of our number allowed enthusiasm to outstrip discretion and followed its leaping attempts at escape some hundreds of yards outside the barbed wire which surrounded our camp. He was arrested by the guards, who announced their intention of shooting him out of hand.

We could see him tied up to a post outside the guard hut. Night was falling. If he was to be saved, swift action had to be taken.

Every man in the camp at once thronged the parade ground opposite the guard hut and indicated that if any violence was offered the frog hunter they would tear the guards to pieces. The guard commander, therefore, agreed—for the first time—to hear our commanding officer's version of the frog hunter's story. And when he did (surprised that it was not an escape attempt he had foiled), he promised that the captive would be released unharmed.

The commanding officer then came over to our mass of men (about a thousand) and told us that all was well—a verdict which was received with frantic enthusiasm as the crisis had been a real one (one cannot murder Japanese guards and get away with it). The officer, with a cheery smile, then said, "All right, gentlemen, break off," and, for the second time in our gaol-bird career, we were caught. We broke off. And for the second time we were abused roundly for our presumption in so elevating ourselves. But this time we ignored the indignant command to stand fast. We continued to break off, the Number One Gentleman leaping up and down with rage as the parade ground gradually emptied itself of the thousand men who, having gathered spontaneously to save a comrade's life at whatever cost, now withdrew to their huts without the formality of a Dismiss.

Hard upon this episode came the year's best rumour. The Russians were in Greece! For about six hours the camp seethed with excitement at this overnight advance from Stalingrad to Athens. Then the sad truth was unearthed. It appeared that the Japanese proposed working us on extra shifts from that day forward in their attempts to victual their island campaigns. For that purpose, for the moment, *the rations were increased.* Sadly we settled back to a war which was still largely defensive.

The remainder of our stay in the Valley consisted of bomb loading for the Japanese and stealing for ourselves—highlighted by such incidents as the sudden craze developed by Australian soldiers for tattoos (a craze catered for, with complete lack of artistry but the usual regrettable permanency of all tattoos, by one of our more businesslike companions who at once bought ink and needles from the natives and proceeded to desecrate many a hitherto unblemished forearm).

As well as that, I remember reading *Winnie the Pooh* three times (to the great disgust—at first—of my friends). When at last, however, they could stand my frequent bursts of laughter at the antics of Ee-ore and the poems of Pooh no longer, they began furtively dipping into it themselves, and eventually it went round both tiers of our overcrowded and verminous hut. *Winnie the Pooh* is a book which all adults, particularly those whose lives have become difficult, should read.

I also remember the ritual of several men who daily collected one matchboxful of bugs and carefully cast them into the guard hut as they marched past and out to work. I remember the Irishman called Geraghty who, being responsible for guiding a Jap driver on a bulldozer, had quite deliberately waved the Nipponese gentleman on over a forty-foot drop and then persuaded the senior Jap engineer that the accident had occurred because the driver was drunk! Result —one shattered bulldozer: one equally shattered driver. I remember that one day some British Other Ranks were charged with a completely trivial breach of regimental discipline and—to our universal astonishment—sentenced to cells and only one meal a day by our own officers. There being no cells available, they were incarcerated in a filthy wooden shed. There being no room in our lives for such nonsense, we tore the shed down, released the prisoners and used the timber so gained for firewood.

Harry discussed the matter, as he lit a native cheroot purchased with the illegal winnings of a frog race. He lit it from the end of a long length of smouldering rope. Matches had vanished and the everlasting search for a "light" had become quite a dominating factor in our lives, so that a hut which contained its length of slow-burning rope was the object of a steady pilgrimage of smokers from all over the camp.

"These *chuis,*" he said ("chui" is Japanese for "officer"), "ought to take a pull at themselves." He exhaled a cloud of smoke and looked quizzically at the cheroot, his mouth crooked. "Bloody horrible," he declared. "I've smoked tea leaves and chopped-up cane and papaya leaves, but this is the most bloody horrible of all. Now where was I?" he asked.

"The chuis," he was reminded.

"That's right," he agreed, "the chuis. They ought to take a pull at themselves. Someone's got to give orders and they're the blokes that should give 'em. But if an order don't make things better for all of us when you've done it, then there's no point doing it because we've got plenty to do for Nippon anyway." To indicate, however, that there were no hard feelings, he offered his cheroot to the duty officer (who had been in on the whole debate) and said: "Have a drag." The duty officer had a drag, coughed in agony and handed it promptly back.

"For Christ's sake," he said, "where'd you get that?"

"Bought it off a boong for fifty cents," Harry told him.

"Well, he saw you coming," was the officer's retort. Then he started coughing again so Harry and I thumped his back for him. "How are the legs, Russ?" I showed him my legs, which were ugly with the lime burns and the year-old sores on my feet which wouldn't heal. He grunted sympathetically. By way of reciprocation, I asked: "How's your gut?"

"Lousy," he assured me, "went twenty-eight times yesterday and well on the way to beating that today."

It was a sign of the times that man's main preoccupations in those days were the inhalation into his lungs of smoke, the filling of his stomach and the evacuation of his bowels.

The Coral Sea Battle was won, the Japanese endeavouring to cover up their defeat by fantastic claims in the *Syonan Shimbun*[1]—claims which involved the sinking of more Allied vessels of war in one clash than were ever listed in all the copies of *Jane's Fighting Ships*. Perhaps because of the open derision with which these propaganda efforts were greeted by us they staged a sudden search for secret radios. They found none—although one lay in the rice store, one in an open dust box in a hut casually camouflaged with rubbish, and one in the bottom half of an Army-issue water bottle.

This latter had more than once caused us heart failure as its

[1]Singapore had been renamed Syonan-to: *Shimbun* is simply a "newspaper."

owner always wore it to work. That, of course, was the logical thing to do, since we all wore our water bottles to work.

Where our friend, we felt, went too far was in making a point of offering the guard a drink out of it each day. Though it held water in its top half, we couldn't help feeling that the bluff was a little cold-blooded.

Nevertheless, it bore dividends. It was our practice, when we had emptied our water bottles of water, to fill them with anything that we could steal. Thus, in the last days of our sojourn at River Valley, we found ourselves in a go-down where, as well as bombs, there were palm oil (for the manufacture of soap) and bicycle parts. Accordingly, in between carrying bombs and evading the "Speedoes" of our guards, we all filled our bottles with oil, which we drank and (for good measure) popped in as many ball bearings and other small bicycle parts as possible—these to be sold later to the Chinese.

Exhausted by his non-stop screaming, the guard suddenly found himself in need of a drink. He accordingly, and to our great horror, picked up the first water bottle he set eyes on and drank. He drank three large gulps of Singer machine oil and about eighteen inches of bicycle chain! When he had eventually clawed the chain back out of his gullet and frantically swabbed his tongue free of lubricant, he was extremely displeased. As if it were not enough that he himself had suffered considerable discomfort, the I.J.A.—faced with a fuel shortage because of their inability to repair the wrecked oil wells of Borneo and the Dutch East Indies—regarded bicycles as war transport and theft of bicycle parts as sabotage.

Consequently, we were all lined up and our water bottles, one by one, emptied. As each was upturned and its contents fell to the ground, its owner was punished. But when the guard came to our friend with the wireless in his bottle, he remembered the daily offer of a drink and said: "You O.K.," and merely patted him affectionately on the shoulder—which was silly of him because of that moment, as well as a radio, the bottle contained hundreds of connecting links for which the Chinese were prepared to pay a small fortune. Thus we petty pilferers returned to camp covered in blood and disgrace, whilst the arch-villain of us all marched brightly back, arm in arm with his guard, singing "Dinah, is there anyone finah," and smoking one of the I.J.A.'s Kooah cigarettes!

8 BORE-HOLES

A few weeks later we returned to Changi—returned to celebrate our first Christmas in captivity and almost a year in which for most of us no word from us to home or from home to us had been heard.

8 BORE-HOLES

Changi was much the same. Officers still looked gorgeous and wore pips on their bosoms so that no one might mistake them for anything else. Orders of the day were promulgated (as the hideous word was) with abandon and were usualy superfluous. The all-embracing cover-up for multidinous sins was that they were "good for morale." Japanese guards were seldom seen. All the work that was required of the men in camp was what was necessary to keep the area spotlessly clean, the gardens growing and the kitchen fires burning.

The Australian Concert Party had developed from a rather polished purveyor of vaudeville corn into a group who already gave signs of becoming the backbone of Changi entertainment—which entertainment was to be a key factor in maintaining our high morale in the ensuing years and for the preservation of which our command (to whom I have not so far been excessively kind) must be awarded the fullest possible praise. Whatever demands the Japanese made for workers, the Concert Party was always preserved intact. No better investment than this was ever made on our behalf. There are few men who were captured on Singapore in 1942 and who survived till 1945 who do not now remember, and will not always remember, the skill of John Wood, the songs (topical and tuneful) of Slim de Grey and Ray Tullipan, the harmony of Geoghegan and Woods and that plaintive cry of our most melancholy comic: "You'll never get off the island." No matter how black the news nor how depressing the atmosphere, Harry Smith, universally known as Happy Harry, had only to turn his long face full at the audience and wail the apparent truism, "You'll never get off the island," for complete hilarity to be restored.

The Concert Party also flourished because it commanded the

enthusiastic support of a Japanese interpreter called Terai. Terai, peacetime professor of English in a Nipponese university, was deemed by almost everyone to be pro-British. He was young, slim, had a pleasant face and was always glad to find in Singapore such improbable commodities as strings for a violin, or women's gowns, or make-up materials or whatever it was that the performers needed. All he asked in return was a little conversation—preferably not about the war, which he hated.

Meanwhile, Changi's irrepressible energy—the energy of ten thousand Britons cooped up without any contact with the outside world—burst out in a thousand different directions. There were courses on every subject and every language: there were societies to discuss every hobby and every sport: there were little theatres playing everything from Shakespeare to *Journey's End:* there were concerts of classical music and concert parties which weren't classical at all. On my first night back in Changi I could have gone to lectures on skiing, contract law, Communism or tiger hunting: I could have gone to any one of four plays or two musical shows: I could have heard Dennis East—peacetime violinist under Sir Thomas Beecham—give a recital. As it was, I went down to the Australian Concert Party, sat on the woodpile and talked with Piddington and his friends about Australian beer and beaches and the possible truth of the prevailing rumour (better known in those days as a "bore-hole"[1]) that all P.O.W.'s were to be repatriated by the Japanese in exchange for a bag of rice per man. Though these bore-holes make extraordinary reading now, it must be realized that they formed a strong part of the fabric of our lives and that, whilst to most of us they were merely topics for pleasant speculation, they were to others—especially those who invented them—subjects about which one must be deadly serious. The most incorrigible bore-holer in the Australian forces was in the habit of betting his paybook on the veracity of his outrageous statements and it is estimated that had all his challengers insisted, at the end of the war, upon

[1]Bore-holes were latrines. They were dug to a depth of forty feet as many as eight side by side. There being no privacy there (or, indeed, anywhere else), one made the most of them and talked amicably with one's fellow visitors. Visits to bore-holes being one of the things that happened most frequently to one each day, they naturally became the occasion for the distribution of every fantastic rumour the camp ever heard, dreamed or invented.

these debts being paid he would have been required to produce somewhere in the nature of a quarter of a million pounds.

In the company of this strange woodpile group, I was to spend a happy few months. They were delightful. Piddington with his passion—which I shared—for travel. John Wood, successful Australian actor of the English stage and films, who was now a signalman but was, nevertheless, the greatest source of stage anecdotes and comic songs that Changi knew. Keith Stevens, a bawdy comic and peacetime advertising salesman. Ernie Ward, who never said anything much but always knew all the news because he kept a radio in his trumpet. Lesley Greener, archaeologist, Arctic fisherman, linesman, artist, traveller, writer. And from the English lines, Harry Witherford, who knew about the stars and production engineering and talked calmly of such unheard-of nonsense as turbo-jet engines: and Mike Cooper, who was a Gurkha officer and gentleman rider. A mixed bag, mixed as to rank, interests and conversational ability, reduced to the one common denominator of a woodpile in the pleasant warmth of Singapore's evening.

Christmas Day came and we ate enormous meals of rice—having saved a small portion of our ration every day for weeks past. This rice was served as rice *au naturel* and as rice camouflaged—in which form it was known to us as a "doover." We also distributed rather pathetic attempts at Christmas cards and such quaint presents as one banana or a little grated-up coconut. The Pommies sang their carols and the entire camp sent toys made of rubber wood to the English children interned with their parents in the gaol a mile down the road. In spite of the Japanese the spirit of Christmas was never stronger.

Apart from the pleasant company and the pleasant surroundings and the pinpricks of incessant regimentation, the two most predominant recollections of that time are the sick parades and the fear of being "sent away."

Sick parades had become a daily factor in almost every man's life —especially the Other Ranks, who, being paid considerably less than the officers, were unable to combat their ailments with purchases of black market tinned food. The universal complaint was lack of vitamins. The universal symptoms a raw scrotum, a raw tongue and sores which would not heal.

Until one has lived with the discomfort of a raw scrotum, the agony of a raw tongue and the revulsion against one's own body that a pair of leprous-looking legs creates, one cannot fully appreciate the significance of these conditions. Perhaps it gives some indication of their impact upon the average man's mind that, though he knew that no treatment did him any good—there being no adequate treatment—he still lined up each day on the sick parade.

From their end, the doctors worked ceaselessly. They created a recipe for making yeast (unfortunately defeated because it could not keep up with the demand upon it and because its distribution managed, unobserved by the administration—whose whole attention was absorbed at that time with the twin problems of saluting and morale—to slip into the hands of racketeers). They invented a machine which extracted a black juice from lalang grass (of which Malaya has a superabundance) and they persuaded us by their own example to drink this juice, though its taste was surpassingly vile. They attempted endless variations and permutations of the available drugs, which were sulphur, eusol, mercurochrome and acriflavine. They circumcised practically every man who was not already circumcised. They never ceased improvising and pondering.

They urged us, with good humour and resignation, to do as little as possible each day because the calorific content of our full ration was—they had discovered—only sufficient to enable one to breathe. If one moved or worked then, if prewar medical standards were to be believed, we must all surely die.

This interesting piece of information we accepted as dispassionately as we accepted fatigues to kill flies, and weevils in our rice, and sleeping on floors, and never seeing any women. We merely suggested that it might be as well if they—the medical pundits—contacted first our own authorities (less they kill us all off with compulsory saluting) and then the Japanese, who appeared to have totaly different ideas about calories and plans as to how they were to be consumed.

But even the doctors had their blunderers—two in particular come to mind. The first called a full parade of the men who were unfortunate enough to be on his "panel" and addressed them. He told them that they were suffering from pellagra. Pellagra, he pointed out, advanced in three stages. First, skin diseases from which, as he rightly declared, we all already suffered. Second, a raw tongue—also already upon us. Third, madness! This, he asserted confidently, was (*a*) coming, and (*b*) incurable. He looked at the parade gravely, revelling in his drama. Regrettably, the Britisher has little time for drama and his grave warning was greeted with prolonged and uncontrollable laughter.

The other M.O. who distinguished himself was the one who called a similar parade and threatened it with universal, perpetual and imminent sterility if it did not at once and regularly thenceforth eat plenty of hibiscus leaves! For months, though no one took him too seriously—for he was known as a doctor who would make a good plumber—there was not a hibiscus bush in Changi to be seen upon which sprouted even the smallest shoot of green.

Fear of being sent away on a working party was also a very real psychological factor in those times. It sprang from the strange unwillingness we all experienced to move anywhere once we had settled, and it was especially strong in those who, so far, had never worked outside Changi—that is, had never worked for the Japanese. It resulted in endless intrigue and string pulling—and there were plenty of strings to pull—which was probably more exhausting than the work it was designed to avoid. That it was a fear for which there was considerable basis, however, is not to be doubted. One has only to look at the annihilation which befell the party sent to Borneo, the drowning of shiploads of men en route for Japan, the decimation of the railroad workers in Thailand and Burma, to realize that, intuitive though the fear was, it was a most sensible one.

So, to the accompaniment of endless sick parades, rumours, apprehension about the possibility of one's being sent to the Kra Isthmus to dig a canal across it and the news that abroad the Germans in Africa and Russia were now steadily being pushed back, the first months of 1943 passed.

Possibly it was the B.B.C. news (now for the first time encouraging since the war began) which inspired the most fantastic of all Changi's episodes. The Australian 30th Battalion, in the middle of a prison camp, under the very nose of an enemy notorious for his shortness of temper, was ordered to start drilling again. This it did on the Selarang Barrack Square, marching to and fro armed with dummy rifles. As if this were not enough, our command instituted courses in unarmed combat and bayonet attack. None of this was done with particular discretion and it seemed inevitable that Nippon, silly as he could be at times, would soon wake up to what was being done—especially since we were cursed, then and in most camps at most times, with the presence of Indonesian troops who, wretched as Allies, as our fellow prisoners were the Japanese' best source of inside information as to all our activities.

In any event, the phony captivity ended with a sudden bang when a terrific search was staged for radios, suspected operators were whipped off to Outrim Road Gaol (where they endured ghastly conditions), the national anthem was banned and the camp was warned that parties were to be made ready to leave Singapore for Thailand. Those who remained, it was rumoured (correctly), were to build an aerodrome below Changi where now there was only a swamp and two hills.

The Thailand parties, the Nips said, were to go to comfortable camps with plenty of rations. They pointed out that Thailand—unlike Malaya, which imports half the rice it eats—was self-supporting. They urged that sick men be included in the party lists so that they might convalesce. They suggested sweetly that band instruments—even a piano—might help to while away the leisure hours of those who were transplanted.

Thus, midst a welter of contradictory reports, bribery, corruption, faked sickness and genuine attempts to transfer hospital cases to better conditions, the first party—known as F Force—left Changi. It left with a large proportion of men who came direct from their beds in hospital, plus the piano, plus all sorts of paraphernalia suitable for a convalescent camp under a civilized foe.

A short time later a second party was conscripted with Terai as its interpreter. Hugh was put on its list, though still a bed case in the hospital. I, after much heart-searching (for I felt that all was not well with this Thailand venture), decided that I should go with him. I therefore severed all the strings which were being pulled so industriously on my behalf and, on the eve of H Force's departure, asked that my name be added to its numbers.

Next day we were crammed, thirty men and all our possessions (as well as our share of the force's cooking utensils, medical panniers, agricultural implements and guards), into each truck. As the train chugged erratically over the causeway, back towards K.L., I found myself thinking that all this was most inauspicious. My thoughts were interrupted by a thunderous shouting, all along the train, from British and Australian throats alike, of Harry Smith's now immortal cry: "You'll never get off the island."

Thirty seconds later Singapore lay behind us and we steamed into Johore We were to know no further peace of mind or body until, a year later, the fortunate survivors would cross that causeway again and get back onto the island.

3

1 "BRING YOUR PIANO"

The journey to Thailand was unpleasant. It took five days and our cattle trucks all seemed to be equipped with innumerable protuberances which stuck into one's back as one squatted (there was not room to sit), or into one's head as one crouched under a roof which was too low to allow standing. By day the steel carriages scorched with the heat of the sun: by night they were like iceboxes. Perhaps once a day men were allowed out of the trucks to stretch their legs and attend to the various demands of nature. Nature, unfortunately, did not understand this arrangement and made her demands much more frequently, which—in crowded trucks on a jolting train—required all our patience and tolerance of one another.

Water was the main difficulty. One could overlook the absence of food, but in that intense heat thirst became an obsession. We soon learnt to steal out whenever the train stopped and fill up one of the dixies from the engine—greasy water, but boiled, so consumable. Usually the two men who went on this expedition were caught and thrashed, but the expeditions, being necessary, continued.

At one such stop Terai, the interpreter, came down to our truck. I was reading.

"What are you reading, Mr. Braddon?" he asked quietly.

"George Bernard Shaw," I told him.

"Like it?" he queried.

"Some of it," I said. At that he launched into a long dissertation on *St. Joan* which was only terminated when the two men with the dixie were dragged back by three guards and savagely punched for leaving the truck. Terai watched the bashing with evident distress.

"This is very unpleasant," he said, "I am sorry."

"We have to get water," I explained.

"Why not some other way?" he demanded. "Why not ask?"

I laughed at that. His eyes flickering up at mine and then down again, Terai repeated: "This is very unpleasant," and left.

We crossed the Thailand border and found Thailand no different from Malaya except that its natives were rather more energetic—especially in their thieving, at which they were most adept. And eventually the train ground to a halt and we were ordered out, to the accompaniment of the usual endless bellowing, onto a rather dreary-looking platform.

Anxiously I took stock of my possessions. One water bottle, one mess tin, one spoon, toothbrush and razor; the complete works of G.B.S., *Mein Kampf* and an *Oxford Book of English Verse,* given to me just before our departure by Harry Witherford, the British officer who knew about the stars and turbo-jets. Having made certain that they were all there, I bundled them into the rice bag I used as a haversack and, with the rest of the party, started off down a filthy dust track towards the promised convalescent camp.

I wondered how Hugh was. Ironically enough, I hadn't seen him since we got on the train at Singapore, where the authorities had suddenly been smitten with the bright idea that it would be more efficient if the whole force fell in in alphabetical groups. Consequently, men found themselves separated from their inseparable friends and one of the few comforts of our lives was removed for a five-day journey and the ensuing march.

The dirt road led through a Thai town called Bam Pong. There our presence as we marched roused interest only in the native traders, who—led by their yellow-robed, predatory, Buddhist priests—clamoured to buy anything we possessed. It was a sign of the times that the participants of Nippon's Greater East Asia Prosperity Scheme were now prepared to buy anything rather than keep the Jap paper money in their pockets where it became steadily more worthless every minute. Though the Thais allegedly remained independent, their economy was so hamstrung by the Japanese Occupation that in that country, as everywhere else in the Far East, blackmarketing with prisoners of war was one of the main and most vigorous industries. As a nation we found the Thais excessively dishonest and thieving. We reciprocated wholeheartedly.

The Convalescent Camp turned out to be native huts made of attap, mud-floored, littered with excrement, seething with flies, and in that condition of unspeakable filth which only Asiatics can attain. It was bad enough for those of us who were fit, but for the men who had been uprooted from Changi's hospital it was like a death sentence. The five-day train trip had not improved their condition. The sour, fermented rice and the greasy water of those days had brought on fresh bouts of dysentery to almost all of them. They looked drawn and one felt fearful for them.

Without warning, the Japs swept down on the camp and searched it—searched it for everything from weapons to wireless sets. Though they found nothing it was only at the expense of our dumping all grenades, bayonets, daggers and machine-gun parts (of which there were more than a few) down the camp well. The radio, being secreted in an accordion which the gentleman who owned it played gaily and with no tune at all throughout the search, was not discovered.

The Japanese, through Terai, then ordered us to fill our water bottles and fall in for a night march.

"How far?" we asked.

"Twenty miles," was the answer.

All that night we marched with our respective sacks and packs on our backs; the qualis and dixies and axes and other tools slung on poles and carried by pairs of men in turn; the sick, as they collapsed, being supported by whomever was nearest. The Japs at the head of the column, marching with only a rifle, set a brisk pace which they refused to ease: and the Japs at the rear used a liberal rifle butt to ensure that this pace was maintained. I soon found myself slipping into my prison habit of counting. Each step I counted. Thousand after thousand—even though I determined dozens of times to stop—until I nearly went mad. The sun was scorching down again before we reached the next camp high on the water-eroded banks of a swift-running river.

Without any hesitation, and in spite of the bellows of our guards, we squatted on our heels and glissaded down the almost sheer forty-foot clay bank of the river and into the coolness of water. For a few moments the cares of our coolie existence fell from us. The sensual pleasure of swimming on a hot day in rushing water quickly washes away memories of such nastiness as the existence of the Japanese. But the Japanese are not a race who will happily allow their existence to be forgotten. Shots from the bank above indicated that they were not pleased. And when we looked up we saw why. In the torrent of the river we had all been washed some three or four hundred yards downstream and were still moving steadily on. Hurriedly we fought our way to the bank. There a further problem presented itself. We had no means of drying ourselves: the banks were almost sheer clay: our wet feet and limbs turned their practically vertical face to grease and we were completely unable to make the ascent. One would get a few feet up and then hurtle backwards into the river again. No good the guards screaming (which they did with gusto), we just had to wait at the bottom until we were dry. When we did at last clamber up to the top, the guards gave practical demonstration of their extreme displeasure.

The day was spent bartering briskly with the Thais to obtain as much food as possible to sustain us over the next night's march, which we had now been told we were to undertake. Anxious about Hugh, I searched him out and found him in the hands of one Harry Peck.

Harry, as a thirteen-year-old Cockney lad, had decided that he would emigrate to Australia. For months he pestered his family to sign the necessary papers. For months they boxed his ears and refused. But Harry was persistent and at last they agreed. Harry was on his way.

He landed in Sydney dressed in the height of Cockney fashion, complete with check suit and heavy cap. This garb stunned the locals—especially the Reception Committee—who thrust him on a country-bound train as quickly as possible, much to the amazement of the other passengers.

At Parkes in New South Wales, Harry, in checks and cap, got off the train to meet his new employer—in a khaki shirt, wide-brimmed hat, Army boots and dungaree pants. They gazed at one another in mutual astonishment. Then the farmer said: "Get in," so Harry hopped aboard the buggy and they jogged out to the farm.

There Harry lived in a galvanized iron hut with primitive furniture. Lived quite alone except for the company of a large carpet snake, which slept in the rafters over his head eating mice. He was terrified of this snake.

He learned to plough a straight furrow, to ring-bark a tree, to sink fence posts, to stretch barbed wire. He knew no one except the carpet snake and, as soon as he had saved a little money, he left the farm and farming and the carpet snake for good and went into the nearby town.

There, with his savings, he bought a small share in a vegetable shop. Soon he had enough to buy out his partner. Then he bought another shop, and became a Mason, and flourished. When war broke out Harry was earning two thousand pounds a year and had great plans for the future. But he was still the same Cockney as had first landed in Australia—simple, stubborn, generous to a fault—and the war left him in no two minds as to what he should do. He gave up all his plans and volunteered for the A.I.F. A year later he was handed over to the Japanese by the capitulation of Singapore. Little more than another twelve months found him on the banks of a river in Thailand looking after Hugh.

With his penchant for trade, Harry had bought some coffee and sugar from the Thais and he and Hugh were now doing a brisk business selling the brew at ten cents a cupful to thirsty marchers. Harry's wide grin on his sweating rugged face was cheering in those dismal surroundings. His sparse, sandy hair stood up on end and was full of cinders and ash from his fire.

"No wonder they call you a nation of shopkeepers," I observed. "How are you doing?"

"Fine," said Harry. "Fine—have a cuppa coffee."

"How much?" I demanded cautiously. Harry looked offended, and, as Hugh approached, said: "Give the gentleman a leggi cuppa coffee, Hughie." Hugh grinned and doled it out into my mess tin and asked what sort of a trip the A's to D's had had. I said not too bad and enquired about the M's to P's—at which Harry looked up from the fire, which he was blowing lustily, his face scarlet, and answered: "Bloody atrocious."

Then the whistle blew for a parade and I had to leave. "See you next stop," I said to Hugh and he grinned again, but looked much too frail to be doing another twenty-mile march that night.

"I'll look after the kid," Harry promised.

"Good on you," I thanked him. "See you later, Harry. Bye-bye, Hugh, thanks for the coffee," and I made my way back to where my section was already falling in.

To my enquiries as to what it was all about, I was told that there was another search on. Almost immediately Terai appeared with some guards and our few possessions were once again ransacked. Terai flicked his way, with academic interest, through my book of Shaw.

"Do you like *Pygmalion?*" he asked. I said I did.

"And this book of verse," he continued, flicking over the pages of the Oxford edition which Witherford had given me. I said I liked that too.

"I am sorry," said Terai, "but you had better leave these here with me."

"You mean you're confiscating them," I said. Terai shrugged apologetic shoulders. I asked what about *Mein Kampf*. Mr. Terai indicated that Nippon would not take it amiss if I read *Mein Kampf*. But Shaw and the Oxford book of verse—again that apologetic shrug.

Ten minutes later the march started again and I slung my bag across my shoulders—a bag about seven pounds lighter now that the complete wisdom of Shaw and Oxford's distillation of English verse had been removed from it—and strode off with the rest, realizing irritably that thenceforth my mental companion for however long we remained in Thailand was to be none other than Adolf Hitler.

The second night's march saw further casualties from exhaustion and the Nips' bad temper and when, in the morning, we reached a flat, parched piece of scrub, at which the guard called a halt, we just dropped where we stood and slept. After a few hours the sun beat down so fiercely that everyone was compelled to crawl under the spiky bushes that grew dotted around the clearing—stunted and filthy with the rubbish of previous native forces though they were—and we slept again.

When we woke we found that the Thais had been most active and stolen everything that was not closely guarded. This included much of our officers' kit (about which we were not unduly upset since officers' trunks tend to become heavy on a twenty-mile march) and any other movables which had attracted the Thais' roving eye. The place, we were told, was called Kanchinaburi, which was pronounced Kamburi. It was an old walled city (and, indeed, now that we looked, we could see the city with ancient walls a mile or two away on our right) and was the last spot of civilization before the jungle belt that makes Thailand such a hellhole of fever and Nature at her most savage.

We asked about previous parties, F Force, for example. The Thais pointed, grinning amiably, straight into the heart of the jungle and mountains. So at last we knew for certain. The Convalescent Camp was a complete fiction. All the men in Thailand were to be used on the long-rumoured construction of a railway connecting Bangkok with Rangoon. Japanese losses at sea round the Malacca Straits and the Indian Ocean had been so enormous of late that they now proposed a land line of supply to their forces in Burma instead. We were to build that land line. Remembering that the British, who first surveyed the route, had abandoned the prospect as impossible, because of the cost to human life involved in those fever- and plague-stricken mountains, it was difficult not to feel a little sick at heart.

The Japanese gave us a cursory medical examination and a test for dysentery (a crude affair carried out with a glass rod and designed rather to humiliate than diagnose—certainly we never once heard any results of these tests). Then they vaccinated each man by slashing his arm with a lancet and splashing serum onto the cut. Finally they injected a few c.c.'s of something which they declared was anti-cholera serum—cheerful thought—into one's arm. Then, without more ado, amid torrential rain, we set out on the march. In a few minutes we left the road and puddled our way into the jungle. For the first time in my life I heard a British column start off on a long march without the cheerful sounds of singing. There were no marching songs that night nor for any of the rest of the seven nights of the ordeal. Indeed, there was nothing to sing about!

Those hundred or so miles through the jungle are very confused now. They were repetitions of vicious bashings from guards to those who fell, of the plundering by Thais of stragglers, of slogging along through knee-deep mud in blinding rain and inky darkness, of counting either consciously or subconsciously until my mind became frenzied with the interminable progression of figures. And each morning we would come to a staging camp, each successive camp more primitive and foul than the last—attap shelters which leaked and whose mud floors were littered with filth of every kind and here and there a dead native.

There were highlights, of course. The way when any man fell his comrades, however exhausted themselves, at once picked him up and carried him until his strength returned sufficiently to enable him to carry on alone. The way men accepted their share of the impedimenta and carried it for their allotted time and then passed it on, with never a complaint or a thought of cheating on their shift throughout the whole march.

Above all, there was the extraordinary courage and gentleness and the incredible endurance of the medical officer, Major Kevin Fagan. Not only did he treat any man needing treatment to the best of his ability; he also carried men who fell; he carried the kit of men in danger of falling, and he marched up and down the whole length of the column throughout its entire progress. If we marched one hundred miles through the jungle, Kevin Fagan marched two hundred. And when, at the end of our night's trip, we collapsed and slept, he was there to clean blisters, set broken bones and render first aid. And all of it he did with the courtesy of a society specialist who is being richly paid for his attention and the ready humour of a man who is not tired at all. With Padre Duckworth of Kuala Lumpur, he is the most inspiring man I have ever met. Some twenty thousand British and Australian troops share my view.

"That man," observed a complete moron called Rocky Ned, who normally appreciated nothing, "is a bloody saint." When a personality impresses itself upon the mentality of Rocky Ned, and when an Australian is so far overcome as to call anyone a "saint," then, indeed, you are in the presence of a great man.

Like all worth-while saints, however, Major Fagan possessed a goodly streak of earthy realism. On our first night in the jungle a nuggety little man with close-cropped hair and a cauliflower ear suddenly dropped moaning in front of me. My companion at that time was a lad called Roy Death. Anxiously we surveyed the body at our feet and asked it what was wrong.

"It's me legs," gasped the fallen man, "they won't move." By this time the end of the column had passed us and a guard was already waving his rifle round in a most disagreeable manner.

"Is it a cramp, Smokey?" asked Roy.

"No, it's me legs," said Smokey again, "they won't move."

Roy looked at me and said: "Jesus, we'll have to carry him." I am not a charitable person and Smokey was one of the men on the force whom I liked least. Even I, however, realized that Smokey could not be left to the tender mercies of our guards and the Thais, so we divided his gear between us and then picked him up and for two hours we carried him, his paralyzed legs dragging in the slush between us. Finally we managed to catch up the tail of our column and in a few moments the ubiquitous Fagan appeared alongside us. With a swift glance at the three of us, he said: "All right, sonny," to Roy, "I'll take your place." For this I was grateful. Roy had dysentery and carrying Smokey had been difficult for him. Fagan slipped Smokey's arm over his shoulder and then said, as we jogged along, Smokey's feet still dragging stiffly through the mud: "Now, laddy, what's the trouble?"

"Me legs," said Smokey piteously, "they won't move."

Quickly Fagan laid him down and looked at him. Then he crossed to me and said: "Kick him in the seat of the pants. Hard," he added. I thought it very sad that our best officer should have to go mad at this juncture and looked at him in dismay. "Go on," urged Fagan, "boot him." Mad as a March hare, I thought, and did nothing. Impatiently Fagan strode over to the prostrate Smokey and applied a vigorous boot to his paralyzed posterior. With a howl of pain, all symptoms of paralysis vanished. Smokey leapt to his feet and fled.

"Playing possum," Fagan explained. Roy Death looked rueful. "Guess that's the easiest couple of hours' march he's ever had," he said.

At the next halt we dumped his gear and waited hopefully for Smokey to come and collect it. We had words which we wished to say to Smokey. But Smokey was not so silly as that. He remained hidden in the mass of men, somewhere at the head of the column, and when we started off again he still hadn't claimed his gear. We decided that if the Thais got it it really didn't matter and rejoined our squad, leaving his possessions in a small pile at the side of the quagmire which was our track.

On the night of our march to Tarsao—probably the foulest of all the staging camps—it rained with increased fury and our casualties became serious. Early in the piece one of our number collapsed and could not be revived. We collected a stretcher and took it in turns to carry him, one man on each handle of the stretcher. This meant roughly a quarter of an hour's carrying and a half hour's rest throughout the night.

Just before dawn our leading guard took the wrong fork in the jungle track and we covered about four miles (twelve thousand exhausted paces) which had then to be retraced. I have seldom seen such desperation as when the order came to go back on our tracks to that fork.

It was dawn when we reached it. Roy, myself and two others were carrying the stretcher. Just before our time ran out we sighted the squalid huts and bamboo compound fences of Tarsao. We decided to finish the journey with the stretcher. About ten minutes later we laid it down in one of the huts and called a doctor over. He unwrapped the patient out of the gas cape in which we had rolled him to save him from the rain and looked at his face. A few deft prods at eyelids and pulse and he glanced up. "Dead," he pronounced, "been dead for hours."

I was filled with fury at this man who was selfish enough to allow us to carry him for twelve miles and be dead all the time. Roy laughed. The other two looked at one another and demanded of each other: "Wouldn't it?" The M.O. glanced up sharply and brought us back to our senses.

"Take him over to the mortuary," he instructed, "they'll fix him up over there."

"Mortuary?" Roy queried. "What the hell have you got a mortuary for?"

"Because," replied the M.O. grimly, "we can't leave bodies lying round the place and there's no one to bury them till the working parties come back each night." Silently we carried our burden to a small ramshackle shed and laid it among the five other bodies which, wrapped in hessian sacking, awaited the return that night of the working parties.

"Mortuary," muttered Roy despondently as we left it.

Tarsao had a river and, to get rid of the mud of the march and the sweat of our exertions and the stench of corpses, we made our way down to it. On its banks Thais did a brisk trade buying the clothes men stripped off to go swimming. Already starvation had become sufficiently real to make food infinitely more important than clothing.

We dived into the brown water and, sighting Hugh in midstream, I swam over to him. Revived by the water and in his element in it, for he swam like a fish, he looked surprisingly fit.

"How are you doing?" I asked.

"Fine," he replied.

"Where's Harry?"

"Making coffee," he said, and we laughed. I took a mouthful of water, spat it at him in the friendliest manner possible and swam slowly back to my clothes (now receiving unhealthy attention from a nearby squatting Thai). Hugh followed me in, backstroking leisurely. We sat on a rock to dry off. Hugh's emaciated legs and blistered feet I pretended not to notice; and about my own revolting extremities he tactfully said nothing.

Hugh dressed and picked up a four-gallon petrol can.

"What's that for?" I asked him.

"Water for Harry's coffee," he told me, "he's boiling a brew back at the camp." It was half a mile uphill back to the camp, so I said I'd give him a hand, and a few minutes later we set off together.

Halfway up the hill a rather harassed-looking lieutenant passed us and glanced at the water in the tin.

"Make sure you boil that before you drink it," he said, "that river's full of cholera." I remembered the mouthful of water I had spat at Hugh, the mouthful practically every man in the party had spat at someone or other in their pleasure at having sufficient liquid available to be able to afford the extravagance of spitting it. We finished our journey back in silence, Hugh and I—no use talking about it, but we were both thinking the same thing.

Our party filled in what was left of the day in a rather sombre silence. The officer who had passed Hugh and me with our can of water had, it seemed, gone down to the river and there—too late—exhorted everyone to keep their heads well clear of the cholera-infested water. The effort of not thinking about this and of not talking about it flung the entire party into a restless gloom.

We were not closely guarded. In fact, we were hardly guarded at all. It was not necessary—there was nowhere to go. The countryside for hundreds of miles around was rugged jungle, uninhabited, fever-ridden, devoid of food. To flee from any of our stopping places, or even from the march itself, was simply to die alone in the jungle.

Accordingly, we were left in peace until, late in the afternoon, a Japanese doctor decided that he would like to examine our feet. The party lined up, to the accompaniment of much mutinous comment, and filed past, displaying its feet for the edification of Nippon. To our dismay, he treated every blister by cutting off the entire swollen surface with a lancet (which got steadily filthier as the examination proceeded) and then pouring iodine onto the resulting raw surface. The operation was both bloody and painful and did more to infect and cripple than anything else we had so far experienced.

When the party set out that night, climbing steeply up a rain-drenched mountain, the gait of even our most sprightly members could only be described as a hobble.

Because this was the last night of the march, and an especially long leg, the guards were more than ever noisy and violent. In the rain it was impossible to discern any track, so one merely followed faithfully in the footsteps of the man immediately in front. If he fell, you fell: if you fell, a hundred men behind you, one after the other, fell. The best that could be done was to pass warnings. Thus, if a man hit his head on a bough, he would halt and, to the man following, say: "Duck: timber!" And all down the line, hundreds of times, the phrase would be repeated: "Duck: timber . . .," "Duck: timber . . .," "Duck: timber . . .," and each man would duck his head to save it from the blow of a bough he could not see and, turning round, repeat: "Duck: timber!"

Apart from mud and its splashing, the darkness, the sounds of the guards' voices screaming "Speedo," "More Speedo," and the occasional bashings, the march had little that can adequately be described. Altogether it was a miserable affair. Being too wet for too long, and walking too far too quickly, is never enjoyable. The jungle, though invisible, made its presence felt with vines that tripped and bamboo spikes that pierced, but most of all by a faint all-pervading stink of leaf mould, bugs in the bark of giant trees, fungus and stagnant water. No place that smelt like that could be meant by God to be inhabited by man.

But if the jungle lay heavily round us, shrouded in murky gloom and vapours, the character of the marchers themselves—from Fagan downwards—shone out brilliantly through all their dark progress.

In a hundred ways the carefulness of those men for one another and their willingness to lend a hand to whomever needed it impressed one. Whilst I was filled with peevish anger at the outrageous blows of rocks, logs, trees and rifle butts, they plodded stolidly on, punctuating their muddy plunging with remarks like: "Stump on the left . . .": "Are you all right, mate?": "You horrible little bastard" (this to the guards, who thoroughly deserved it) . . . and occasional fulsome oaths of such richness and vigour that, peevish or not, one found oneself laughing.

But it was in the watery light of that next dawn that all laughter was killed for good in Thailand. A handful of grey men working on a Japanese truck (which had been manhandled the hundreds of miles thus far and was now inextricably stuck in the mud) turned out to be members of the force, F Force, which preceded us. They were emaciated, seemed indifferent to everything, and their faces were stamped with a misery that was too awful to look at. Their eyes, inches deep in the sockets, looked mad. F Force, they told us, had been smitten with cholera and was being obliterated. We marched another five or six miles in a despairing silence heightened by drenching rain. These were the first fruits we had seen of Nippon's promises of convalescent camps—skeletons with purplish skins, teeth that looked huge in shrunken faces and haunted eyes.

Within three weeks we were all to be reduced to the same travesties of men.

With only three kilos to go—the Japanese measured all distances by the metric system—we halted for a short rest, a "yazumé." We halted in a sudden bare patch of swampy ground at the foot of the mountain we had just crossed. It was a mere saucer of treeless mud in the middle of the high-flanking, jungle-covered mountains. At its far end a track ran out of it past a palisaded camp on the right and a native camp—in the usual state of indescribable filth—on the left. The palisaded camp was deserted, having been recently vacated by the Pommies. The native camp seethed with Tamils. The track led into the mountains and to a place known to us as Kanu II. Kanu II was our destination, according to Mr. Terai.

We sat in the mud, midst sick and dying and an agglomeration of dixies, axes, changkols and kit bags, and looked up that track. How much better, or worse, than all this would Kanu II be?

Terai moved sympathetically among us and spoke for a few moments to the officer in charge. That worthy then detailed a dozen of us to stay in this saucer of mud and, on its tree-flanked border, just before the deserted Pommy camp and almost opposite the Tamils, to cut out a headquarters for our Japanese guards and the Japanese administrative officers of H Force.

Objecting violently to being separated from our friends, we collected our kit and fell out from the main party. I said good-bye to Hugh and Harry and Roy Death and a dozen or so more. Then they all marched away up the track and into the mountain. It was the last time we who remained were ever to see most of them or that they were to see most of us. But there was no time for reflection. A short, stocky guard, by name Kanemoto, came bellowing over and within thirty seconds—though we had just marched twenty miles—we were working, hacking down trees and bamboo from the jungle. Our labours in Thailand had begun.

2 KANEMOTOSAN

Kanemoto proved to be an unpleasant little man with exaggerated ideas about the amount of work one Australian can or is prepared to do in one day. I, on the other hand, had long since conceived it as my duty when working for the Japanese to do as little as possible and that only of the most inferior quality. It was, therefore, fairly inevitable that, on the subject of building railway lines through Thailand, First Class Private Kanemoto and Gunner Braddon should eventually clash. We did so, with great and mutual ill-will, the day after our arrival.

For a fortnight thereafter Kanemoto endured our shortcomings with considerable lack of patience. In that time we cleared a patch of jungle to a depth of about fifty yards and along a front of almost a hundred. In the process we killed numerous highly venomous snakes and disturbed a family of baboons who withdrew themselves in high dudgeon to the top of a far-off tree from which they screeched their disapproval. Their voices are high-pitched and sufficiently human to sound demented. At night it is an unpleasant noise.

Having made a clearing, we were then sent into the jungle to collect bamboo. This grew in huge vine-entangled clumps of anything up to forty lengths of bamboo, each length anything up to fifty feet in height. Cutting it was a task made doubly unpleasant by its protective carpet of needle-pointed spikes and by its wilful refusal to fall even when every single stem had been severed. Lashed together by the tough jungle vines, the bamboo would remain obdurately upright. When eventually, by shinning up the centre of a clump and hacking at the vines with a parang, the stems were freed and fell, one still had the task of weaving a forty-foot-long stem nine inches in diameter through the tangled undergrowth of the jungle. It was a tiresome task rendered none the easier by the fact that the cavity running down the centre of each bamboo was filled with water, nor by Kanemoto's hoarse shouts of "One man one" and "Speedo."

Having collected sufficient lengths, we were then required to erect the scaffolding of a hut—uprights, floor supports and roof supports—and then to lay attap on the roof and slats of split bamboo on the floor and walls. Crosspieces were bound onto uprights with wire: attap was secured to rafters with vines. It was a primitive, but effective, method of construction.

In that first fortnight all twelve of us succumbed to malaria—more familiar to us as "The Bug"—a fact which maddened Kanemoto, who kept pointing out that he did not get malaria, so why should we. By way of answer, we pointed to his protective clothing and our own G strings, to his mosquito-netted bed and our little nests in the mud, to his bottles of quinine and atabrine—of which we had none. He did not accept this at all graciously and kept us working until one either collapsed or one's temperature reached 104° by his thermometer (of which he was inordinately and childishly proud), whichever came first.

It was a combination of that thermometer and the third hut (an especially lavish affair designed to house Terai and the two senior Jap officers of H Force) that led to my final clash with Kanemoto. I was squatting astride a crossbar, entrusted with the task of splicing the next crossbar along onto its upright support, when it occurred to me that if I arranged the wire binding so that it merely *looked* as if it were firmly secured then I would save myself considerable exertion (always to be desired) and at the same time contrive the distinct possibility of the crossbar's collapse, at some future date, onto the skull of someone from Japan. At the very least, I thought, whoever it was, it would give him a shocking headache.

At that moment, my own head swam with the afteraffects of the previous day's fever and the man beside me grabbed me to stop me falling off my perch. Observing the commotion, Kanemoto looked up, his face surly, and grunted "Currah!"

I said I was "*biyoke* [sick]."

"*Biyoke-ka?*" queried Kanemoto.

"Hei," I assented vigorously, assuming my best sick look.

As Kanemoto produced his beloved thermometer, one of my fellow workers handed up a mugful of freshly boiled water in case I felt dizzy again. Kanemoto passed the thermometer up and indicated that I was to put it in my mouth. As soon as his attention was distracted I seized the opportunity to pop it into the water—still very hot—instead. The result was most gratifying. The mercury rose right up to the top of the thermometer and read a temperature the likes of which no mortal had ever survived before. I was certain that my Japanese friend would be impressed. And in this I was not wrong.

Kanemoto looked at his thermometer and gasped with astonishment. Then Terai and Kanemoto took it to their colonel, who looked at it and then at me with open admiration. Then came my undoing.

"Again one time," ordered the colonel, pointing first at the thermometer and then at me. And at once the obsequious Kanemoto swarmed, with that gymnastic skill which all Japanese soldiers possessed, up an upright and onto the crossbar next to mine, the better to take my temperature. My sham wire binding lasted about three seconds—then, with a rending crash, the crossbar, and Kanemotosan, plunged to earth. As he glared furiously upwards from where he lay, the mugful of nearly boiling water fell neatly over his head. At a single blow the quality both of my work and of my fraudulent medical practices had been revealed.

2 KANEMOTOSAN

After a short interval during which, with the aid of a webbing belt, he attempted to convince me of my follies, Kanemoto informed me that next morning I would be sent three kilos up to Kanu II.

"*Kanu taxan cholera,*" he said balefully. "There's a lot of cholera in Kanu." I knew exactly what he meant.

Next morning, therefore, our small party was lined up and Kanemoto confronted us to conduct a purge of those to be banished to cholera-ridden Kanu II. He was in a difficult position. He disliked all of us and had now to decide upon just whom he disliked most. Remembering the events of the day before, I was not surprised when I was seeded number one. Terai, who had been most friendly over the past fourteen days and who now stood at the gateway of the clearing watching this culling, solved the problem of meeting my gaze by turning his back.

Eight of us at last were honoured with the stamp of Kanemoto's especial dislike and fell out to collect our gear. I put my eating-irons and my toothbrush and my razor and my copy of *Mein Kampf* in my sack and was ready to go. Kanu next stop.

Kanu was not a nice prospect. When the remainder of our force had arrived there they had found only mud and jungle. They had been compelled to hack a clearing out of this jungle and at the same time send out every man who could walk to hack a cutting through a mountain. The cutting was deep: the tools—sledge hammers, crowbars, wedges, a small quantity of gelignite, changkols and baskets. They worked sixteen hours a day, then returned to do more work in the quagmire of their camp. Draining, digging latrines, building a cookhouse, collecting rations from the barges on the river more than a mile down a precipitous track below them. Cholera had broken out and every day more men suddenly vomited a greenish fluid, their bowels melted, their flesh withered off their bones and—looking like strips of potato that had been baked to a crisp in an oven and then allowed to go cold—they died. They had no drugs. Their only sustenance was the tireless strength and devotion of Major Fagan.

There also, as in every camp along the whole length of the proposed railway, they were harassed by camp administrations under the control of Japanese junior N.C.O.'s, or even privates, and by Korean guards—Koreans who, knowing nothing of the refinements of the 38th Parallel and acknowledging no difference between those of their countrymen who came from the north and those who came from the south, were quick to implement with the utmost violence the demands made upon our men by the Japanese engineers (than whom God has created no nastier breed).

And at the moment when we eight should have marched out of the gate and up the mud jungle track to Kanu II, a Nip surveyor arrived from down the line and demanded workers for a special task in his area. Almost disappointed, Kanemoto surrendered us to him. We were to go and live in the centre of the small saucer of swamp that lay a quarter of a mile away. We were to work there collecting fuel and water for the Japanese reinforcements marching through Thailand up to Burma; we were to bury the natives who died so untidily and so regularly all round this particular area; in our spare time, we were to work on the cuttings and embankments of the line that would run from Tarsao to Kanu.

As we marched out behind our new guard, his stocky, puttee-clad legs taking quick short strides, Terai said: "I am sorry," and glanced downwards, whilst Kanemoto, endearing to the last, mocked at us: "*Di-sana taxan malaria. Ashita mati mati* [Down there is much malaria—tomorrow you will be dead]."

One of our number, a round-faced, curly-haired little man of about forty, glared at him aggressively. "Cheerful little bastard you are," he commented.

Our new abode was not savoury. It consisted of the weather-battered fly of a tent beneath which was a rough flooring of split bamboos raised a few inches off the mud by more bamboo logs laid flat. It was neither rainproof nor windproof and it hummed with mosquitoes—those mosquitoes whose parasite-laden bite had kept the interior of Thailand barren and uninhabited for thousands of years.

Between our tent and the jungle on the right lay two huts in which lived the Japs. To our left a small stream—nothing more than a drain—wound sluggishly across the mud and separated us from the greater part of the swamp and the jungle which lay beyond it. In this stream the Indians from the camp just up the track were accustomed to wash, drink and excrete—a charming triple practice from which nothing could dissuade them.

In consequence of it there were always two or three of them lying on the side of the track in their death throes. Their fellow countrymen apparently felt no compassion for them as they lay there, foam on their lips, dying. They provided them with no water, nor attention, nor comfort—just padded past as if there were no one there. And when, hours later, they died, Nippon ordered us to bury them just across the stream from our tent. So we carried these graceless corpses and interred them in shallow graves because a foot was the deepest the guards would allow. And when it rained the covering soil washed off them and arms and legs—contorted and stiffened in death before we had found them—pointed skywards out of the black mud. Pointed until they decomposed or the vultures ate them.

Against this background of guards on the one side, exposed corpses on the other, the railway approaching from Tarsao behind us and the annihilation that was befalling Kanu II ahead of us, we settled down till September of 1943.

3 "ULCERS AND BUSHIDO"

Once again time ceased to have any significance. For almost a year no man knew what day of the week nor what week of the month nor even what month of the year it was. It was just 1943 and the Railway. If one were to survive it was essential not to acknowledge the horror that lay all around, still more not to perceive the effect it had upon oneself. It was not wise ever to look in a mirror. Life accordingly evolved into a blur of continuous work, people dying, guards bellowing, heavy loads to be carried, fever which came in tides of heat and cold on alternate days, dysentery and hunger. All those became the normal. Upon them, occasionally, an event superimposed itself with sufficient violence to be remembered.

There was little scope for planning one's own way of life. To preserve my health, I vowed to wash whenever it rained, lying under the dripping edge of the fly, and to clean my teeth every day, using the toothbrush Piddington had given me and ground-up charcoal for powder. Charcoal was also useful as a medicine against dysentery. To preserve some dignity, I vowed I would shave at least once a week if only I could remember the days. To preserve my self-respect, I vowed that whenever necessary I would make the latrines or bust; and to preserve at least some mental agility, I determined to learn off by heart one page a day of Mr. Hitler's *Mein Kampf*. As the days succeeded one another for the rest of that black year, this particular vow became increasingly difficult, but I managed never to yield to the temptation of excusing myself from my task—and in return derived a perverse pleasure from the daily assimilation of so much vile prose.

Terai arrived one morning from the headquarters camp just up the track. He said that he had bad news. Roy Death had died and Harry Peck was dying. He was sorry.

I thanked him for letting me know. He shrugged and asked was there anything I wanted. Remembering the huge Japanese stocks, and that the Netherland East Indies were its source, I said: "Yes, quinine"—to which he replied apologetically that quinine was difficult, and with that he left.

We went to work in a cutting. High above, at the cutting's top, stood the guards, Koreans and Japanese, throwing stones and young boulders at the men who slaved below. In the cutting men worked in pairs, one holding a rock drill, the other hitting it with a sixteen-pound sledge hammer. All day long one swung the hammer, the other twisted the drill. Hit, twist, hit. All day long in turns, and at night some more by the light of bamboo and resin flares—and a most prompt thrashing for any pair who stopped for so much as a second for any reason. So it went on, hit . . . twist . . . hit, with every now and then fingers crushed with the sledge hammer, or heads split open by irritable guards and legs cut by the rocks which they shied down from above—cuts which in a few weeks were to develop into the huge ulcers that caused even more misery than cholera.

When the holes had been drilled deep enough by this process, known as "hammer and tap," gelignite was inserted and the area blasted. The shattered rock was then carted in baskets, or man-handled in skips, to a cliff and there thrown over.

An English lad collapsed on the edge of this cliff and fell far down onto the jagged pile of broken rock at its foot. The guard peered over. "More one skip," he ordered. No one moved. With an impatient heave he dragged the lever of the skip himself and a ton of rubble crashed down on the body below. Only two men spoke. One looked the guard squarely in the eye: "Your turn'll come, you rotten bastard," he said quietly: the other, glancing down at the pile of rubble which was now a grave, spoke an epitaph: "Half his luck," he said, "half his luck."

The philosophy of "half his luck" was one which, though I could readily understand it, I could not accept. I had not the quiet fatalism about my impending extinction which these other calmly courageous men had. And yet, there being no room for optimism in Thailand—there being in fact no such thing as optimism in Thailand—some such insulating philosophy against the physically and mentally corrosive circumstances in which we existed was essential. Mine, which I found effective enough, was simply "It didn't matter—nothing matters."

The deaths of my friends, the ugly diseases that beset us, the constant reduction of rations that already seemed impossibly small, the bestiality of guards—against all these things, whenever they seemed likely to impinge upon my mind, I flung up the conscious barrier of "It doesn't matter—nothing matters."

It was a kind of narcotic, a self-induced drug, and no doubt—like all drugs and narcotics taken habitually—damaging. The fact remains that, starting in Thailand, and continuing on right through my captivity, and stopping I'm not sure where, I withdrew into the ostrichlike burrow where "nothing mattered," and there, mentally secure, I remained.

Terai visited us again. He was very sorry, he said, but Hugh Moore had cholera, Harry Peck was still dying, Reg Dudley and Dan Winters (the two friends who had been so unsympathetic about the grenade under Jack Mullins' throat at Parit Sulong) were dead. I thanked him for his news and he said he had brought me something to help. "Quinine?" I asked hopefully, for all eight of us now suffered from fever every alternate day; but he replied, "No, quinine is difficult," and gave me his present. When he had left I looked at it. A small, expensively produced book called *The Japanese Art of Arranging Flowers.*

We were taken to an embankment built by natives and there required to drive spikes, known as "dogs," into the sleepers laid along it. This was done, at Nippon's instructions, in tune to a chant of "*Ichi ni san-i shi*" (which means only "One . . . two . . . three four," and is not, therefore, a very interesting chant). I found swinging a sledge hammer with seven others to the endless accompaniment of "*Ichi ni san-i shi*" dull in the extreme and wherever I was so employed the quality of the Thailand Railway became very inferior indeed.

It therefore came as no surprise to us that the first train to push its way up from Tarsao towards Kanu was derailed on one of the more precipitous bends where we had worked. Its accompanying sentry was severely injured. We were called out of our tent late at night to help extricate this warrior. On seeing him, securely pinned under the wreckage, we recognized him as a gentleman of whom we had no cause at all to be fond, so we worked with great clumsiness and lack of speed. His completely abandoned screaming throughout this operation once again gave the lie to Oriental stolidity.

Having finally disentangled him, we marched back towards our tent—only to be confronted, at the entrance to the swamp, with a Nisson truck which had optimistically been driven up beside the railway and was now almost irretrievably bogged down in the mud. Not quite irretrievably because Nippon already had thirty prisoners from other camps on the end of a tow line and when we appeared he added us to their number and made it quite clear that there we stayed until we lugged the truck free.

Waist-deep in mud, we jerked the truck forward an inch at a time. At first the guard insisted on his absurd "Ichi ni sani-i shi" chant, but we very quickly abandoned that and reverted to the Australian "One . . . two . . . HEAVE." Eventually the Nisson was manhandled about forty yards to a small patch of dry soil. The sun was just rising. It was time to start work.

As we shuffled over towards the guard hut to get our orders for the new day's shift I noticed that the suction of the mud during the towing of the truck had dragged the soles off my boots. The rest of my stay in Thailand was spent barefooted.

The oldest member of our party died of what looked suspiciously like cholera. Another fell ill and followed him shortly afterwards. We were now six and I found that my limbs no longer functioned very well. There was an angry swelling in my feet which made them look like purple balloons—the toes were cocktail sausages attached to them like teats on an udder.

As I looked at them one of the others, pointing at my bloated extremities, asked: "What's the trouble?"

"Edema," I told him.

"Christ!" he said, much impressed; then, cautiously, "What's that?"

"Swelling," I told him.

"Silly bastard," he laughed, "why didn't you say so first time?"

But, edema or swelling or whatever the cause, my legs now ceased walking either easily or quickly and whenever any weight was put on my back they folded up. Since Nippon's only object in bringing us all to Thailand had been to put weights on our backs and then get us to carry them elsewhere this condition of mine did not bode well for the future.

And, in truth, things would have gone very badly indeed for me had it not been for the generous help of the men with me. At all times they covered up for me so that the guards did not realize how slowly I worked. And when they had finished their own quota of work, then they would do mine too.

In this respect one Snowy Bernard did most. He was unfortunate enough to have paired up with me when we first started work. Now that my arms seemed to have no strength with an axe he would chop down his own timber, then mine. When my legs crumpled under the weight of carrying the timber—particularly the long bamboos—back to camp, he would deliver his own, then come back and deliver mine. And never was there any suggestion of condescension but only that inexhaustible readiness on the part of the ordinary man to lend a hand whenever it was needed.

And all the time that Snowy and the three other men carried me so steadfastly, I became more and more of a burden. The swelling spread up my legs so that ankles and knees vanished into two water-filled columns of suet. Then my trunk began to swell with that same ominous suggestion of liquid beneath the skin tissues and even my eyes became merely two slits in a puffy sphere. I was constantly surprised by the slowness of my movements. I was not aware of being slow, but my companions and I had only to start walking and in thirty seconds I was thirty yards behind them. Then Snowy would stop and come back and shove me firmly along until we caught up—whereupon, left to my own devices, I would at once flounder to the rear again.

The guards began to take an unconcealed interest in my condition and daily showed their surprise that I was still alive. "*Ashita mati mati*," they would say, pointing towards the crop of arms and legs that protruded from the washed-out graves beyond our tent, and drawing a mocking cross on the ground. If I had required any stimulant to prevent me from succumbing to the beriberi that so bloated me those daily jibes by the guards would have done the job perfectly. Nevertheless the morning at last arrived when I found that not only could I not walk as fast as the others, I could not walk at all. This was disconcerting and I decided that I must see an M.O. Accordingly that night I left the tent on my hands and knees, eluded the guards, and crawled towards the headquarters camp. As I covered that quarter of a mile I found myself completely at a loss to understand why babies should spend the first twelve months at least of their lives propelling themselves in quite such an exhausting manner. The moon rose. In the powerful light it shed I decided that Thailand must be the only place in the world where all that moonbeams bring out is decay and mud and the demented high-pitched love song of baboons. My musings on this subject were interrupted by the M.O. himself, who spotted me ploughing—infant-like—through the mire and wanted to know what the hell I thought I was doing.

I replied that I thought I was coming to see him. He parried this with a question as to whence I came. When I told him he pointed out that, that being one of the most cholera-ridden areas in Thailand, I was extremely unwelcome and would I kindly stay where I was.

I said: "What, out here in the mud?" and he replied: "Yes," as if that were the most reasonable thing in the world. I was deeply aggrieved and said so. He, however, was adamant and eventually he persuaded me to remove my unwholesome presence altogether by throwing me a small jar. It landed about ten yards up in a pool of slime. I crawled up and retrieved it and, wiping it clean on some leaves, looked at the label. "Marmite," it read.

"You have beriberi," he shouted.

"I know," I replied from the mud.

"Take a spoonful of that a day," he advised.

"Will it do any good?" I asked.

"Might," he replied, and, returning firmly inside the palisade of the headquarters camp, indicated that the subject was closed. I crawled back to our camp, where I found the guards very cross that I had eluded them. I took a spoonful of marmite and, exhausted, fell asleep.

The railway nosed its way into our swamp and along with it came about forty tents to house the batches of natives who, impressed in Malaya, were shipped daily up the line. Thousands upon thousands went up into the heart of Thailand and Burma. It is thought that 130,000 of them died. The Japanese preferred them to die rather than return to Malaya and tell the truth about Co-Prosperity.

Each night, therefore, we received forty tentfuls of natives—about a thousand men, because the Japanese worked on the principle of at least twenty men to an English Army four-man tent—and each morning we buried the dead they left in those tents when they moved out. They were feckless, gutless, selfish and careless of anyone but themselves, those natives; but one could not help feeling sorry for them as they moved up in daily droves to be slaughterd.

One thing they did have, though, that we could well use—money. With their infinite capacity for commerce, they had all arrived in Thailand with thousands of dollars. Here, it seemed to me, was an opportunity to repay my companions for something at least of what they had done for me.

I sold my only pair of shorts—they would no longer fit my swollen body anyway—to a Thai for $3.75. Then, on the first dark night, armed with the $3.75 and a stick round which I twined my left leg, I started off. A pace forward with the right leg: then swing the stick, and on it my left leg, in a looping arc forward: then a pace with the right again. I made quite good speed in the dark and was well pleased with myself. About three hours later, having eluded all guards and patrols on the way, I reached the next camp down the line where the Thais sold cigarettes. I bought $3.75 worth and then returned, looping and pacing, to our own camp, reaching it just before dawn. I sold the $3.75 worth of cigarettes to the natives for $7.00, and next night repeated the operation. In a week we had $37 in kitty with which to buy any food available from the barges down at the river. I felt a little less of a liability.

We were sent down to the river and then given one hundred and twenty pounds each of rice to carry. The track up the mountain, being clay and wet, was murderous. To our surprise we carted the rations not to Kanu but past it to the next camp, about eight kilos up.

Outside Kanu, in the small stream that trickled down from the mountain above, lay a naked man. When asked why he lay there, he pointed to his legs. Tiny fish nibbled at the rotten flesh round the edges of his ulcers. Then he pointed inside the camp. Other ulcer sufferers, reluctant to submit to this nibbling process, wore the only dressings available—a strip of canvas torn from a tent and soaked in eusol. Their ulcers ran the whole length of their shinbones in channels of putrescence. Looking back at the man in the stream, it was impossible to decide, even though he was insane, which treatment was the best.

We reached the next camp and found it practically deserted—almost all the original inhabitants were dead. There were proud signs of the struggle for survival those men had put up. Carefully constructed latrines, spotless surrounds, an overhead pipeline made from bamboos which brought cholera-free water from its source two or three miles away and hundreds of feet up at the top of the mountain. This pipeline led to a shower centre with a bamboo floor and separate cubicles (pathetic symbol of man's desire for even a little privacy) and to a cookhouse that was all clean wood and carefully swept packed earth. All of these were refinements installed after gruelling sixteen-hour shifts of work at the expense of sleep and the recharging of their energies so vital to the next day's shift. But none of this had been enough—flies carried the cholera germs and mosquitoes the malarial parasites. Starvation and slavery did the rest. Now, as we set out back to our own camp, there were only a few skeletonlike travesties of humanity left and the big fire where they burnt their dead.

These fires flared at every camp where cholera struck. They lighted the way out to work in the dark before dawn: they guided the men back through the dark wetness of the jungle long after dusk. And always, lying round them in sticklike bundles, were the bodies that awaited cremation—bodies at which the returning men peered closely as they came in to see if any of their mates lay among them. And every now and then, as they filed past, came that muttered: "Half his luck."

About these fires a strange story was told. At one camp the task of attending to the pyre and of consigning the bodies to the flames was given to an Australian who, being without brains or emotions or finer susceptibilities of any kind, was more than happy at his work.

He stripped the dead of their gold tooth caps: he stole fearlessly from the guards, who dared not touch him lest he contaminate them: he cooked what he stole—for one only stole food, or something that could be bartered for food or tobacco in those days—on the fire where he burnt the bodies. He was the complete moron.

It was his practice before dealing with the fresh batch of bodies that arrived each morning to boil himself a "cuppa cha" and watch the working party fall in to be marched away to the cuttings. He liked watching the working parties fall in to march away because *he* stayed at home by his fire where, even in the monsoonal rains, he could keep warm and do his cooking. Upon one particular morning he sipped his tea out of the jam tin that served as a mug and watched the parade. As he watched he rolled some tobacco in a strip of the tissue that clings to the inside of a bamboo: then, his fag completed, he picked up a body and tossed it easily from yards off (for it was only light) onto the fire. He enjoyed the revulsion this caused. He did it every morning just before the workers marched out. Grinning at them as they glowered angrily, he then shambled to the fringe of the fire to light his cigarette.

As he leant forward to pick up a faggot the body he had just tossed into the flames, its sinews contracted, suddenly sat bolt upright, and grunted, and in its hand thrust out a flaming brand onto the cigarette in the moron's mouth.

With a scream of terror the man who had burnt hundreds of bodies with callous indifference fell backwards, his hands over his eyes. When the workers reached him he was jabbering and mad.

They took him to the hut that housed the sick, an attap roof draped over a patch of mud in which—all over one another—lay hundreds of men. For days he lay there silent, knowing nothing. Then one night he suddenly remembered and screamed, screamed piercingly and long so that, even though it was forbidden, the medical orderly lit a resin flare and rushed down to where he lay to see why he screamed.

Then, as the orderly leant over him, the moron sat up. Flare and moronic face were abruptly within inches of one another. With a scream more wild and piercing than ever the moron dropped back dead.

Terai called again and we had a strange conversation. He was sorry, he said, but many hundreds of my friends had died at Kanu. Too many to remember the names.

"Moore?" I asked.

"No," replied Terai, "not yet, nor Peck. But many hundreds of others. Arthur Farmer is one." I found it difficult to understand why he bothered with these condolences, but he interrupted my thoughts.

"You have read the book?"

"What book?" I asked vaguely, at which he looked hurt, so that I remembered the expensive little volume on flower arrangement and quickly said yes, I had read it.

"You liked it?"

I said that it was quite interesting but impossible to reconcile with the atrocious mentality of the guards we had struck in Thailand.

"They are only coolies, you must understand," explained Terai, "I am sorry that they behave badly."

"They're pirates," I pointed out, "you are an officer: you could stop them if you were really sorry."

"It is difficult," Terai explained.

"Like the quinine," I suggested, and he allowed anger to flicker for just a second in those intelligent eyes. Then he glanced down again and repeated: "It is difficult. I have brought you another book." Realizing that an awkward subject was thus being closed, I said, "Thank you," and added that it would make a pleasant change from *Mein Kampf.*

"Why do you read *Mein Kampf?*" Terai enquired.

"Mainly because you confiscated my Shaw," I told him.

"Socialism is not good in Nippon," Terai explained. Then: "Do you enjoy *Mein Kampf?*"

I told him that I didn't, but that it served its purpose as I learnt off by heart a page of it a day for the good of my memory, if not of my soul, and that I reckoned that that should see me over the worst part of the war.

"But, Mr. Braddon," he demurred, "the war will last a hundred years."

"Ah so-ka?" I answered him, using a common Japanese expression of surprise. "A hundred years? Six months ago it was all going to be over by the fifteenth of August of this year. Why the change?"

"It will be a hundred years," he repeated stubbornly, "but Britain cannot win."

I told him that on one of the most recent pages of *Mein Kampf* that I had committed to memory Mr. Hitler had written that the British Empire could not *lose* a war.

"Hitler is a fool," Terai snapped.

"He's your ally," I pointed out.

"He is still a fool."

"I'm glad," I told him, "that we don't think the same about Mr. Roosevelt."

Terai flushed darkly at this and there was silence for some seconds. Then, with a bright smile, he slapped his sword hilt and said: "I must go.

"By the way," he added, as he prepared to leave our tent, "I am writing a play."

"In English or Nippon-go?" I asked.

"English," he said proudly, "you must read it when it is complete and give me your criticism." I promised that I would.

"*Sayonara,*" he said, in farewell, and left—a slim, good-looking young man whom I didn't understand at all. I glanced at this last book he had given me. It was entitled *Bushido or Japanese Chivalry.*

By this time the fluids of the wet beriberi which swamped me were flopping round in my chest, having crept up from my legs, and a most unwelcome sound it was. The Nips now abandoned their drawing of graves and crosses on the ground and instead mimed a man drowning. I had become indifferent towards many modes of death, but drowning could never be one of them. The only preventative I could think of was to consume sufficient Vitamin B tablets (they would have, of course, to be stolen from the Japs) to overcome the deficiency which caused the beriberi.

A large force of Japanese reinforcements came sloshing up the jungle trail, shoving mountain artillery along with them. Their hoarse, rhythmic shouts of "Esau, Esau" as they pushed mountain guns along mud tracks sounded harsh and bad-tempered. They were not misleading.

Though we had just finished a particularly heavy shift we were routed out to light fires, boil water, cook food. An officer thrust his waterproof cape at me and indicated that I was to dry it. I was shivering with a malarial rigour.

Standing in front of the fire with the cape, I found it impossible not to sway on my unstable legs. Soon the inevitable occurred—the cape caught alight. Before I extinguished the flame one large corner of the gentleman's garment had vanished into a tiny heap of ash and a black cloud of pungent smoke.

The gentleman himself was not slow to notice any of these things. With a hoarse "Currah," he leapt up. He kicked, leaving a perfect impression of his toecap in my sodden flesh for hours afterwards: he swiped with his bayonet, cutting open the back of my head: and he then, for good measure, shoved me firmly into the fire. Bloated as I was, I was slow to move. I was surprised to notice that, though the skin bubbled and the flesh smelt singed, I felt nothing. The beriberi had at least done that for me, I reflected gratefully. On the other hand, however little it hurt, one couldn't afford to remain sprawled in a fire for long. Snowy solved the problem by ignoring the officer's bellows and dragging me out. It was all over in seconds, but it did nothing to heighten in my mind my impressions of *Bushido or Japanese Chivalry.*

Muttering to himself, as Snowy brushed me free of embers, the officer took his charred cape and placed it resentfully over his other possessions. Following his actions with a wary eye, I noticed that from the top of his haversack there protruded a large bottle of Vitamin B tablets.

When I left the guardhouse, so did the bottle. That night I sat up and ate solidly the small brown tablets of bran so rich in Vitamin B. They did not make easy eating, but I was a man who for a hundred days had been mocked by the Japanese as a perambulating corpse, so I continued munching. By morning the bottle was empty. I did not require my small ration of rice.

About two days later I reaped the profits of my theft. We had just gone to our bed spaces and I was laboriously scrubbing clean (with a few drops of water in my mug and my toothbrush) the burns I had received on my hands, arms and legs as a result of being booted so unceremoniously into a fire. It suddenly became necessary to urinate. I crawled the thirty yards to our makeshift urinal and obliged, and started to crawl back to the tent. I had only gone half-way, however, when it became necessary to reverse. Eventually, I stayed there and every ten minutes or so for two days fluid poured out of me. My chest no longer looked puffy: my stomach lost its thick pregnant look: my knees reappeared: then my ankles: then my toes. The beriberi bloated pudding was gone. In its place stood a skeleton which had never in all its life been so pleased with its physical condition than at this moment, when, according to the Japanese quartermaster's scales, it weighed eighty-one pounds.

The death roll all the way up the line was at this time so appalling that even more violent representations than usual were made by the British officers commanding each party to the Japanese administration. The representations were received by Colonel Fukuda, upon whose good will we all depended for food and drugs.

"The Japanese," he said, "are prepared to work: you must be prepared to work. The Japanese are prepared to eat less to save the strain on a difficult supply route: you must be prepared to eat less. The Japanese are prepared to die: you must be prepared to die." When, to this specious argument, the British officer replied that that was all very well, but in actual fact the Japs did no work: ate as much as ever, and—by virtue of regular doses of Vitamin B, quinine and anti-cholera serum—did *not* die, the honourable colonel merely shrugged his shoulders and replied: "There are plenty more prisoners of war."

That was his final answer.

I lay alone in the tent one day, shuddering with the uncontrollable animal shivers of fever. We had been given a quota of rock to carry and the rest of the men had sent me packing.

"Have a spine-bash, Russ," Snowy said, "we'll get it done without you."

Much of the day passed in a haze of shivering—nothing, it seemed, could ever induce warmth again. Then, suddenly, the sweat broke through, the coldness vanished and raging heat consumed everything. By noon I had drunk all the water in my bottle. By midafternoon I was looking with longing eyes at the water bottle in the kit of a man who slept next to me—a lad called Jimmy. Five minutes later I had furtively uncorked that bottle. I knew what I was doing. I was stealing water, more precious than gold, from a man who at that moment was doing my work. Breaking the one hard and fast rule—that every man is responsible for providing his own water. I drank a mouthful. Then, with what little will remained, I forced myself to recork the bottle, put it back where it had been (where exactly had it been? I felt sick at the prospect of being so easily discovered) and then crawled outside away from temptation. I spent the rest of the day and the night until my companions returned crouching by a fire, watching the vultures eating the latest disinterred native corpse and hating the environment that had reduced me to water stealing.

As soon as they came in, I called Jimmy over. "I pinched some of your water this afternoon," I told him. He stared at me squarely and I felt like squirming. "Didn't you have any of your own?" he asked. "Yes," I said, and he looked a little angry: "but I drank it all." For a moment Jimmy was silent. Then: "That's the trouble with the Bug," he said, "makes you mighty thirsty." He stooped and entered the tent; put his hand down instinctively to where his water bottle should have been; groped for a second and then came out.

"Didn't even put her back where she belongs, you bastard," he grinned, as he straightened up outside the tent flap.

"Had an idea I hadn't," I confessed miserably.

He passed the bottle over. "There y'are," he said, "have a good swig." And as I hesitated: "Go on . . . be in it. I'll boil some water up later and we'll fill *all* the bottles." So together we finished off his water: and then, armed with two petrol cans, one on either end of a pole slung across his shoulders, Jimmy plodded off into the night towards the watering hole half a mile away.

The drive to get the railway completed suddenly heightened. Everything became dominated by "Speedo." All requests for "yazumés" were greeted with the answer *"Yazumé nei"*: all requests for more food were greeted with the answer: *"Messi messi nei."* By day and by night parties of men, naked except for their G strings and the canvas bandages round their ulcers, marched to the cuttings and the embankments and the bridgeworks of the railway. Their joints stood out grotesquely as they walked stiffly by, all grace and rhythm gone from bodies which, though still young, looked as old as Death itself. Their eyes glowed deeply within gaunt faces and the skin over their thighbones—thighbones which protruded like axeheads—was worn through in great red patches of flesh where they slept on their sides.

Terai came down to give me a list of thirty names of men who had died within the last few days. He was, he said, very sorry.

"There are so many," he said softly. There were indeed. With relief I noticed that both Hugh and Harry were still alive. "They must be putting up a good fight for it," I said, almost to myself.

"Who?" asked Terai.

"Moore and Peck," I told him.

"They are very lucky," Terai declared; then, before I could point out that in Thailand there was no such thing as luck, he went on: "Mr. Braddon, why are you so yellow and thin?" His grimacing face conveyed the impression that I was hideous, which more or less confirmed my own views.

I told him I was no thinner than most of his prisoners and that we were all thin because a diet of a few ounces of rice a day plus some dried seaweed for sixteen hours' work was not enough. I told him I was yellow (and as I said the word I grinned, because it seemed such an odd question for a Nip to ask: but at once his lips tightened and I knew that this was not a safe subject for grins, so I continued quickly), I was yellow because for four months on every second day I had been shaken with fever and had had no quinine to suppress it. Terai opened his mouth to speak, but I forestalled him: "I know," I said, "quinine is difficult." I felt that that round went to Braddon.

Mr. Terai, however, proceeded smoothly to ignore all this unpleasantness. Clicking his sword up and down in its scabbard as he stood before me—I sat on the bamboo floor of the tent killing lice—he said: "Well, I have some good news for you at last." I wondered what it could be. The Emperor of Japan dead or Colonel Fukuda boiled in oil or an extra ounce of rice a day on our ration—dozens of things flashed through my mind as I looked questioningly up at him. Banging his sword with an air of finality back into its scabbard, he announced. "Italy is out of the war."

This was a great disappointment to me. I—in fact, everyone in Thailand—had known for two days, via our illicit radios and the grapevine, that Italy was out of the war. It would not, however, be wise to say so. So I just said: "Is it? That's good to hear."

But Mr. Terai was no fool. "You are not surprised, Mr. Braddon," he observed. This, I realized, was a point. Although I had not said "I know" to his news, I had not looked surprised at it. That had been a mistake. I must retrieve it.

"No, I'm not," I said, "they're lousy soldiers."

"But Italy has not just lost a battle," Terai pointed out, "she is out of the war." He paused. "And you were not surprised. You must have known. How did you know, Mr. Braddon?"

This was nasty, but I stuck to my guns. I did not know. I was not surprised. They were lousy soldiers.

Terai repeated that, if I was not surprised, I must have known. Where had I heard it? Who had a radio? Perhaps I had better return to headquarters till the matter was cleared up.

Still repeating that I had heard nothing about it until he told me and that the Italians were all lousy soldiers, I left the tent with *Mein Kampf*, my razor, my toothbrush and eating-irons in my sack, and my water bottle tied round my waist. Mr. Terai and I walked amicably along the fresh laid track of the railway to the headquarters camp. As we entered, Kanemoto scowled savagely at me and I—feeling that I might as well be hung for a sheep as a lamb—allowed myself the pleasure of scowling savagely back.

3 "ULCERS AND BUSHIDO"

For several days thereafter Terai and a friend of his from the Kempe-Tai[1] questioned me gently but firmly about how I must have known about Italy's surrender not to be surprised at the news: and I, in my turn, gave them the line that the Italians, as soldiers, were so lousy that no one possibly *could* be surprised.

Meantime, a swift surprise search had been conducted for radios in all camps up the line, and several suspects had been arrested. Others were severely bashed. Then the uproar subsided and my own case—to my vast relief—was dropped. I had not cared for the idea of more intensive Kempe-Tai questioning as to where P.O.W.'s got their news. I was, however, retained at the headquarters camp, where Terai was most agreeable. But I no longer felt at all confident of Terai.

The days succeeded one another and the railway nosed its way well past the headquarters camp and into the mountain that led to Kanu. The atrocious project was nearing its completion.

Half a dozen of us were sent up just beyond Kanu to lay some lines. The "Speedo" was on at full pressure and this particular section lagged. We marched along the newly laid track past Kanu—a shambles of rotting tents and decaying bamboo huts which spewed out rotting and decaying bodies only distinguishable from corpses because they breathed and moaned for water. Past a British camp on the right where very few were left and those mainly incapacitated with ulcers that snarled at you, the lips of flesh drawn back and baring shinbones and pus. They were dressing these terrifying wounds with the inevitable canvas (used and reused a thousand times and by successive sufferers as each last one died) and water in which was dissolved a minute quantity of salt.

We worked until the required section was completed. Then only did our Korean guard grunt "Yazumé all men," and we lie down to sleep.

We had not been asleep long, lying on the track itself, when someone shook me into wakefulness. "What's that?" he asked: and at the same moment I heard a demented, high-pitched, near but not quite human screaming, piercing and prolonged.

"Baboons," I reassured him. "Horrible ruddy noise, isn't it?"

[1]Japanese Gestapo.

"That's no baboon, mate," he argued, "I heard plenty of baboons and I seen 'em. And that ain't no baboon." We listened again, and again the shrill shriek cut through the jungle darkness like ice run across the back of your neck.

"Christ, that's horrible," said the other. Then, as the sound came weirdly at us again, "C'mon, mate. That's no baboon, that's a man."

Though I didn't want to go with him and find what caused a man to make a noise like that I lacked the courage to say so. We stole down the line, my companion sure-footed and determined: I constantly irritated by the universal law of railway lines that no two sleepers shall lie at an interval that shall fit either one walking or one running pace.

We covered a quarter of a mile and the sound now came from our right. We cut into the jungle, our progress now noisy and difficult, but still dominated by that demented voice. It seemed soon to lie ahead of us again. I called to my companion: "It's no use," I urged, "it must be a baboon. Keeps moving round."

"No, it don't, mate," he replied simply, "we do"—and he pushed on. So I followed and almost immediately we found the source of the noise. The wreckage of a man, mere bones, skin and hair, stood clutching a railing, his mouth wide open, screaming, mad, inhuman.

Two figures suddenly appeared beside him and carried him away. He appeared not to notice and the screaming continued. My companion and I followed them until they placed him on the ground in a small hut with four or five others.

"One of your blokes?" I asked.

"Yes, chum," said the Pommy, an R.A.M.C. orderly.

"What's the matter with him?" demanded my companion, his voice husky.

"Cerebral malaria," the Pommy told us. "He was trying to get down to the water. It's got a fascination for 'em."

"Many like that?"

"No, not so far," said the orderly, "but if we don't get quinine soon, we'll all be like it."

"Bloody lovely thought that is," my companion said.

"How old was that bloke?" I asked.

"Twenty-two. He's not dead yet, you know." We started to move off. "He will be soon, though," he added. "What we need is quinine."

But then quinine, I knew, was difficult. Wearily we two Australians threaded our way through the jungle, on to the rail track with the sleepers that didn't fit any step and back to the little group of sleeping men. Slightly apart from them the Korean lay on a groundsheet, his close-cropped skull pillowed on his haversack, snoring gently. My companion picked up a sledge hammer and looked thoughtfully at the black bristly skull.

"Forget it," I said, "it wouldn't make any difference anyway." Dropping the hammer beside the recumbent Korean, the other man nodded and brushed his hands together absent-mindedly, as if he'd just finished a job.

"You could be right, mate," he said, lowering himself onto the ground. "Happy dreams."

The line was finished. From Bangkok to Rangoon it ran uninterruptedly—except that the Royal Air Force blew up the odd vital bridge at strategic intervals so that no train ever got through. But, for the moment, it was completed and the Japanese decided to open it with ceremony.

At this ceremony the senior British officer on the line was invited to speak. He refused abruptly, saying that neither he nor any prisoner of war wished in any way to celebrate the official opening of a railway line whose every sleeper on its whole four-hundred-mile length had cost one human life. The Japanese were in no way put out.

The I.J.A. were now confronted with the problem of what to do with the wreckages of humanity which were the survivors of their railway. These did not look like men; on the other hand, they were not quite animals. They had feet torn by bamboo thorns and working for long months without boots. Their shins had no spare flesh at all on the calves and looked as if bullets had exploded inside them, bursting the meat outwards and blackening it. These were their ulcers, of which they had dozens, from threepenny-bit size upwards, on each leg. Their thighbones and pelves stood out sharply and on the point of each thighbone was that red raw patch like a saddle sore or monkey's behind. All their ribs showed clearly, the chest sloping backwards to the hollows of throat and collarbone. Arms hung down, sticklike, with huge hands, and the skin wrinkled where muscle had vanished, like old men. Heads were shrunken onto skulls with large teeth and faintly glowing eyes set in black wells: hair was matted and lifeless. The whole body was draped with a loose-fitting envelope of thin purple-brown parchment which wrinkled horizontally over the stomach and chest and vertically on sagging fleshless buttocks.

That was what the Japanese and Koreans did to the men who went on Forces F and H and lived. Of the total number who left Singapore, about half had survived. Now, what to do with this wreckage? And when they looked at it, even the Nips were a little unnerved.

The first thing they did, therefore, was to collect most of the survivors at Kamburi—that same Kamburi which had been the last town before the jungle commenced on our march up. We were loaded onto trains and shipped down. There were several longish stops on the way to allow those who died to be buried.

Finally we steamed into the flat fields of Kamburi.

As I staggered off the train, cramped and ravenous, for we had had no food for two days, I noticed that beside the line ran long rows of huts separated into two areas. In the one were white men: in the other black men. Both lots looked shocking. The fence that marked the dividing line between railway and camp was draped with white men only. The natives no longer took any interest in anything. Therein lay the difference. And, as I shambled towards this fence, one of the men on the other side crawled under it, dragged me through and greeted me with a warmth I had forgotten existed. It was Harry Witherford. I managed a feeble crack—"How's your turbo-jet?" I asked—but I was a bit overwhelmed. But he, good soul, knew what was required. Leading me firmly round the back of a hut, he gave me bananas and boiled eggs—bought on the spot from a Thai—which I devoured frantically lest they vanish. Though I live to be a thousand the warmth of that greeting and the gift of that food after the sterile months of want that had gone before will never leave me.

3 "ULCERS AND BUSHIDO"

We moved into the huts. They had a raised platform on each side of a centre aisle—as our numbers increased so the amount of this platform available to one became steadily less. It was mathematical. Eventually we had nineteen inches a man and a line of men crosswise at our feet. Nineteen inches is not enough for a man. To this the Japs pointed out that many died each day—soon there would be more room. In this, it seemed, there was great truth, because the day did not seem to pass when twenty men were not buried.

Ulcers were the main problem. They were attacked at once. Whilst Fagan operated all day on a bamboo table in a small cubicle kept free of flies by mosquito net (he cleaned out or amputated as many as forty legs a day, and always there was that gentle smile and the specialist's considerate manner), orderlies and volunteers, armed with common or garden spoons, which were sterilized in boiling water, cleaned out every ulcer in the camp at least once a day. The heroism of those men whose legs were so scooped clean—the flesh pared out like flesh from a melon—was incredible. It was not as if, once done, it was finished. There was invariably the next day. And the next day there was never any improvement. But always, when his turn came, each man would stretch his leg out flat for the orderly, raise himself slightly on his forearm and elbow and, with a friend ready to grab each shoulder should he move, say:

"O.K., mate, give her the works."

Then the orderly would dig his spoon firmly into the stinking pus until he had reached firm flesh and, having reached it, draw the spoon carefully down one side of the gaping wound and up the other. Swab it out: scoop out the few remaining mortified patches: put a bit of canvas soaked in acriflavine over the top and bind it up. Finished till tomorrow. The patient, who had lain straining rigidly backwards and not moving nor uttering more than a few small grunts, would then relax and crumple backwards, his forehead sweaty.

I cannot adequately describe the courage of those men because, having only suffered a few small ulcers myself, I shall never know the pain they bore so stoically. Let me hasten to state, however, that although I clung firmly to a bamboo upright for support I never once had the small craters round my ankle bones scooped clean with that fearsome spoon without either being sick, or fainting, or both. And had it not been for shame at the silence of those others, with the flesh from their knees to their ankles laid bare and their rigid straining backwards, I would have screamed with terror and with pain.

So the day commenced. Next, the night's dead were collected from each ward and taken, in convoy, outside the camp and across the road to be buried. It was difficult not to count them each day: but counting them was depressing, and if one did succumb to the temptation, one pretended one hadn't.

After that the day was one's own, for there was no work to do. If one could walk, one went looking for friends: if not one lay hoping that some friends would come along instead.

All day long a brisk trade was done with the Thais—clothes being the main articles for sale. As soon as the sale was made, the cash was used to buy eggs or fruit—pomelos and limes. The camp authorities—the British ones—were timid about this black-marketeering and forbade it, but we did not think they were serious.

In this, however, we were mistaken. I had just concluded a most satisfactory piece of haggling with a Thai through the back of the latrine—so deep in maggots that no guard would ever dream of coming near it—when an officer arrested me.

He claimed that I was endangering the camp's safety. I replied tersely: (*a*) that I was not; (*b*) that I was selling the trousers of a man who could no longer walk; who, therefore, did not need trousers; but who greatly desired pomelos and eggs because he could no longer stomach rice: and (*c*) that I never got caught anyway.

He replied that *he* had just caught me.

I told him that one did not expect to have to look out for one's own officers exactly as one did Japanese guards. He looked uncomfortable and said he had his orders from the colonel. I said rude things about the colonel. Five minutes later I was marched down for an orderly-room charge.

"Where's your hat, Gunner?" asked an R.S.M., who knew as well as I did that I hadn't owned a hat for two years—which fact I pointed out to him.

"Get a hat," he ordered. So I wandered off, and when I returned with a hat on, I was called to attention, right-turned, quick-marched, left-right-left-righted and called to a halt. To all of this nonsense I paid not much attention, being preoccupied at the time with plans for selling my own shirt next morning.

I was then ordered to remove my hat.

"But I only just got the ruddy thing," I complained. Apparently, however, that is exactly why one has a hat for orderly-room charges —so that one may be ordered to remove it lest one should strike the presiding officer with it.

"Wouldn't it," I asked, "be easier not to have a hat in the first place? Then you couldn't hit him whether you felt like it or not." I was instructed not to be flippant and, after some absurdly superfluous questions about my name had been asked, the charge was read out. If I had murdered a hundred or so of my comrades in their sleep, it could hardly have sounded worse.

Asked if I had anything to say, I replied that if the court had not as yet appreciated that our diet as O.R.'s required supplementing, if we were to continue to live, I hoped that someday it would. The court then found me guilty of the hideous charge it had heard and fined me a dollar and a half, which I did not have. I said so, and was instructed to pay it within the week—presumably by selling something on the black market.

As I left the "court," an officer, Pockley by name, grabbed me. "What did they fine you?" he demanded fiercely. I told him a dollar and a half. "Fools. Bloody fools," he shouted and, thrusting two dollars into my hand, added: "Here, go and pay them off."

I walked back into the hut which was the "court" and plonked down the two dollars. Great excitement, and everyone on the "bench" wrote things on various bits of paper. I stood silently and watched. Finally, one of my judges spoke. "All right, Gunner," he said, glancing up impatiently, "what are you waiting for?"

"My fifty cents," I replied. Irritably it was handed over—five tin-like coins with holes in the centre. Still I stood my ground.

"Well, what is it now?" snapped the Court.

"My hat," I replied.

"Oh yes," said someone sheepishly, and produced the potentially lethal headgear. I then left and outside met Pockley again.

"O.K.?" he asked.

"Fine, thanks, Dick," I told him, "here's your fifty cents change."

"Keep it, man," he said, "buy yourself an egg," and limped off on his badly ulcered leg to his own hut.

So I bought an egg and took it back to my hut along with Exhibit A, the pants. I sat down on the "chung"[2] beside the man who owned

[2]Bamboo platform.

the pants and told him the story in mixed German and Malay, for he was an Amboinese soldier of the Netherland Forces and they were our only common languages.

"Aber ich kann nicht Rice essen," he said. "I can't eat rice."

I said I was sorry. I would try to sell his trousers the next morning and buy him pomelos.

"Ja," he said eagerly. *"Pomelos sehr gut,"* and, in case I hadn't understood, added, *"banya bagus."*

Next morning I limped over to his bed space and found an orderly rolling up the trousers, and the space empty, and on the floor a broken egg.

"What happened to Joe?" I asked.

"Died last night, chum."

"What of?" I asked.

"Starvation, the M.O. said, chum. He hadn't eaten anything for a week, you know." As I walked away, I was very angry—not because the orders themselves were so silly but because they were applied with such silly rigidity.

Hugh and Harry I found quite early—Hugh obviously on the mend, though fearfully torn by the fires of cholera: Harry, equally obviously, doomed. Hugh and I spent quite a lot of time with him, but his bowels kept failing him, and we were never sure that our presence wasn't more of an embarrassment than anything else.

Finally, however, he sent for us. Hugh was on a hut-sweeping fatigue, so I went down to the dysentery hut where Harry lay. In the callous—necessarily callous—fashion of those days, he had been laid on the floor because, in his extremes as he was now, he was constantly fouling himself and on the floor it didn't matter. When two hundred men evacuate about forty times a day each and there are only two orderlies with half a dozen crude half-bamboo bed-pans ("boats" they are called), to cope with that day's eight thousand calls, it can readily be seen that no care should be wasted on a man who is dying. So Harry lay on the floor, a wizened-up little heap of rag with two clawlike hands and a tuft of dirty hair on his head.

I knelt beside him.

"How are you doing, Harry?" I asked.

"Won't be long now, Dig," he replied weakly, but steadily.

"Don't come that on me," I argued, "you've got too much to do back home."

"No, lad, no," he said, "I'm on the floor. I know what that is. I'm finished. Like you say, Russ, it doesn't matter. So long as I'm not alone, I don't care."

I tried to rouse him. "Sell you a cup of coffee for a dollar," I said. He knew what I was up to. He turned his grotesque head with its tuft of dirty hair and grinned. For a fraction of a second the eyes were Harry's again as he grabbed my hand in his two claws. Then they dimmed again, bluish-glazed like a newborn pup's.

"Just so long as I'm not alone, I don't care any longer," he said.

"You're right, Pommy," I told him, "you won't be alone."

I needn't have worried, though. Harry had already gone where all good shopkeepers go.

Kamburi turned out to be a hotbed of M.T. malaria—M.T. stands for Malignant Tertian and wreaks fearful havoc among sick men who are not safeguarded with nets and quinine. The death roll, which had been slackening slightly, speeded up again under the stimulus of M.T. malaria.

As was inevitable, my turn came and I found myself too weary with fever to move, or eat. Hugh was a tower of strength. He collected cupfuls of water and washed me. He fed me my rice until I was sick. He did everything possible until I got so hot that I no longer knew whether anything was being done for me or not. Instead I thought I read a book. A book I had written myself full of sonorous phrases and magnificent sentences. It was a most excellent book, except that it made no sense, and when I reached out my hand to turn over the page it was not there.

When that happened I would return to reality—but only for a second. Then I was off again, reading. A hundred times I reached out to turn pages. And a hundred times I awoke with a jerk to the truth of Kamburi. But the book always won—until one night I was very hot and my mother came to put cool cloths on my head. I knew she should not be there, but when I argued, she just laughed and called gently and my sister also appeared.

Now I was in trouble. Both my mother and sister in Kamburi! All night I led them between huts and behind trees and across streams—particularly streams: how cool they were—using all the skill in outwitting the Japanese that the last two years had taught me. And, at the last moment, we found a small boat. I handed them into it, and they sat down. As they sat a guard leapt upon me, seizing my wrist: so, with one kick, I shoved the boat out into the stream and it rushed quickly away with the tide, with my mother and sister sitting quite still facing me, dry-eyed, and the dog jumping up and down asking for its ball to be thrown.

The grip on my wrist tightened and so, confident that they were safe, I turned to deal with my assailant. "It's M.T.," I heard a voice say, "he's not too good. Give him some of that atabrine or we'll have another cerebral case on our hands," and another voice said: "Pulse is fast," and the grip on my wrist vanished.

Cerebral malaria. The noise like baboons, only it was men. That dispelled all my dreams. From that moment I ate everything and eagerly awaited my half tablet of the precious atabrine a day and went to sleep only grudgingly lest my control of consciousness should slip again. I did not want to shout like a baboon.

A few days later it was all finished.

"You're a bright one," said Hugh with a grin, "silly as a two-bob watch you were." And when I asked how I'd managed to get so much medical attention, he explained that Dick Pockley and Theo Walker had badgered the doctors until they came to me. The longer one lived, it seemed, the greater the number of generous people one met.

The Indians in the camp next door, meantime, died like flies and were buried as, or just before, they died in huge communal graves. Those who had ulcers were unceremoniously bundled into a special charnel hut and there locked in to starve to death. These, especially, were unhappy and noisy.

Their lot being a sad one and they not blessed with the moral fibre to stand up against difficulties, they decided, in droves, not to endure it any longer. So when they heard the train coming up the track, they would rush out and lay their necks across the line. This effectively solved their problems but would stop the train if there were too many of them because the wheels became slippery. The habit attracted hosts of vultures from the district all around and these lived in the trees in our camp. They are loathsome birds.

One day, as we carried out the body of a youngster who had died the night before, one of these vultures swooped and tore at its chest. We were too quick for it though, dropping the body as the bird swept down so that it missed on its run-in with its curved, tearing beak. But we hated it, the four of us who carried the boy, for daring to attack him. So we picked up stones and sticks and followed the vulture to its tree near the fence that divided the camp from the line. Then we hurled the stones and sticks at it, and, one of our number being an American sailor off the *Houston*, and a baseball pitcher as well, hit the bird, which came shrieking and tumbling down.

"What'll we do with it?" I asked.

"Eat the bastard," retorted the Yank. And within a half hour it was stripped, boiled and eaten. The tables, I felt, as far as that vulture was concerned, had definitely been turned.

The dysentery huts rang to the urgent shout of "Orderly, Orderly. Bring the 'boat' please!" and a few seconds later: "Too late . . . bring the shovel." The beriberi ward grew steadily more and more crowded with bodies that bloated first and then drowned and the ulcer sufferers went through the daily ordeal of the spoon, and the scoured flesh always refused to granulate and heal (although now that the Japs had been persuaded to donate a little M and B 693 and some iodoform as well, there seemed more hope). Fagan continued to operate up to forty times a day. Then a new scourge hit the sick men of Kamburi.

On that red raw patch over the thighbones where they lay on their sides, the flesh first mortified and then swiftly developed into an abscess. In a matter of days this abscess swelled till it covered the whole thigh—big and deep as half a football. It had to be opened and drained, and for so swift an incision, albeit so agonizing, the camp could not spare any chloroform. Not while there were so many amputations waiting. So each day they were done, the abscess sufferers, without anaesthetic. A swift stab, a moan, a gushing and dripping into a kidney bowl—and on to the next man.

That sharp moan hurt to hear.

In the camp was a Dutchman called Elser. Small, dark, with curly hair and round eyes behind thick glasses. He spoke bad English and was at the same time both nondescript and arrogant. He was a hypnotist.

One day he sought, and obtained, permission to use hypnosis on the Dutch cases whose abcesses were that day to be lanced. His technique was brilliant and the Dutch—a superstitious race—were most susceptible. One after the other, as he passed, each man fell backwards onto the chung in deep, hypnotic sleep. And one after the other their abcesses were lanced. In the whole ward there was not one of those sharp moans that hurt to hear. It was a miracle.

I had never been readier to admire a man in all my life. But I did not admire Elser. He came out of the ward, his birdlike face wreathed in smiles of self-satisfaction—*not* because he had saved men from suffering: *not* because that sharp moan had been silenced, but because Elser had been glorified. "They vill vorship me now, those men," he said, "because my vill is stronger as theirs." I must have looked my contempt.

"*Ja*," he repeated, "is right. My mind," and he tapped his forehead at the side of his big glasses, "is stronger as theirs."

"*Than* theirs," I observed.

"*Ja natürlich*—than theirs," he amended.

"I doubt both statements anyway. It's very sad," I told him, and walked away.

"*Was?*" I heard him shouting. "*Was ist?*" but I ignored him. Elser, I knew, would not trouble to save Kamburi any more pain. And, in fact, he didn't. The miracle of the abcess ward was never repeated and the following year Elser himself, the man with the strongest mind in Thailand, achieved the astounding and unequalled feat of contracting scabies, falling into a decline of misery thereat, and dying.

3 "ULCERS AND BUSHIDO"

Volunteers were requested for duties as medical orderlies. Only knowledge necessary—how to empty a bedpan or boat. Tired of being useless and bedridden, I handed in my name. I thus entered the strange world of people who stay awake at night and watch while others sleep and die.

It was a little eerie, that night duty, with only a small coconut-oil wick for light in a fifty-metre hut. It was also touching. The gratitude of men for a drag upwards as they tried to rise, or a restraining arm as they fell back too quickly. The supreme pathos of two hundred dying men who, relaxed and unself-conscious in their sleep, looked like children—when the oil got very low and the light very dim, like babies. The whispered "Thanks, mate," when you took them a boat. The offers of a cigarette because they had nothing else to give—and even that they had been given. They were good lads.

For a while it worried me that some of those who died should do so asleep and without warning—they seemed so unprepared. But then when I saw those who knew exactly what was happening and lay patiently *waiting* to die for hours: and when they, too, saw no heavenly hosts nor had any comforting visions (of the type much vaunted by priests) but had only their own courage and humour to bear them over those last minutes—then I ceased to worry about those who died in their sleep. They did not have to face this waking wait, with its prospect of oblivion. I felt happier about those who died in their sleep—so long as I found them before the cold stiffness of death had set their legs and arms in the careless, childlike posture of their last sleeping moment (seldom suitable to a dignified burial).

I learnt to undress the dead, tidy up their belongings, straighten their legs, fold their hands across their chests, close their eyes. If the lids were reluctant to shut, a little cold water on a piece of cloth, and, after a few seconds, the eyes were closed and peaceful. All this and much else I learnt—even to dressings, so long as they involved the patient in no pain, in which case I felt sick. Most important of all, I learned to sit on the edge of the chung near any man who couldn't sleep and, while I waited for the next hoarse urgent whisper of "Orderly . . . boat, please," to talk with him about those sudden thoughts that come at night to men who are far from home. Voices low-pitched, sporadic phrases and long, companionable silences. It was some comfort that the war had at least taught me to like my fellow men and that, for all of us, there was more than a little to be said.

Rosie—the bombardier-solicitor of the slide rule, the carefully considered answers, the seasick pills and the cutthroat razor—Rosie died. And shortly after him, Robbie, Piddington's rickshaw mate. But Robbie had almost a hundred boils and, though he smiled cheerfully all the time, his release from them must have been a mercy. All the threads with the past seemed to be snapping. There was, of course, no future. No one with any intelligence allowed himself in those days to contemplate the future.

In Kamburi water was always the difficulty. When it rained everyone crawled out and stood or lay under the pouring eaves of the huts and scrubbed themselves clean. But when it didn't rain, then even to get enough water to drink was a problem.

It was in this matter that a small group of officers started and carried out (always more difficult) a most generous scheme. Playfair, Le Maistre-Walker, Mackissack, MacLeod, Knox, Pockley and Gibson (there were others, doubtless, whose names I forget) collected a basin and a kerosene tin. They would fill the basin with clean, clear water collected from the well some distance outside the camp. Then they would send one of their number up to one of the huts and he would select someone to whom he would say: "There's a tub of water for you down at our hut if you want it," and that was all. When you went down to the hut, the basin stood outside with a small piece of soap. No one there. No questions asked. It was restoring, that free bath, after days of sweating with fever and parching heat.

Nor did the group stop there. With their limited officers' allowance, they made gifts of fruit, eggs and money—usually when one slept, so that one awoke to find it there beside one. They dropped in to each hut almost every day, each one of them, to yarn and see how things went. They pestered the hard-pressed medical staff if they saw a case that needed attention.

Let it be said here and now that almost all of us had experience of such groups and that without them things would have gone very hard indeed.

Not only these officers, however, understood the value of water. My duties as a night orderly were abruptly terminated by a second attack of M.T. malaria in the course of which I returned to my "book reading" with renewed vigour, not even the absence of a page to turn, as I reached out for it, bringing me back to my senses.

At that time Kamburi had had a rainless week. Water was at a premium. I needed gallons of it.

One day I became aware of the soft clang of a mug against tin, then the splashing of water. At first I thought this noise, so close to my head, was as non-existent as my "book." But finally, unable to stand it any longer, I turned my head and looked.

There, in the aisle between the two chungs, stood an Australian—Snowy, we called him. In his right hand he held a four-gallon can of water: in his left a mug, which he constantly filled and poured slowly back into the can, filled and poured back.

"Want a drink, mate?" he asked. I explained to him that if I had to choose between a bagful of diamonds and a drink of water at that stage, I'd take the drink. He grinned understandingly.

"Give us your mug then," he said. I struggled upright and found my mug in amongst *Mein Kampf* and all the other junk. He dipped his own mug into the water . . . cool, it looked . . . and held it over mine, ready to pour. My tongue curled dryly, like a roll of sandpaper, back against the roof of my mouth. Then:

"Got ten cents on you, mate?" Snowy suddenly asked.

"Got what?" I asked, my mind still on the water.

"Ten cents," said Snowy. And, as I looked uncomprehendingly at him, added: "It's ten cents a mug, you know." He looked at me shrewdly, his eyes hard as I rebelled at the thought. He poured the water slowly back into the can. "Only ten cents a mug," he said, "it's worth it. You're thirsty, ain't you?"

"You know I'm thirsty," I told him, "else you wouldn't be standing there pouring that water in and out of your blasted can."

"Take it or leave it, mate," he said. "Ten cents ain't much and a man's gotta live. I mean I gotta get dough for a smoke somehow, ain't I?"

"I haven't got ten cents," I told him, which was true, "so shove off." I lay back again and tried to think about lemons which, I'd read somewhere once, was a very thirst-quenching thought. The water splashed, a long slow trickle again, just behind my head.

"You could give me an I.O.U., mate," the flat nasal voice urged. "I got one here. All you gotta do is sign."

"I haven't got a pencil," I said. I was struggling against the temptation of this usury. I didn't want any part of it. Except the water. And Snowy knew that; and he knew he had me because he'd caught so many hundreds of fever and cholera sufferers before me.

"I gotta pencil," he said, "indelible," and thrust onto my chest a grubby form and a pencil. I read the form:

> I the undersigned hereby promise to pay on demand the sum of 10 cents or upon the return to Australia £1 (one pound).
>
> *Signed* . . . .

One pound for a mug of water!

"Snowy," I told him, "you're a good businessman," and signed. He replied: "Thanks, mate, one pint of misuwa[3] coming up." He took his pencil and I.O.U. and passed me my mug. I drank deeply and felt better.

Altogether, during that rainless period and my high fever, I bought, or Snowy managed to sell me, £112 worth of water.

When, two years later, I got back to Australia, one of the first letters I received was a demand for £112. I wrote Snowy a polite note saying that I should be enchanted to pay him, every penny of it, so long as he would meet me in Sydney where we might both be photographed by the press—I giving him a cheque for £112, he handing me a receipt for £112—money paid for water received. I thought that as a tale of comradeship in arms it would read well in the dailies.

Surprisingly, I received no answer.

I had just recovered from this latest bout of fever when into the hut strode Terai—a Terai resplendent not in the usual rather drab I.J.A. interpreter's uniform, but in a dove-grey tunic and breeches

[3]Japanese: "water."

and glittering black boots to his knees and his hand on his sword. I had seen other Japanese officers wearing this uniform, but they had been members of the Kempe-Tai—not pro-British war haters as Terai was thought to be.

"Hello, Mr. Braddon," he said, "I am glad to see you again. But you are still so yellow and thin."

"Still got malaria," I told him.

"Ah so-ka," he agreed, "I am sorry." Then, more cheerfully, "I have finished my play."

"Good stuff," I told him. "Got it there?"

"Yes," he said, digging into his dove-grey tunic and dragging out a roll of typescript, "here it is. You will read it and tell me your criticism." I nodded. "I will return tomorrow," he said, and, with a smile, left. "Christ," said my neighbour, "who was that . . . Hirohito?" I said: "No, just an interpreter."

Slowly I unrolled the neat typescript. Strange bloke, this Terai. Pro-British, some said. Got violin strings which were scarce as all hell for the Concert Party; but couldn't ever get quinine, of which there was tons, for the railway workers. Went to a lot of trouble to keep you informed about your friends in other camps; then spent days trying to trick you into admitting that you got news from an illicit radio. A professor of English classics who pressed on you booklets about Bushido and the art of arranging flowers.

I skipped the title page and the cast list, my eye flying direct to the introduction. It observed that British, American and Dutch prisoners of war had worked with Nippon on the glorious project of the Thailand Railway. By completing it, they had both atoned for the accumulated sins of their forefathers in the East and had imbibed sufficient culture from their guards to raise themselves onto an altogether higher spiritual plane.

I grunted at that. Either this Terai was the most superb satirist of Japanese propaganda or he was the most fanatical—and cunning—purveyor of it. I started on the play itself.

An hour later, with difficulty, I finished it. The dialogue was hopeless: the English poor: the plot fatuous. It concerned Allied P.O.W.'s who, after working with a noble Japanese guard on the railway, became convinced that the Japanese way of life was quite the best and the British way of life quite the worst. It was a very bad play.

Mr. Terai arrived next day and I was no longer in any doubt

about him—even though this time he wore his colourless interpreter's uniform and looked quite gentle and innocuous.

"You have read my play, Mr. Braddon?" he asked. I nodded.

"And . . . ?" he queried.

"Lousy," I told him—and enjoyed it.

"Lousy, Mr. Braddon?" His face was questioning, although a glimmer of angry understanding lurked in his eyes.

"Yes, Mr. Terai. Lousy! *Warui, tidak bagus,* Number Ten." I elucidated in all the other languages, including his own, that he was likely to understand. I held out the rolled typescript and, with carefully suppressed fury, he took it . . . slowly.

"Nothing personal, of course, Mr. Terai," I added, sweetly.

"Of course not, Mr. Braddon. I am most interested in your views," he said, "most interested," and left.

I didn't see Terai ever again: but when the war ended with Japan's unconditional surrender, he was, I am told, one of the lamentably few who obeyed the Nipponese injunction never to be captured alive. He attempted hara-kiri—which was an odd thing for a man who was pro-British and anti-war to do.

As the weeks rolled on at Kamburi the incredible mental resilience of the men who lay there reasserted itself. They were rotten with ulcers, heavy with beriberi, torn with dysentery and fever, yet slowly the haunting numbness of the past year vanished from their eyes and the future came to have some meaning.

And one night—the best night I remember in Thailand—quite late, the Pommies in the next hut, without warning, suddenly started singing. Not just one, but the lot. Good, clear, young voices. Young—that was it. It was the first time for many months that it had occurred to me that we who looked wizened enough to be a thousand were still young. They sang the inevitable chorus in their warm men's voices:

> "There's a long, long trail a-winding,
> Into the land of my dreams . . ."

and, when they finished that—and in the silence you could hear every man in the camp listening—they swung by some strange mass instinct, with barely a second's hesitation, into:

"When they sound the last all-clear,
How happy, my darling, I'll be . . ."

and at that the next hutful of Pommies joined in with them, and the next with those, and the worst of Thailand was over.

Thereafter there were nightly singsongs and quizzes and lectures. Entertainers became popular and names like Bill Williams and "Professor" Roberts will always be remembered. Bill Williams had a tiny portable organ. This he would cart into the centre of one of the huts and there, squatting on a box, he would pedal furiously and sing cabaret numbers to men who died, and shouted, "Orderly, boat, please . . . too late . . . bring the shovel," and lay bloated or raddled listening to him. He was a delightful artist. To the accompaniment of his boogie and point numbers men forgot their ulcers and straining bowels. When he plays his point numbers nowadays in the luxurious floor show at the Berkeley Hotel in the West End of London I wonder how often his mind goes back to the days when those same fingers, that same indolent voice, that same wide smile enchanted the shattered men of Kamburi. Bill Williams was very much a vital part of those mad days and nights.

And then, suddenly, on one of them, the Japanese said: "All men go to Singapore," and without the smallest compunction we got in trains and left the vultures and graves of flat, mosquito-infested Kamburi. Not even the vile five days that followed in that train could dampen our pleasure because now at last we were going home and nothing could ever, after Thailand, be bad again.

4

1 A HOME TO BE BUILT

The trip down, like the trip up, was tedious. Towards its conclusion, as the train chugged onto the Johore end of the causeway (where a very inadequate crater bore witness to the feeble attempt at blowing it made years before in the face of the Japanese advance), a shout went up, as it had last time we crossed the causeway.

"You'll never get off the island," the shout went, and very ironic the shout was.

From Singapore station we were transported in trucks, trucks noticeably the worse for wear in the last year, to Sime Road—where once there had been a golf course and now there was a camp.

At Sime Road we stayed for several months, recuperating and licking our wounds. Nothing much happened at Sime Road. General Saito, who commanded us, ordered that all men should be able to count up to one hundred in Japanese and that all orders on parade should be in the same barbaric language. Whenever he or his aide, Lieutenant Takahashi, appeared, we were all to shout "*Kirray*" and stand up to attention and salute.

Saito and Takahashi frequently did the rounds of the camp to enforce this rule. They and Saito's pet monkey on a leash became quite familiar signs to us, though, of the three, the only one we liked was the monkey.

Then one day the monkey on its leash leapt round the corner of a hut and the first occupant who spotted it shouted, "Kirray," realizing that Saito and Takahashi would be close behind. But, as the whole hut stood up and saluted, Saito and Takahashi were not close behind. They were, in fact, standing on the crest of a hill a hundred yards away. And what they saw was block after block of prisoners of war screaming "Kirray" and saluting a monkey as it bounded down the lines. The implication was unmistakable. There is no subject on which the Nip is more sensitive. That night Saito chopped his pet monkey's head off with his large Samurai sword and next morning Takahashi issued an order that any other pet monkeys in the camp were to be destroyed.

The next event of significance was the collapse of Kevin Fagan. Exhausted by fever and a year's superhuman effort on behalf of others, he suddenly folded up. It was a brilliant morning that the story flashed round the paths and slopes and huts of Sime Road Camp. "Fagan's ill, unconscious, they say he's dying."

And, if any proof were needed, that moment decided the greatness of the faith that the men of the railway had in the slim, greying M.O. To the fibro-cement room where he lay, from all over the camp, came an endless pilgrimage of soldiers bearing tinned food, money, oil, soap, clothes, all their most cherished possessions. "Brought this for the major," they would say, "thought it might help," and then wander off. No other man in the entire Malayan Force could have won so spontaneous a tribute of such treasures.

For days his progress was followed with even closer attention than the B.B.C. news. When it was announced on parade that he was off the D.I. List, the ranks of men rumbled with pleasure. When he was first seen up and walking again, the camp gazed proudly upon him as a hospital does upon its star patient. In the light of the total and inexplicable absence of official recognition, since the war ended, of his devotion to his men and his selfless courage to help them, it is pleasant to recollect that at Sime Road, when he fell ill, we were at least able to pay a small part of the tribute so long owed him.

The final event of importance at Sime Road was mail from home. It had come through the Red Cross and was sixteen months old. But it was from home. Hugh and I both received our first letters. Mine came from my sister. It said:

> Dear Russ,
>
> Mum's puddings are still as lumpy as ever. Oodles of love from us all.
>
> Pat

I read it over and over. If twenty-five words was all the Japanese would allow our folk to write, then that letter told me all I wanted to know—that the family did not accept that I was "killed," as posted: that the old household jokes about my mother's rather abandoned cooking still flourished: that home was still home.

A lean figure leant disconsolately against a post opposite me.

"No mail, Dig?" I asked.

"Nope."

"Like to read this?" I offered, as casually as possible because I knew the hurt that came when you missed out on the Red Cross mail, which arrived only once a year.

"Do you mind?" he asked. I waggled my head from side to side. "Don't mind if I do," he said cautiously, so I passed him the card and, as he accepted it, he said: "Ta."

He looked at the address, at the Japanese frank, at the colour of the ink. Then, very carefully, he read it. And then again. After about ten minutes he handed it back.

"'Oodles of love,'" he said, "that's nice. That's a nice letter." A pause for thought and then: "Pat's your sister, is she?' I nodded.

"What's your mother like?" he asked. I said tall and good fun, but a lousy cook.

"Thought from that she might be," he laughed. "My old woman is too. Trouble is, she don't know it like yours." For a few moments there was silence, then he said: "I'll get one one day, mate, don't you worry. I had a baby coming just when Singapore chucked it in. Got to find out whether it's a boy or a girl yet."

"Fussy?" I asked.

"Aw," he said, "I reckon I like me teapots with a spout on 'em." He stood up straight from the post and strolled off. After a few yards he turned and shouted back: "Thanks, mate, do the same for you sometime."

Quite soon after that we were informed that all P.O.W.'s on Singapore were to be concentrated inside Changi Gaol. Once again we prepared to move. At least, we felt, we would meet a lot of friends.

So, at Changi Gaol, were concentrated about seven thousand men—the remnants of F and H Forces, the workers of Changi Aerodrome, the Changi Administration.

The gaol from the outside was tall and grey and its barred windows had a blind, un-looked-out-of expression. Its walls breathed isolation and sterile retribution. It was said to be modelled on Alcatraz, only better. It was the sort of building the very sight of which was so unnerving as to make one resolve never to break laws. Once inside, one realized the skill with which its architects had combined humanitarian principles of accommodation with an atmosphere so oppressively penal as to deter all but the most anti-social.

And once inside, one knew why the barred windows looked blind and un-looked-out-of from the outside. They *were* un-looked-out-of. They were so placed that they admitted light and air—but they were too high for their inmates to see from within the free world beyond the walls.

And once inside, one appreciated the sinister envelope of the gaol's double walls. Like a layer of specially thick insulation, these two walls, and between them the girdle road, which ran right round the four sides of the gaol, isolated the gaol community from the world beyond. They cut off all hope of escape—both to the convict and to the prisoner of war.

This, then, was the position. Changi Gaol was one of His Majesty's most modern prisons, proudly surmounted by a gleaming concrete tower, which in its turn was surmounted by a radar screen which did not work, which in its turn was surmounted by a flagmast bearing the Japanese flag. It had been designed to hold six hundred native felons and to cater for their needs with a steam kitchen supplied by oil-burning boilers, and latrines with cisterns. The oil burners no longer worked because there was no oil: the cisterns no longer worked because most such refinements, after a few years of Japanese use, usually don't.

In other words, into a ferro-concrete gaol for six hundred, without sewage or cooking facilities, on the one day, marched seven thousand men. To transform this ferro-concrete shell into a home they had the following natural or man-made materials to hand:

Rubber trees
Coconut trees—the fruit as well
A few augers
Some steel filing cabinets, removed from Changi Barracks in transit
Palm oil

1 A HOME TO BE BUILT

Bamboo
Barbed wire
An infinite capacity for stealing
Their own inexhaustible imagination

With these materials, and these only—for the Japs offered no help—they transformed the gaol in a few days.

The oil-burning boilers were, by some sapper's miracle, translated into wood-burning boilers and a wood-cutting party grubbed stumps out of the nearby swamps, split their iron roots into lumps and had fuel ready for the burning. Thereafter, with a good head of steam up—and the R.E.'s always had a good head of steam up—the rice for our seven thousand was pressure-cooked in a matter of seconds.

At the same time the augers were flung to work—a steel tripod twenty feet high, from the apex of which hung a shaft whose nose was a sort of triple shovel. Through the shaft ran a bar and on each end of the bar three men pushed . . . round and round . . . until that triple-shovel nose or bit at the end of the shaft was full of clay. Then haul it out, empty it, and start again. Working in shifts, the holes sank, one after the other, in every gaol courtyard, forty feet deep. Those were our latrines—and, used in rotation, they never failed in their purpose.

And while hundreds of squads of six men in shifts kept the augers turning; and whilst others carted away the raw red clay that the augers churned, and spread it where gardens were to be planted, or banks made, or ground levelled: and whilst the woodcutters lugged logs into the cookhouse courtyard for the hungry maw of the R.E.'s boiler—while all this went on, others cut palm fronds and separated the bladelike leaves and hung them over thin saplings about four feet long. Enough of these, like flat grass skirts, and one could make a rainproof roof or wall.

Rubber trees were chopped down for uprights and bamboos for roof supports: and barbed wire was straightened for bindings and its long spikes were shaped into nails. Then, with attap over and around the skeleton, huts quickly sprang into being—two or three in every courtyard. Huts one hundred metres long, with earth floors.

So, by sleeping four or five in every cell meant for one: by sleeping on the safety screen that covered the well on each floor between the cells: by sleeping in the huts, and under the washbasins that didn't work, and in the corridors, every man found shelter. And, with the bore-holes functioning so perfectly, no dysentery epidemic broke out. And, with the cookhouse producing our rice within a matter of minutes, no one starved. And the Japanese—who had looked rather sardonic as they herded so huge a number into so small a space with no facilities—were surprised.

But Changi had not finished yet—not by a long chalk. Parties that went out to work stole lengths of inch-piping and, with it, showers were installed in each courtyard. And the engineers made the taps at the washbasins work, by some weird magic known only to engineers.

And, by stripping the hard spine out of the leaf of the palm frond and binding bunches of these spines together, birch brooms were made. Shorter lengths were stuck, in harsh, evenly clipped tufts, into a wooden head—stuck with pitch torn off the roads—and hard brooms of first-class manufactured appearance were the result. Likewise were nail brushes for the doctors and medical orderlies made: and, with the softer fibre from the outside of coconuts, soft brooms and toothbrushes.

And with the palm oil and some potash from the boilers, and a complex machine made of empty drums and stolen pipes, soap was made. A cake of good, soft soap for each man in the gaol, once a fortnight, to use under the showers.

And with the grass that grew, and water, and potash, and some trays cut out of the filing cabinets, paper was made to write on—very expensive, high-class paper, as is only to be expected when it is hand-made!

And with the latex that came out of the rubber trees—latex which the Japanese regarded as useless because the wicked British Imperialists had destroyed all the coagulant as they retreated—with this some planters soled boots and shoes. They coagulated the latex—crudely but effectively—by urinating in it. Poor Nippon! A little sand added to the hardening fluid, and there was a tough sole for a shoe.

With the same material, they devised a means of patching clothes—cotton having vanished from our lives—and of preparing an adhesive tape for medical dressings.

And with the soft white wood of young rubber trees those who had no boots fashioned themselves clogs so that the gaol's concrete corridors rang to their clip-clop all day and all night, and one came to recognize one's friends by their particular note and tempo—this especially when, later on, many men, because of vitamin deficiencies, became so blind that faces were indistinguishable to them.

Also, there was a workshop where the green filing cabinets were transformed into dixies and mugs and spoons. And another workshop where filing cabinets and rubber trees were wrought into artificial limbs—beautiful pieces of work which their owners (the hundreds of amputees from Thailand and Burma) preferred after the war to the products given them by a grateful government at home. They were light and walked without squeaking and the young craftsmen who made them were happy to modify and modify until the stump of the leg fitted snugly and without chafing into the socket of the artificial limb.

And one man made a small engraving machine which could be used to inscribe "Rolex Waterproof" on the back and face of even the cheapest watch so that it became worth thousands of dollars on the black market.

Another man, carefully, patiently, with infinite labour, contrived from nothing a small hand lathe—every piece in it he made himself. Then, on this lathe, he turned an exquisite chess set in bone: and General Saito saw it and demanded it as a present. The man refused. So General Saito just demanded it. The man refused. So General Saito suggested that the whole camp might suffer if the man did not give him this exquisite chess set, so the man gave it to him and used his lathe thereafter only for medical instruments and parts of wooden legs and things that General Saito would *not* fancy.

Meantime, every floor of the gaol had been equipped with a small coil which, when one pressed a button, glowed red hot so that cigarettes (made out of papaya leaves wrapped in pages of the Bible) could be lit. The eternal search for "a light" was thus solved. And every day salt water was collected from nearby Changi beach—which water was boiled down, yielding a few ounces of salt to each gallon of water, so that the rice would have flavour and our bodies might replace the fluids lost by sweating.

And finally, within the earliest days of our occupation, gardens were planted. An area of rubber outside the gaol was sought from—and granted by—the now bemused Saito and Takahashi. It was cleared, terraced and planted. Wells were dug and pumps were made. Every day and all day an antlike swarm of men pumped water and dug with changkols and tended the long rows of native sweet potato, the ubi kaya ("wooden potato," or tapioca), the papaya, the bayam. Every drop of urine passed by all seven thousand men was carefully conserved and carted out to these gardens and mixed with the water from the pumps and poured on by the endless stream of men. Buckets and cans had to be made—the Engineers made them. The life-giving green leaves (potato, bayam and araminth—bitter and teeth-staining) flourished. Two inches a day, they sprang up under Changi's unflagging care. So the beri-beri was kept at bay and blindness was contained within the lesser sphere of dimness.

Such was the background of our own domestic arrangements in Changi Gaol. But, as they stand, they present a false picture. For *they* were only the second theme of our life. The main theme—predominating everything else—was the Aerodrome. For this, every day, from the day we arrived, the Japanese required every fit man. And thus, in the grey light of each dawn, every fit man marched round the girdle road between the gaol's double encasing walls, out the main gate—upon which the mark made by the Royal Crest could still be seen, though the Japanese had long since removed it—down past the gaol, through the hospital lines, through a half mile or so of bush (at which time the sky was just growing pink) and then—at the water's edge—onto the air strip. A chaos of narrow-gauge lines from the water's edge, into which tailings were tipped from the skips, ran back to the bitten-out surface of a hill where men worked in thousands, nibbling away to fill the skips.

That bite out of the hill ran straight as an arrow its whole length, white-faced like the cliffs at Dover, until the hill curved and dipped. Then the bite vanished only to start again a few hundred yards farther on where the hill rose softly once more out of the marsh. It was four thousand metres long and the white clay and stone of that bite into the hill face, along with the pulverized flat of the air strip at its foot, stretching sideways to the sea, glared and glittered sullenly in the unending heat. The thousands of men who worked there day after day, all week and every week, were black with the sun and this mirrored glare.

So, while the men who could work slaved down on this aerodrome, those who couldn't stayed in Changi Gaol digging boreholes, making brooms, growing gardens (these outside the gaol as well), grubbing wood and dragging it to the cookhouse, building, scrubbing and sweeping.

Nineteen hundred and forty-two may have been the phony captivity, and the administration may have been maddeningly unrealistic in its approach and manner. But 1944—though frequently still maddening as to manner (but what authority, at times, isn't?)—1944 saw our administrative officers do a magnificent job. The Japs were kept quiet without our people appearing conciliatory: the labour available for domestic use was employed with incredible economy and efficiency: the whole gaol energy was devoted to the realities of the situation and to overcoming them as ingeniously and swiftly as possible. Changi Gaol in that year was a triumph of improvisation and pulling together—even the men dying in the hospital huts sat on their chungs with a heap of palm fronds and tore out spines for brushes, or separated the leaves for attap, or plaited them for screens to be placed round showers, urinals and latrines.

For the thousandth time in my captivity, I felt pride in my fellow men.

A third theme that went to make up the Changi Symphony was the existence and maintenance of radios. These the Japanese still frowned upon. On the subject of B.B.C. news both Takahashi and Saito could, through our interpreters, for they denied that they spoke or understood English, wax most vehement. On the other hand, the demand of seven thousand men for news, instant, up-to-the-minute, fully detailed and reliable news, was clamorous and not to be denied.

Thus, when, in Sime Road, the British administration did once deny us news—on some quaint pretext of security or old-womanish caution—a group of O.R.'s, headed by a Canadian called Thompson (who had been head of Ford Motors in Singapore) and an Australian called Wall, made themselves a "pirate" set. This set, created out of parts stolen from Japanese trucks and all the technical skill of all Thompson's friends, quickly sprang to life. Once more we received our news. In a Pacific island-hopping war, as it was at that moment, news was vital to our peace of mind. When it did come we found, as had been suspected, that the meagre snippets of information being passed on to us at that time by our command were all about a month old. Very irritating.

Command, upon realizing that we had up-to-the-minute news, uttered fearsome threats, demanded the instant surrender of the set and in the meantime outlawed it. This caused much merry laughter among the men concerned and Thompson, Wall & Co. carried on regardless. Not only were they *not* discovered, but eventually, when command's radio unexpectedly died on them, they became the sole source of news. They were, therefore, hurriedly, though tacitly, unbanned; the fearsome threats were swallowed and the outlaw became the fair-haired boy.

Similarly in Selarang and Roberts and all the other areas that went to make up the seven thousand who finally thronged Changi Gaol. And when they did throng Changi Gaol, they all brought their radios. It then depended upon *whom* of the various commanders the fickle Saito, advised by the unpredictable Takahashi, would appoint as gaol commander. If it were the Sime Road C.O., then the Sime Road radio would become the official one: all the others "pirates." If it were the Australian C.O., then his favourites would become the official news purveyors: all the others—British and Sime Road alike—illicit dealers. If it were the British C.O., then the Australians would be the outlaws.

All this could have been most confusing had anyone—except the succession of commanders appointed by Saito—worried anyway. As it was, no one did. All sets flourished while they could, seldom certain whether they were black or official; and, in consequence, all official attempts at the censoring or suppression of news (not infrequent, and an insult to camp intelligence) failed. There was no section of people in the world so thoroughly, regularly and accurately informed upon the daily events in all theatres of the global war of 1944 as the soldiers who were confined in Changi Gaol. The man who could not give an accurate résumé of the day's Allied bombings of Germany and the war on the Russian, Burmese, New Guinea and Pacific fronts: of the political movements in the House of Commons and Congress: of the latest extravagances of San Francisco radio and the points at which Radio Delhi differed from the B.B.C.—that man was simply not worth his salt! To such a pitch had listener intelligence risen after three years of life in a society where radios and the B.B.C. news were the subject of a death sentence.

2 THE AERODROME

2 THE AERODROME

Work on the aerodrome continued with unabated fury, we of the railway now taking our lead (in black-marketing and evading the worst guards) from the more experienced Changi-ites, who had been "on the drome" for over a year.

The veterans of Changi had organized things well. Though to the beginner, and to our guards, the air strip appeared to be flanked with solid walls of jungle and swamp, the experienced prisoner of war could take you to certain bushes and, if you bent down and crawled under them, you entered a long tunnel through sun-warmed lalang grass and low shrubs. And halfway down these tunnels, facing you and lying happily on their stomachs (for they are a lazy and indolent race) would be waiting native traders. Youths with a ready grin and an infinite capacity for haggling. Thus you lay in the tunnel with the object of the transaction between you—perhaps food that you wished to buy or a magneto stolen from a Japanese truck that you wished to sell—and for half an hour or so you bargained. Then at last, the transaction complete, you would slither backwards towards the strip through the tunnel of grass—your progress watched with idle interest by the Malay who lay there waiting for his next customer. And when you reappeared on the task, if the guard had noticed your absence (not uncommon), you said:

"*Benjo,*" and if he still looked suspicious, added: "*Zuzu* [Belly-ache]."

Nothing, however, could detract from the tedium of the work itself. Digging out the white, gritty, glaring face of that hill, shovelling it into skips, pushing the skips to the other side of the strip and emptying them onto its swampy fringe—gradually filling in and levelling. Then, as a small corner was finished, uprooting all the lines and the sleepers and carrying them to a fresh corner and laying them again. Long lengths of rusty steel lines and the difficult business of lowering them onto the sleepers so that no fingers were caught. The dread of working with Dutch Indonesian troops, who never bore their share of any burden and always dropped their end too soon so that the line sprang into the air again and fractured jaws and broke legs and severed fingers.

Fortunately, tedium was an old friend of ours now and we all had our various ways of dealing with it. Some, like Hugh, worked steadily without ever stopping. Just a rhythmic shovel and throw, shovel and throw, for however long the shift lasted. Others stole with an abandon and recklessness that was terrifying and yet seemed never to get them into trouble. (One even removed the machine gun from a crashed Japanese fighter before the Nip mechanics could get it.) Others spent the entire day planning their postwar future—usually leaning reflectively on the handles of their shovels. This did not please Nippon, but the bashings of Nippon no longer terrified. One becomes immune to anything—even the Japanese. My own recipe was the mental exercise of trying to recall to mind the second movement of Bruch's violin concerto and the proof of Pythagoras' theorem about the square on the hypotenuse of a right-angled triangle. For months the air was made sad with a plaintive approximation of Bruch, whilst thousands of square yards of the air strip were defaced with the complex lines of Theorem 74 drawn with the blade of my changkol in its white dust. Regrettably, I never did manage to prove Mr. Pythagoras' statement and when I was one day arrested for drawing the plans of a wireless set on the ground (nothing for hours would induce the guard to believe that the hundreds of lines he saw were related to anything so innocuous as geometry), I devoted my whole mind to the less dangerous problem of recapturing the strains of Bruch. It is remarkable to recall how many of my friends did *not* know how to prove the Pythagoras theorem and could not whistle to me the second movement of the violin concerto by Bruch.

The amount of work done by men who now weighed about eight stone instead of their usual eleven or twelve (and who sank to as low as five or six) was remarkable. The heat had no effect on them. They worked without headwear, they wore only G strings, they ate less each day than international prewar scientists had declared to be the amount on which a man could continue to live, and yet they contrived to plug along for ten or twelve hours on end, shifting tons of obstinate tailings in that time.

In one respect they did suffer more than ever. Skin diseases, never given a chance, by sweat and rain and working in bogs, to dry up, became worse than ever before. Scrotums were once more raw—legs once again covered in sores—hundreds of them. The doctors had obtained a purple dye, a green dye, a red dye and acriflavine, which was yellow. They painted these sores with all these dyes in turn and, though this had no effect at all on the sores, it was at least most colourful.

The doctor who treated me took a tireless interest in my legs—especially the three-year-old holes in my foot which still refused to heal—and tried everything. He scalded them clean with water in which he maintained he could insert his own elbow without discomfort, though I never saw him do it. He prepared a culture from the matter in my wounds and pumped it into me in ever-increasing doses, though always with precisely the same ineffectual result. He scraped them clean till they all bled each day. He bound them up and allowed them to stew under the same dressing for a week. It made not the smallest difference. Always there were hundreds of nagging sores and always they flourished.

Finally he decided that a shock to the nervous system might clear them up. He therefore produced a very large and not especially sharp hypodermic needle with its attendant syringe. He plunged the needle into the toughest vein in my right arm and drew out fifteen cubic centimetres of my precious blood. He then immediately rolled me over and, plunging the same needle into my reluctant thigh, pumped the fifteen c.c.'s of my still warm blood straight back into me. Nothing could have been better calculated than this barbaric thrust to produce shock—nervous or otherwise. I trembled: I went bright grey: I felt sick: I saw three of almost everything: my head swam. Finally, I fainted. When I revived, my first thought was for my legs. They must, I was convinced, be cured. Eagerly I gazed down. From thigh to toe, they were covered in sores and remained so for a year. After that I worried no more. Most people in Changi Gaol had the same experience.

I finished my self-imposed task with *Mein Kampf*, having committed to memory its last vitriolic page. Now I must do something else to keep my mind off my revolting body with its weeping legs and its raw crutch and its tendency to beriberi and dysentery. I flung about me for fresh fields of mental activity—there was plenty of scope.

There was knitting. Quite a lot of men now knitted—and with great agility, too. They stole Army jumpers from the Japanese, unwound them into balls of wool and knitted them into socks which they then sold back to the Japanese for ten dollars a pair.

Or there were carving and engraving—the main material being perspex from the windshields of crashed Japanese planes. The Japanese seemed not very expert at landing their planes on the new aerodrome we had built for them and many hit the trees at the commencement of the 4000-metre runway. When they did P.O.W.'s were always quick to strip the wreckages of perspex: and although its absence worried the Japanese salvage squads they never solved the mystery of where it got to. I realized, however, that I had no talent and less patience for perspex-engraving, so that was out.

There were also languages. In Changi every language, every language known to man, including Esperanto, was taught by someone. I thought I might easily learn a language—perhaps two.

And there was *Exile*—Ronald Searle's beautifully illustrated monthly magazine. His cartoons were a delight and he drew his articles widely from all sections of Changi's population. I thought I might write. Then I lost my nerve and thought that I wouldn't. Finally, I did and wished that I hadn't. Writing is always like that.

And finally Piddington lured me into a nightly practising of some simple exercises in telepathy. These exercises would swiftly have languished had it not been for the patronizing eye cast upon them by Elser, the Dutch hypnotist. I disliked him so intensely that I determined to succeed. And when Piddington and I eventually demonstrated these experiments publicly, some said that it was a hoax, and quoted the *Road to Endor;* and some said it was genuine, and quoted their own psychic experiences in the various cases of their old dead uncles and aunts and other relatives; but Elser, Elser to my unqualified joy, said nothing, but practised secretly himself each night, though with no success at all.

Thus Changi life regained its rhythm. Work, on the aerodrome, on the bore-holes, in the kitchen, all day: lectures or lessons or talk or knitting or a concert at night, in those first cool hours: then sleep—

usually in the open courtyards, lying flat on one's face on the ground. Flat so that those thighbones did not wear through the skin and cause an abscess. The human body seems able to adapt itself to anything. Even sleeping a full night's sleep on bare concrete under the stars, confident in the knowledge that in Malaya it rarely rains at night.

My circle of friends eddied a little and swelled. Hugh I worked with each day on the aerodrome, but as well there were those who shared the courtyard in which I now slept—a courtyard at the end of which stood a huge building forty feet high which was a stage with a wide proscenium: a courtyard whose space was mostly taken up by seats in the open air made out of coconut trees split down their centre and placed flat side upwards. This courtyard was Changi's theatre—the Playhouse, as it was called.

And with me there lived Piddington, with whom, like Hugh, I had shared so much. He was now wraithlike, but his smile was as wide as ever, for all that he weighed only seven stone, and he was consumed with a febrile energy which meant that life with him was never dull. Philosophy—"a philosophy of life"—and travel were his two main themes of conversation. Together we made many plans. His footsteps when he walked the corridors in his clogs were swift and sharp and impatient, like his voice with its stammer.

Then there was Chris Buckingham. He knew a bit about electricity and a bit about the stage and a bit about other things, but nothing very much about anything. This dissatisfied him and because he had abscesses which required frequent lancing—an operation he endured in stoic English silence—he decided abruptly that one day he would know a great deal about medicine. All the time in Changi, while we philosophized and assured Chris that the only way to endure this life was to say that nothing mattered—all this time Chris resolved that one day, although now not even matriculated, he would know all about medicine. He is now a doctor and won gold medals all the way through his course.

Also there was Ronald Searle. Ron was young, dark-haired, blue-eyed and listened keenly, but not with much air of being impressed, to everything that was said. He was an artist.

He had left England with the 18th Division and travelled halfway round the world so that at the last moment, when all was already lost, he and his comrades might be flung into our tropic campaign in their English winter uniforms. Ronald's interest in things military seemed to have died on that day. His only interest thereafter lay in training himself to be an artist so that when the war ended he might make his mark in England. He therefore drew assiduously, and criticized his own work mercilessly, from the first day of the captivity to the last.

In Thailand, as a rapidly improving artist, he had proved himself a lamentable builder of railways. The Japanese were not slow to observe this fact and beat him on the head many times. With the ingenuity of the born cartoonist and the unself-consciousness of the true artist, Searle took to wearing a hat stuffed full of lalang grass. After that, when the Japanese beat him on the head, he would sag a little but remained unbent.

Then the Japanese realized that he was an artist and commissioned him to draw them dirty pictures, giving him pencils and paper, and eggs to eat. He ate the eggs and with the pencils and paper he drew everything but dirty pictures—thereby greatly irritating the Japanese but (he declared) much improving his economy of line.

He fell ill in Kamburi and when I saw him was covered from head to foot in a foul creeping skin disease. As well his innards were torn with dysentery and his left hand—his drawing hand—holed with ulcers. He lay in a coma. But whenever he regained consciousness, he would crawl upright and draw—with his right hand, since his left was useless. He should have lost that hand. He should have died—everyone thought he would. And now he lived in the courtyard and drew incessantly on the back of prewar prison records—economizing with his lines (whatever that meant) and evolving further atrocities for his schoolgirl cartoons.

As well as that he designed and carried out the sets—décor, I believe is the word—for all the Playhouse shows, which ranged from Coward to pantomime and which in quality and production could easily have taken their place in any of London's West End theatres. No man ever looked to the future with a more steadfast and determined eye than did Ron Searle with his wide blue ones. His present-day ranking as Britain's most popular cartoonist is no surprise to anyone who lived with him in Changi.

Spice was added to our company—and its conversation—by the presence of one Hap Kelly. Hap was a Yank from Texas. He had been sunk in the naval battle in the Sunda Strait, between Java and Sumatra, in 1942.

Hap had joined the U. S. Navy as a trumpeter. He was short, lean, thirtyish; had the rubbery features that so many Americans seem to have, and a wide mouth like Joe E. Brown. His wide mouth constantly grinned and his bottom, in the Yank style, bespoke self-confidence. He had joined the U. S. Navy as a trumpeter because he liked playing the trumpet and band business was bad. He had no desire, in the U. S. Navy, to do anything except play his trumpet.

Imagine then his wrath when, in the first days of 1942, he was abruptly thrust into a smoke-filled steel coop and told to help. A shell was dumped in his arms and he passed it to the next man and at the same time demanded to know "What the hell?" "The hell," it appeared, was a gun turret in the *Houston*—now committed, with a token force of Australian and Dutch vessels, to a suicide battle with a Japanese fleet.

"Say," protested Hap, "I didn't join this goddam fleet to load guns. I joined to play a trumpet." But no one heeded him and the whole scene became very noisy and smoky, so Hap gave up and carried on loading guns.

Then the walls of the turret began to get pink, so, in the uproar, Hap asked why the walls of the turret were pink.

"We're on fire," Hap was told.

"Well say," asserted Hap, "I didn't join no Navy to be burnt at sea. I joined to play . . ." but no one was listening, so Hap just carried on loading the gun.

But then lights glowed and whistles blew and there was great commotion.

"Say," asked Hap, "what's all the fuss?"

"Abandon ship," he was told, "you gotta swim for it." That was too much for Hap.

"Look, Buddy," he said, "I joined the Navy to play a trumpet and I can't swim." But at that moment his buddy flung him overboard, so he had to.

Coaxed and coached by his buddies, Hap struggled on. Bits of wreckage helped as ship after ship around them in that circular holocaust—for the Allied ships had deliberately steamed into the centre of the Japanese fleet and then opened up—sank. Slowly, one at a time, Hap's companions floundered and drowned. Finally, next day, Hap, the U.S.N. trumpeter who couldn't swim, landed alone on a beach fourteen miles away in Java. He was captured in the jungle and shipped to Singapore. He now played the trombone—rather brilliantly—in the Playhouse orchestra.

"How's your swimming now, Hap?" I asked him, when we first got this story.

"Say," he said, "I went down one day on the salt-water party to Changi beach, you know?" We said yes, we knew. "And I jumped in the water and I swam. And, do you know what?" We waited, entranced. "I sank like a goddam stone!" He grinned. "I guess," he added, "I'm a trumpeter, not a goddam swimmer."

An academic flavour was given to our conversations by the inclusion of three of the strongest-minded men in Changi—Alec Downer, David Griffin and Tony Newsom.

Alec was the son of Sir John Downer, one of the architects of the Australian Federal Constitution. Oxford-educated, wealthy and gifted, Alec found the social restrictions imposed by his rank of "gunner" irritating and unjustifiable. He therefore modelled his prisoner-of-war life carefully upon the principle of knowing "people in high places" and making sure that they did what he wanted them to.

Griffin was a barrister, a scratch golfer, a witty talker and a sergeant. He, too, saw the virtue of knowing people in high places and played his hand with skill throughout the war.

Newsom, short, incorrigibly cheerful and possessed of a riotous laugh, was exactly what he should have been—the senior representative of Kolynos Toothpaste in South Australia.

These three men, the scholar, the lawyer and the salesman, from the first days of Selarang in 1942, ran the library. Irked beyond endurance by the "officers-must-be-saluted-and-treated-like-tin-gods" nonsense of 1942, they called everyone who came to their library—be he colonel or private—"Mister"! In this atmosphere of almost prewar courtesy, they studied their readers' tastes, persuaded men who never had read to start, urged everyone to steal books and contribute them to the library, ignored the nastiness that was

Nippon and—whenever trouble arose with any of the minions of officialdom—promptly had it squashed by their tame "people in high places."

The library which, between them, these three ran for all the days of our captivity was one of our main consolations and there could have been no better men to run it. Though their books (and they accumulated a very respectable collection) became full of bugs which dropped onto your chest or crawled onto your fingers as you read and raised huge lumps with their bites: though the backs broke and had to be rebound with banana leaf and latex and a little canvas: though the battle with the late borrower was endless . . . they nevertheless managed, through all those days, to maintain a centre where the cultured tones of Oxford chanting about the seats of the mighty, and the caustic wit of the Bar, and the infectious cackle of the perfect *bon viveur* could all be heard at once, as if the absurdities of war had never intruded upon their carefully guarded lives.

And, as the last touch to our background, there was added the bizarre company of the officers of an Italian submarine. This submarine and seven others had left Vichy France for Singapore, each carrying technicians and duplicate blueprints, in the hopes that one, at least, might run the gauntlet and reach the factories of Nippon.

One did. And only one. It surfaced—after a harrowing trip—in Singapore Harbour in 1943. It was greeted by a Japanese admiral who informed its crew that Italy had, since their departure from Europe, surrendered.

Would they, the admiral enquired, like to continue the battle from Singapore?

No, said the Italians who, as they explained to us with great frankness, had never greatly enjoyed any battles, they would not!

The Japanese admiral regretted this and, all his powers of persuasion having failed to change the Italians' attitude, he popped them into gaol with us.

This, at first, caused the Italians intense alarm. They had, they told us, been informed by their propaganda machine that Australians ate Italians! On the rations of 1943, there seemed no hope of their avoiding this fate. When, however, at Christmastime the carnivorous Australians quietly deposited a present of coconuts and "doovers" outside the Italians' hut, all fears vanished and international good will became a reality.

In consequence, I met Mario Brutti Liberati. He had about eight other names (most of which seemed to be girls') and was a marquis as well, but this we ignored. To us he was Mario.

Mario was an authority on classical music, naval engineering and women—in the other order. He spoke excellent, though at times quaint, English. He was generous, amusing, widely travelled and enterprising. He taught me Italian and introduced us to the art of cooking snails in palm oil. Mario was a stimulating talker in anybody's language.

This immediate circle, with others not so close but just as good, with the Playhouse and *Exile* and the daily B.B.C. news, was the mental stimulant which stopped me—after ten hours a day of Nippon—from going cuckoo.

The first real news of our new gaol life came rushing through the cells and corridors and courtyards one lunchtime in a carefully concealed gust of enthusiasm. It was June, 1944. The Allies had landed once more in Europe. Into the eyes of every man came a gleam of anticipation. We had passed the blackness of 1943. Nothing would ever be bad again.

"Soon," said Piddington, stammering eagerly, "this bloody war will end.

I nodded. Chris nodded. Ron Searle just went on drawing—he was drawing a cat. He had drawn it fifty times. It was a cat we intended eating when he had finished drawing it, but apparently he was using too many lines. So whilst he, detached and determined, started his fifty-first drawing of the cat we three sat and thought about the miracle of the end of the war.

3 THEATRE

The Playhouse undoubtedly deserves more mention—there is not a Changi Gaol-ite who does not remember it vividly and with gratitude.

First, the building. Leslie Greener, when the seven thousand poured into the gaol, designed a stage. It was the complete and perfect stage. Broad, deep, plenty of space for scenery to be flown above and for sets to be manoeuvred from the wings. Altogether, it was a very large building. He therefore drew his plan on a very small piece of paper. Relying on this mild deception, it was submitted for approval to Saito and Takahashi. They assented—on condition that no aerodrome workers were employed.

But Greener & Co. (mainly a gentleman called Daltry) had thought of this. A swarm of officers, young and old, swooped upon the courtyard and in no time at all had graded it so that it sloped upwards away from where the stage would stand, and they then started upon the construction of the stage itself.

From every quarter of Singapore, from every job the working parties did, materials were scrounged. Galvanized iron, wood, plywood, wire, canvas, globes, screws and paint.

The engineers made pulleys out of wood and nails out of wire—and suddenly, swiftly, up shot the scaffolding; round it went its clothing of galvanized iron; onto its floor went innumerable stolen boards; footlights and floods were fixed; the stage—forty feet high in all—was complete.

Takahashi, gazing first of all at Greener's small piece of paper, and then at this monstrous edifice born of O.R.'s thefts and officers' labour, remonstrated mildly. "I gave permission," he said through our interpreter, "for a stage to be built—*not* a skyscraper." Daltry, at whom the remark was directed, merely turned and smiled that vague smile which English gentlemen can smile but which means nothing. That was the kind of answer Takahashi understood and respected, so he went away without further complaint and the stage —henceforth to be known as the Playhouse—remained.

For its material, the Playhouse drew on the old Australian Concert Party as augmented by any British talent that could be unearthed. Because of the Australian commander's unalterable policy of preserving his Concert Party intact, come what may, Changi now had a seasoned group of performers who, led by John Wood, could tackle any task with confidence.

The early brashness and crudeness of the Army performer had long since vanished under the polishing influence of John's London West End experience and the increasing demands of the audiences. The shows they gave had acquired a reputation for sophistication and originality. Those who did not have genuine talent at least acquired good technique. There was also a competent orchestra with a sound knowledge of theory and a willingness to work hard on arrangements and rehearsals—a willingness which was greatly encouraged by the inclusion of Hap Kelly of the U.S.N.

They had, as well, an efficient stage staff, including set builders. When, to this nucleus, was added the brilliance of Searle, the battle, as far as presentation was concerned, was won.

To mould this material, with the good will and blessings of all—even Takahashi—came Daltry of the gentlemanly smile.

Daltry had been a major in an artillery unit. He had sufficiently impressed everyone during the campaign itself to be selected as one of a special escape party on the eve of Singapore's capitulation. As he stood waiting for the boat to take him from the island, a shell fell at his feet, blew off a leg and removed an eye. He remained on the island.

Thenceforward, Daltry allowed nothing to worry him. If anyone asked him he invariably assured them that he found life in Changi quite delightful. He was a fluent and outrageous conversationalist. He emphasized all his points by thumping his stump and pointing a long finger. His blind eye he ignored.

He was well equipped to produce Changi's entertainment, having, in the days before the war, run the Westminster Theatre in London. He swooped, therefore, on long crutches upon the Playhouse and, to the astonishment of all, opened its season with *Autumn Crocus*—a gentle love story which the near-destroyed souls of Thailand and the aerodrome-scorched workers of Changi found thoroughly delightful. Having started his career in Singapore's sterile gaol by staging a story of love in the cool heights of a mountain, the outrageous Daltry settled down to months of exhilarating production.

4 "HARRY THE HAWK"

Two elements arose to enliven our work on the aerodrome. One was a new guard; the other was the inception of a regular reconnaissance by Allied planes—Superforts which, thirty thousand feet up and serenely deliberate in that brilliant sunlit sky, gleamed silver and almost translucent, like fairies. They were very pretty, those reconnaissance planes. The Japanese hated the sight of them.

At first when they arrived, their beautifully even purr making itself heard long before they could be seen, everyone would down tools—changkols, picks, baskets, sledge hammers and lengths of line—and shout excitedly: "Here she comes," and gaze upwards. Meantime, from the other end of the drome, all the Nip planes, fighters and bombers, would take off as hurriedly as possible and scuttle away in the opposite direction.

But soon the guards came to dislike our cheers and the shouts of "Here she comes"—and if they heard anyone commenting, or saw anyone look up, then they beat him severely. So then it became necessary to comment upon the purr of those engines without saying "Here she comes," or looking up. Walking boldly into the enemy's camp, we took his own word for aeroplane—"sikorki"—and, using rhyming slang, called the recce plane "Harry the Hawk."

And so, in the midst of emptying a skip, the keen-eared would suddenly mutter casually: "Harry the Hawk's with us again," and you could glance at your guard, remember the day's news of the Pacific campaign and the advances in Europe, and think: "Your day, my lad, is coming to its close."

When Harry the Hawk or, as he was alternatively known, "The Boundary Rider," swooped insolently low so that not even the Nips could ignore him, the guards would scream, "Currah! Currah!" and refuse us our break in the afternoon, saying: "*Yazumé nei!*" and adding vehemently: "War last one hundred years. Nippon Number One."

Our new guard—the second enlivening element—was a delightful little gentleman called the Ice Cream Man. He was called the Ice Cream Man because he was rather less than five feet tall, wore a white topee, which covered most of his face except a chin with a lamentable tendency to recede, sported a white linen coat and white gloves and shouted incessantly. After the first glance the British troops were unanimous—he was the Ice Cream Man. He was never referred to as anything else. Not, at least, till he came to recognize the sound of those three syllables and to infer, quite accurately, from their contemptuous inflection, that they applied to himself. Then, because if he heard them he bashed the man who uttered them, he became Mr. Peters to the Australians and Mr. Lyons to the Pommies, which was much the same thing.

The Ice Cream Man was now in charge of our work on the aerodrome. As a second-class private that was a power he enjoyed. He would assemble our squads each morning in the pinkish light, the Australians, the British and the Dutch, in three separate groups. Then he would announce: "Nippon Number One. All men say 'Mastah,'" and point to himself. Then the British squad would shout out all their favourite terms for the Japanese—except Master. And the Australian squad in its turn would be riotous with a clamour of "Yellow bastards . . . apes . . . galahs . . . and drongos." And the Dutch squad—the Indonesian troops—would kneel with their hands clasped, as if in prayer, and say, "Master."

At once the clamour would break out afresh among the British and Australians—this time directed indiscriminately both at our heroic allies and at Nippon.

"Papaws," we would taunt the Dutch troops—papaws being green outside (like the Dutch uniform), yellow inside and a strong emetic as well. "You syphilitic little monkey," we would roar at the Nip. It was all very noisy and undignified, but gratifying. Also, it used to waste twenty minutes every morning when otherwise we might have been working.

Then the Ice Cream Man, screaming with rage, his eyes bloodshot, would point angrily. "You," he would say, "come heah," and motion a man forward with that peculiarly Japanese downwards flap of the outstretched fingers. Then again, "You, come heah." And again, and again, until he had six or seven Englishmen and Australians. These he would beat unconscious with his short truncheon-like cane. And then, the Ice Cream Man having established the superiority of Nippon, we would all march off to work and I would return once more to my mental searchings on the subjects of Messrs. Pythagoras and Bruch.

The day's work over, just as it began to darken a little, we would march back to the gaol—through the scrub, catching snails and frogs on the way; through the hospital lines, with always a glance in to see if Blain, the Australian who weighed only four stone, still lived; through the officers' lines—immaculate, cool-looking men playing chess and eating their evening meal; and then up along the outside of the high wall and in through the big steel gate whose grey front still bore the shadow of His Majesty's coat of arms.

Once inside, the column of men streamed out in all directions and flooded down the various corridors, clattering in their clogs, shouting to their mates in courtyards and cells, retailing to one another the latest outrage perpetrated by the guards or the latest deal on the black.

Then they streamed into the courtyards, all at once, hundreds upon hundreds of naked men milling round the few showers, washing themselves and their G strings. Washing cheerfully but urgently with their lump of gaol-made soap and the water which the Nips left on for only half an hour.

Almost before they had finished these ablutions, the day's mess orderlies were filing up to the central cookhouse—and a few minutes later clumping back, heavily laden with dixies and tubs of close-packed rice, two men to a tub, the back one gaining leverage by bracing his spare hand against the leading man's shoulder.

The tubs would be set out on bamboo tables and the sergeant in charge would stand by checking each man's number off as he collected his "messi messi." No doubling up in those days. And leading up to the tubs of rice, a long queue of newly washed men, who dipped their mess gear in a drum of boiling water as they passed to sterilize it of dysentery. And then give your number, collect the pathetic dollop of rice and the few stewed leaves from the garden and off to wherever your favourite corner was—making sure first that the leggi number was nowhere near your own.

Back in the theatre courtyard, with Searle and Buckingham and Piddington, I would sit down to eat. Piddington and I cultivated a small dried pea—called towgay—in between wet sacks and ate it when its green shoots were one centimetre in length. Each day we had a spoonful, which was good for beriberi and was said to have been all that saved the lives of the survivors of the siege of Kut. We didn't know whether this was true, but we took no risks. As well we added a spoonful each of red palm oil. Meant only for the manufacture of soap, it tasted vile, but doctors assured us that it was nutritious, so each day we ate it.

That was our ordinary meal—rice, greens, towgay and palm oil. But occasionally we would catch a dog or a cat or a snake and then, by agreement with Hap Kelly and Slim de Grey (of whom more later), we would prepare a magnificent stew and eat till we bulged. If they caught a dog or a cat or a snake,[1] then we shared with them. It was a very good arrangment, but since private cooking within the gaol—especially of dogs, cats or snakes—was forbidden by our own authorities, it required organization and cunning.

On the subject of food our own authorities did, at times, tend to be shortsighted. Admittedly wood was scarce and that meant that the kitchen was hard-pressed for fuel. But if men who had done a day's work could be bothered to carry back their own timber for their own fire to cook their own cats or snails or whatever it was, then, it seemed to us, they should be allowed to do so. And, indeed, so we did—orders to the contrary notwithstanding.

Occasionally things came to a head—as when the Australian command issued an order, read to our assembled ranks on the night's check parade in the Girdle Road, that:

"O.R.'s must not in future eat snails and any snails they do bring back must be surrendered to the officers' poultry farm."

The reason: the officers' poultry were dying for lack of just such proteins as snails provide, and from the officers' poultry a percentage of eggs was supplied to the hospital. We, however, made a lightning

[1]For the information of the shrinking reader, snake tastes like gritty chicken mixed with fish: dog tastes like rather coarse beef: cat like rabbit, only better; and snails (Changi-style) like something cut off a tire by Messrs. Dunlop.

calculation of the number of poultry meals enjoyed by commissioned men only: of the minute fraction of the total number of hospital patients who—snails or no snails to the officers' fowls—received eggs: and of the undoubted beneficial effect upon our own scabby legs and weeping scrotums of snail eating. In one uproarious gale of laughter we rejected the order as absurd.

Thereafter, however, our mess tins were searched daily for snails and any found there were confiscated. This meant carrying them back from the aerodrome to the gaol in our G strings. No one who has not walked a mile and a half with a crutchful of snails is in any position to aver that those who have do not thoroughly deserve them.

O.R.'s were not, though, by any means the only sufferers from official interference on dietetic subjects. Though officers, in spite of the fuel shortage, could cook themselves into a pulp if they were so inclined, *what* they could cook was the subject of vehement legislation.

Thus one patient soul who trapped sparrows with a Heath Robinson-like contraption of bricks, strings and grains of rice, was flatly forbidden to convert the feathery bones into a soup. Sadly he destroyed his machine and gave up endeavouring to supplement his meagre diet.

Another, an especially mad Englishman named Lucas, who was a friend of ours, for days stalked a frilly-necked lizard. At length, having pursued it over acres of ground and up many palm trees, he caught it. He was just about to pop it into his stewing pot when an order was rushed down to him by a captain. In astonishment, Lucas read the order:

"Officers will not eat lizards," it said. Lizard eating, it appeared, was *infra dig* for officers.

Lucas, though he was mad, was also very determined. He climbed another palm tree and, from a length of jungle vine, he suspended his lizard so that it hung, just out of reach, outside the office of the colonel who had issued the order.

Two days later, when the office was practically uninhabitable because of the stink, and all efforts to knock down the rapidly decomposing corpse had failed, the order was withdrawn. The next time Lucas caught a lizard, he cooked and ate it undisturbed.

In short prisoners of war in the Far East ate anything which was not actually poisonous—even, in Thailand, the fungus off trees. The only meat it never occurred to the prisoners of the Japanese to touch was human flesh. This may not seem especially remarkable. When, however, one considers that under conditions considerably less atrocious than those of Thailand and Burma the Japanese in New Guinea frequently resorted to cannibalism (and have, many of them, since been proved guilty of the crime and hanged for it), then perhaps the moral strength of the Britisher in situations of extreme and protracted crisis will be better appreciated.

5 THE FOURTH YEAR

Hugh went to hospital with the Bug. We Thailand people seemed constantly to be going down into those attap huts outside the gaol walls with something—dysentery, the Bug, ulcers to have skin grafts, always something. We tended at times to feel sorry for ourselves.

One day Black Jack—the senior Australian officer in Changi—collected all the F and H Force men together in the one gaol courtyard and spoke to us. "You blokes," he said, "had a rough time. We all know that. We're all sorry. But it's over now and I just want to tell you that at the moment you're turning into the greatest mob of rogues, thieves, malingerers and vagabonds I ever set eyes on. Now snap out of it! That's all!" and with that he left.

It did us a lot of good. From that day forward the melancholic sense of the Burma Boys that they were different, that they deserved more of things than other men, died. We became one society—the men of Changi Gaol.

Whilst attending to a radio one night—a radio housed under the boilers of the cookhouse where there was no room to stand and the heat was unbearable—a place the Nips would never look—one of the "news" receivers allowed the sweat to drop off his forehead into the set, and with a brittle snap the hot valves cracked. The set went dead and we, in the gaol, were without news. Though the Playhouse presented Noel Coward's *Tonight at 8:30,* and though lectures were given in all the courtyards, the absence of "griff"—the word "news" was never used—was intolerable.

How the service was restored is a strange story, most of which I got from Hugh in hospital.

It appeared that one day he had left the ward to go to the bore-holes. On his return, at the foot of his bed space on the wooden chung, he found some food and some money. He asked the orderly whose they were and was told they had been left for him by a "young Australian bloke."

Twice this happened and, as well, it happened to other men who were ill; but no one knew who the mysterious benefactor was. Then one day Hugh caught him at it. A slight, dark-haired youth, quiet and pleasant-faced—his only outstanding feature a missing front tooth. Challenged with being the source of so much help, the youngster (then only just twenty-one) agreed. He was on a good thing on the black, he explained, and liked to lend a hand. His name was Paddy Matthews.

Gradually Hugh got his story. It seemed that he stole fearlessly—truck parts mainly—and sold well to the Chinese. And as well he had an interest, purely adventurous, in running radios.

When the cookhouse set broke down, Paddy decided that spare parts for radios were essential. In the course of his prowlings on the aerodrome he had discovered that the Japanese Barracks—the old Roberts Hospital—contained a room on the ground floor which was full of radio parts.

He therefore set out one night armed with a sack and a screwdriver to collect spares. He crawled into a drain which ran under the girdle road and out at the corner of the gaol, its grill having long since been severed. He evaded guards and patrols and made his way down through the scrub to the aerodrome.

Hugging the shadow of the wall that had been cut out of the hill, he walked down the strip until he reached the barracks. Then he slipped inside and, passing between two rows of sleeping Nips, padded quietly to the door of the storeroom. Cautiously he turned the handle. Locked!

At that point most men would have seized the excuse to abandon the project and return home. Not Paddy. He unscrewed the hinges of the door with his screwdriver and lifted the door gently out of its place. He then stepped into the store and filled his bag, systematically, and slowly lest he make a noise, with everything that would be required for the continued running of several radios for several years. Then he stepped out into the corridor again.

And at that moment he heard a sentry approaching on his patrol.

No time to screw the door back on to its hinges, so he merely stood it upright in its place, and then slipped up the staircase onto the next landing.

The sentry came down the corridor slowly, thumping each locked door with his rifle butt, idly flashing his torch. Nothing ever happened to this sentry.

He reached the wireless storeroom, thumped its door, flashed his torch and wandered on, humming quietly to himself and not noticing that the door swayed when he hit it. As soon as he turned the corner, Paddy sped down the stairs again. With sure fingers, he screwed the hinges back onto the door. Then he laid his sack carefully over his shoulders, crept swiftly down between the sleeping Nips and out onto the air strip.

An hour later he was back in the gaol and Changi's radios, whatever the mishaps, were never again short of spares or replacements.

Christmas of 1944 came and with it presents and cards and, of course, at the Playhouse, a pantomime. This pantomime was called *Twinkletoes* and, like all good pantos, was topical, tuneful, colourful and hilarious.

The script was written by Keith Stevens, better known as a red-headed female with an ample bosom and a bawdy tongue, and Slim de Grey. Slim was six foot two inches tall, incredibly lean, and had that kind of wide-eyed appeal which in dogs is irresistible. With Ray Tullipan, Slim wrote all the songs (lyrics and tunes) for the panto.

Slim composed by sitting on the end of his bed, vacant-eyed, his legs swinging, occasionally humming a note or strumming a guitar. Then suddenly he would shout, "I've got it— C'mon, Boardie" (this to Boardman, the pianist), and before he lost it again, not uncommon, the two would rush to the Playhouse piano where, as Slim hummed, Boardman would tinkle and write down the notes.

Tullipan composed more sombrely. Tullipan didn't sit, he lay.

And, as he lay on his bed, he stropped a long and evil-looking knife incessantly up and down the palm of his hand. And as he stropped, he glowered burningly with his dark eyes at those whom he didn't like. Long stares of brooding distaste. Then, as if he had decided upon a victim, he would suddenly sit up and for the moment put his knife away while he wrote down on paper the melody that had come to his mind.

So the panto went on—a riot of clowning and magical sets by Searle (sets created out of canvas and different-coloured muds and crayons) and a fearful hag of a witch who was Daltry, with his one eye and his one leg and a most ungentlemanly screech. But best of all in that panto were the seven or eight new tunes which set Changi by the ears and had us humming happily for months. Even nowadays there are few men who were in that gaol who cannot sing you the words and tune of "Castles in the Air."

It was at one of the shows at the Playhouse that we first met Kio Hara. Kio Hara was a Korean who, with that infallible Asiatic intuition for anticipating economic and political crises, now clearly foresaw the defeat of Japan and wished to witness this event with a clean nose of his own.

Accordingly he had for some time plotted to release himself and his fellow Koreans from the Japanese yoke. Many of them—now anxious to forget their incredible viciousness on the railway and naïvely announcing that they had been forced by the nasty Japanese thus to be vicious—suddenly became quite friendly. About Kio Hara I was never quite certain. On the score, however, that I detested all Koreans and Japanese alike with a beautifully impartial detestation I did *not* trust him. In this, possibly, I was unjust.

In any event one night he cornered Chris Buckingham and spoke most earnestly to him for some hours. Later he did the same with Ron Searle. Finally Chris came to me and told me the setup.

Kio Hara, anxious to get out of Japanese control and to endear himself to what he regarded as the new masters—the Allies—planned to escape. He planned to escape in an aeroplane with a crew of British prisoners of war. He had complete details as to aerodrome drill, guard changes on the drome, times when planes were fuelled and checked, and navigational maps. He required a pilot, a navigator and company—preferably Ron, Chris, Piddington and myself. What, Chris asked me, did I think?

I said I was frightened. I felt that I had had my share of luck so far and was not game for any escape attempt now that the war was ending. I remembered my capture, Van Rennan, the guards drawing crosses in the mud in Thailand. I was still alive, I reflected, and I fully intended remaining so. Shamelessly I announced that I had not the guts to attempt Kio Hara's scheme and withdrew from it. My only contribution was to advise Chris to lay full details of the plan before the most respected soldier in the gaol—Colonel Dillon.

This Chris did and he and Ron (Piddington also withdrew from the plot because he felt it his duty to continue running his absurd wireless set) obtained Dillon's blessing. The plot grew more and more definite—and the danger to the plotters greater and greater. The courtyard in which we lived became a place of tension and whispers and dark suspicion.

Then it all broke. One day Chris talked—apparently casually though in actual fact most earnestly—to Kio Hara in the open ground where the trailers of the wood party were parked. Our own administration—either panicking at his plot or out of sheer inexcusable stupidity (equally culpable in either case)—arrested him for fraternizing with the enemy. To the extreme rage of the entire camp and in the face of Colonel Dillon's approval of the plan from its inception, an English administration cast an English soldier, who was courageously planning to do the duty of every prisoner of war—to escape—into solitary confinement in cells! The solitary-confinement order we ignored, visiting Chris regularly and endeavouring to comfort him. The arrest, however, distressed him considerably and put an end to all ideas in the future of escaping. Escapes are too difficult when as well as the Japanese one must evade one's own command.

The New Year sped on and I celebrated my twenty-fourth birthday. I was touched to receive so many cards. It always does seem touching when other people remember your birthday—though not at all when you remember theirs. And these laboriously produced greetings in a society where any paper commanded a price of a dollar for two square inches (enough to wrap a cigarette) were especially touching. There was also homemade saki (rice and pineapple skin fermented with the sweetness of gulah malacca) with which to drink toasts: and altogether the day was memorable, even if the saki did have a most evil aftereffect.

Then came February and the anniversary of the fall of Singapore and the Nips, as always, celebrated riotously. It was not a celebration in which we displayed much enthusiasm, except that this year, for the first time, we felt: "This, you little apes, will be your last!" Meantime, from Changi Gaol tower, above the radar grill which didn't work, the poached egg continued to float oppressively over our heads. That tower and the flag were always there—symbol of everything we hated.

And one night at midnight when all would normally have been quiet, the gaol was suddenly rent with howls and screams and the banging of tins and the clatter of eating-irons against the wall. Frantically the guard fell out and machine guns were swung round to cover this revolt. But before any shots could be fired, the clamour subsided and everywhere there was silence again. The cause of it all —an Australian with a leaning towards statistics had worked out that that midnight marked our thousandth day in captivity. He and his friends were celebrating.

6 ON OUR RETURN

The camaraderie that had existed in Pudu between Englishmen and Australian, between O.R.'s and officers, began slowly to gain strength in Changi. To this process impetus was added by the "characters" to be found in the various elements of our society.

Men like Alec Downer, the librarian who knew people in High Places and who talked perfect Oxford English—not only talked it but taught it to many an Australian whose flat nasal accents he could no longer stand. Taught it with laborious exercises over those vowel sounds which we Australians tend to murder.

And Professor Roberts, the tiny Pommy with the enormous nose and the acid wit, who lectured to vast audiences on the glories of Communism—and converted not a one but amused them all.

And best of all the two English Indian Army majors, Bartram and Dart—known to all as Bartram & Darto. These two told outrageous Poonah stories all the time about huntin' tigers and spyin' in Afghanistan and snipin' in the Khyber Pass. Invariably, when Bartram told his delightful and monstrous tales, he would add:

"Now you may doubt this, gentlemen, but I know it's true because I was there-ah!" And if he wasn't there, his wife was!

And one day he told the story, complete with the most graphic and frightful details, of the Black Hole of Calcutta. Now surely, thought his delighted audience—especially the Australians—he can't have been there! Not even his wife, they thought, can have been there. Not in the Black Hole of Calcutta.

"Now you may doubt all this," the major stated calmly in conclusion, "but I assure you that it's true. I wasn't there," he explained, "and my wife wasn't there," he continued, "BUT," and here came complete victory to Bartram, "my great-aunt, SHE was there!"

Thus did Bartram & Darto, elderly, moustached, and complete replicas of the classic Indian Army officer, vie with one another, day in and day out.

Finally the Concert Party produced, to the delight of the entire gaol, a sketch in which the two were unmistakably portrayed. Our cup of joy was made full when Darto, at the end of the performance, hastened round backstage.

"That sketch," he roared, "that sketch about the Indian Army fellahs. Damned good, old boy. Damned good. Knew two fellahs in Poonah just like that once!" and stumping out of the dressing room, still muttering, "Damned good," he left.

The Playhouse decided next to stage a cavalcade of song. This commended itself enormously to the Pommy element, who like nothing so well as good old tunes, and even we Australians caught the infection of their enthusiasm.

Bill Williams, the pianist who dragged a small portable pedal organ all around Thailand and played boogie on it in every camp, planned the show. Orchestrations were attacked with enthusiasm by a dozen different men in the band. Searle designed a score of quickly changed sets. The cavalcade was to cover the gamut of twentieth-century popular tunes and to conclude with the latest Changi compositions.

The first night was an elaborate affair attended by the entire Japanese administration, including General Saito. Quickly the show swung into action and as song followed song, set followed set and novelty followed novelty, it became obvious that the audience—Nips and all—were with it, gripped.

The elaborate scene changes went without a hitch, Piddington and Buckingham sweating over charts and property lists. Searle, serious and unemotional, stood in one corner drawing an Indonesian youth as he danced.

Then came the finale, a new composition of Bill Williams'. First of all, with much hooting and smoke, the bow of a steamer sailed majestically onto the stage. It was the full height of the stage and its creation had involved every ounce of Searle's artistry and the carpenter's ingenuity. And, as it reached centre stage, Bill started singing his new song, "On Our Return." The company joined in, flooding onto the stage like voyagers about to embark. The audience was electrified and joined in the last chorus. The curtain rang down and midst frantic applause Saito and his entourage stalked out—in sullen silence.

That was the last show to be staged in the Playhouse. Saito, furious at the title of the song, at its sentiment, at its reception, banned all further entertainment and would barely be dissuaded from having Williams and the entire company executed. The war, he pointed out angrily, would last a hundred years. Nippon was Number One!

Negotiations to get the ban relaxed were futile. Saito stuck grimly to his decision. Not only that, but rations were cut and a search staged for radios. The Nips were obviously extremely put out.

At a final meeting to discuss the matter, all the British administrative officers sat before Saito and Takahashi, who listened to all that the interpreter relayed on to them and looked implacable.

The British officers thereupon uttered some strongly worded comments of their own on both Saito and Takahashi. These the Australian interpreter did not trouble to pass on.

Abruptly Saito indicated that the meeting was over. As was the formality demanded at that time each British officer bowed to Saito

—usually a rather perfunctory nod, for the Britisher does not acquire an Oriental bow with ease. The British colonel, however, believed in doing the job thoroughly and bowed low. As Takahashi surveyed this courtly inclination of the colonel's body, he turned to the Australian interpreter and, in perfect English, remarked: "Rather Elizabethan, don't you think?" which was the only remark he ever made in English and set the entire gaol furiously to wondering.

With the closing of the theatre life came to revolve more around the art of conversation and the consolation to be derived from the company of one's friends. At night then, the day's work done, Changi became dotted with groups in every courtyard who sat and in quiet tones talked of the "griff" and their plans and their homes—whilst all the time the inevitable fag passed amicably from hand to hand for each member of that united group to take a "drag." The smoke would be drawn, one drag, deep down into the lungs, head flung back in satisfaction, as momentarily all cares vanished into the arms of the goddess nicotine. Then, with a plumelike exhalation, the smoke would be blown out, and the tiny cigarette passed on to the next sunburnt hand.

Talk and laughter rippled round those courtyards in low murmurs. Strange that there was never discontent nor anger—always that low confident tone and the plans for the future and the blithe certainty that in six months the war would be won.

Ron talked quietly of Cambridge before the war and the cartoons he planned to sell after it. Chris wondered how long it took to matriculate and whether Norwich would help him with his plans for medicine. Jack Garrett declared firmly that he would go home and win the Australian Professional Squash Championship—and did. Piddington and I planned tours of England, where we would stay for week ends with Daltry and see all the places that these Pommies talked about—the country we Australians always called "Home." And in the meantime Piddington, with Tommy Thompson of Sime Road, ran a radio, which struck me as an extremely dangerous thing to do: and with me gave fairly regular public demonstrations of the tests we had evolved round our nightly telepathy séances.

In the course of those frequent demonstrations we were by no means infallibly successful as far as my reception of what Piddington transmitted was concerned. On one occasion we performed for a Dutch audience and achieved the remarkable feat of getting nothing right—nothing at all—they being the most cussed, unco-operative group for whom we had ever worked; and I, in spite of Piddington's soothing charm, being aggressively aware of the fact. On another occasion a line from one of Shakespeare's plays was written up which read: "And through the instrument his pate made way"; and no efforts of Sydney's would induce me to do more than announce, with a cackle of laughter, that a bald-headed old gentleman had been clocked with a violin. On such occasions Sydney gave me firmly to understand that neither he nor Dr. Rhine was pleased with me. But it didn't matter—nothing mattered!

And so it went on, sometimes right, sometimes wrong, but always causing fierce arguments which (the authorities seemed to think) was a good thing. Certainly it was encouraging to see the response of the men in the hospital huts. The huts themselves were a hundred metres long, earth-floored, attap structures—intensely depressing. On either side of the central aisle there were platforms. On these platforms, side by side, lay hundreds of men, dying, amongst other things, of lack of the interest to live—because there is little point in continuing to survive when life consists only of a starvation diet and bug bites, not to mention the griping pains of dysentery and the agony of constant dressings (always with bandages that have been used again and again over the past three years), of ulcers and sores that never heal, and of the fires of constant fever.

Piddington and I, therefore, were delighted when, after our first show in the T.B. hut, we left about ninety skeleton-like men roused to such a pitch of bitter argument that their eyes flashed again and their poor, fleshless chests swelled with fury. Two of them—both due to die within a fortnight—were, for the first time in months, up off their backs on their feet endeavouring to fight. Even young Norm, the most desperately afflicted of them all, roused himself from his stupor and said: "Don't believe it! Must have dreamed it like everything else!"

Young Norm had become the focal point of the camp's struggle to save these T.B. patients. For two years now he had refused to die. He weighed only about fifty pounds. He ate only occasionally and had no taste for rice. When he asked for any food—from caviare to pineapple cakes—it became a point of honour for outside working parties that day (before he fell again into his coma) to steal it. Every time he dozed off his young face (for he was only nineteen) became utterly peaceful as he dreamed his dreams. And when he woke the orderlies would ask him where he'd been. "Home," he used to say simply. And then they would ask him what he had done at home, and Norm would tell them with the quiet confidence of one who believes what he says implicitly. The orderlies would pass on his dreams to those who brought him stolen delicacies and they, in turn, would pass them on to the rest of the camp. "How's young Norm today?" became as habitual a question with us all at that time as "What's the griff?" And always it was followed by "What's he done at home lately?" because Norm's dreams about home were always so much better than ours.

The battle to save young Norm was fought with all the ferocity that the British sympathy for the underdog infallibly evokes. He achieved a parity of status in Changi Gaol with the Second Front and the possibility of catching a dog for the cooking pot. So when he roused himself from his pleasant fantasies to say: "Don't believe it! Must have dreamed it like everything else," Piddington and I felt almost as proud as if we had brought him a plateful of bully beef and sweetened condensed milk—which, in those days, was our conception of the last word in culinary bliss.

Young Norm died in December and for a moment the whole camp sagged—until those who were with him told the story of how, on this occasion, he had dreamed himself at a Christmas party and, tired, had decided that he must have a sleep. No man in his senses could begrudge young Norm the long comfort of that last after-Christmas sleep.

And after all this lights out and to sleep. The cells full of soldiers now immune to the bugs. The grills over the well of the cell blocks littered with men sleeping with that same childlike abandon that always tugged at your heart. Why should they be so thin and sleep for years in gaols away from home when they looked as helpless as that? I would go down to the footpath in the courtyard, flat on my face to spare those bony thighs, ankles out, feet in, and to sleep till tomorrow.

And one morning we woke up to find that Germany had surrendered. The war in Europe was over. With mocking eyes we looked at Nippon, whose turn was next. "Dammé, dammé," Nippon said, "Deutzel"—they always called Germany Deutzel—"Deutzel Number Ten. Nippon Number One. War finish in one hundred years."

7 THE HIROSHIMA INCIDENT

With the end of the European war to be explained away and the first air raids over Singapore—a hundred fairylike Superfortresses at a time—to add point to the advances in the Southeast Asian war, Nippon did not remain calm.

When each air raid came the Nip Air Force fled till the All Clear sounded: but this did not save their shipping in the docks from destruction, nor their stores from being burnt, nor their dumps from being blown up. And all the time more and more vessels limped into the docks in the Johore Strait for repairs that could not be done. Meantime, Burma was being cleared by an avenging 14th Army and Mountbatten was assembling an amphibious invasion force to retake Malaya.

Angrily the Nips demanded working parties for unknown tasks in Malaya. For the second time in my career I crossed the causeway to work on a project that did not bode well.

We left the gaol in batches of a hundred. We were stripped of everything when we left and radios were consequently *not* part of our equipment when we landed in our new camps in Johore.

Arrived there, we were told that we were to build tunnels for ambushes, earthworks for defences, huge walls for dumps. We were to work until the last minute, carrying ammunition where necessary, then—when hand-to-hand fighting became imminent—we were to be shot.

Under this constant threat we laboured thenceforth. It was not pleasant. Nor was the work. Our group was detailed for tunnelling. We dug tunnels about four metres wide and about four metres high as far into the sides of hills as possible. Dug them into clay with pit-props of green rubber. Soon the rubber rotted in the damp and the clay dropped, a whole hill of it, and the tunnels filled. Often there were men inside. Once the falling clay grips you round the ankles, with its heavy clammy grip, you can't move. You may only stand and wait to see how high the tide of orange earth will rise. Some of us were lucky: others were not. The Japanese seemed indifferent as to what happened to us, so long as the tunnels went in deeply and quickly and the tailings were removed far away so that no indication might be given to the invading troops that an ambush had been prepared.

For weeks we worked thus, returning at night to a gloomy hut in the rubber. Damp and closely guarded. Only once did we get a respite and that was a day at the Johore Barracks, where we were required to move a store of clothing. In the process we found a small toilet stacked from floor to roof with linen bags full of Japanese Army biscuits. Little round biscuits like marbles and hard as iron. All day we stole and munched these biscuits. By nightfall, though our jaws ached agonizingly, we had consumed the lot and felt extremely well fed. The pay-off came on the next day when a Dutch party, the usual native troops, were sent to replace us at the barracks. Just before they knocked off, the theft of the barracks' entire supply of ration biscuits was discovered. The Dutch troops were mercilessly thrashed by their "masters" for having indulged in this wickedness. As they marched past our hut that night it did our hearts good—not a nice, charitable good, admittedly; but nevertheless, good—to see their blackened eyes and bloodied heads.

Then came a rumour that we were to be shot next day. And to settle our fate—for if we were to be shot we had determined to be shot running—the resourceful Paddy Matthews stole a wireless set and listened in that night. That night was August 15, 1945, and Paddy told us not to worry, that he had just heard that the war was over. The Emperor of Japan, overwhelmed by the power of atomic bombs and faced with the prospect of an invasion of Nippon, had unconditionally surrendered.

Three days later even the Japanese themselves admitted that we need no longer work. But the war had not been won: nor lost. It had simply, for the moment, stopped. They ceased to bellow "Currah" and instead bowed politely when we passed. The food which they had recently declared to be non-existent they now produced in vast quantities so that we might eat our fill. Likewise drugs appeared from everywhere and in profusion.

Then we all assembled, thousands upon thousands of men, until there were seventeen thousand there, in Changi Gaol. British paratroopers arrived and were greeted politely by the Japanese. Then Mountbatten arrived and (though we were ordered not to by our administration) a few of us walked the seventeen miles into Singapore to see him accept Itagaki's surrender. At that brief ceremony, when Mountbatten drove fearlessly down through hundreds of thousands of hysterical Malays and Chinese, standing upright in an open car: when Itagaki met him on the steps of the civic hall and handed over his sword—for that brief moment I felt that the war really was over. But it didn't last.

I walked down to the harbour and on board the *Sussex*—where I was fed and washed and given clean clothes by the ever-hospitable matelots of the Royal Navy. I stayed there, smuggled away, for two days: then returned to the gaol in a jeep with eighteen other "sight-seeing" P.O.W.'s.

At the gaol I heard that the Ice Cream Man no longer lived—which didn't surprise me. Also that we were now in the hands of an organization known as RAPWI (which meant "Rehabilitation of Allied Prisoners of War and Internees" and was surely impressive enough).

When, a month later, we still languished on the island impatiently awaiting shipping home, RAPWI was rechristened—in the British manner—Retain All Prisoners of War Indefinitely.

This seemed to sting someone into activity, for at once we were drafted into shiploads and the docks became crowded with transports.

We said all our good-byes.

Mario left, waving an excited Latin farewell, for Italy. Ron Searle and Chris departed for Britain—the one for fame, the other for medicine. Hap Kelly flew ostentatiously and swiftly back to Texas in a Skymaster, sent promptly by an ever-attentive government. David Griffin flew to Sydney and the Bar: Downer to Adelaide and the Federal Australian Parliament. Hugh went home on one ship, Piddington on another, I on a third.

The careful fabric of one's personal life, built up over four years, disintegrated at a single blow. One felt curiously alone as the ship sailed out of Singapore Harbour—except for the moment when old Harry Smith was spotted leaning, as melancholy as ever, against the rail of a ship we passed. As one man, our vessel roared: "You'll never get off the island," at which Harry waved miserably and we laughed.

Then the sense of loneliness returned. All those blokes, Pommies and Australians: all those ties—gone. And then I realized, as I looked back and in the distance saw Changi's tower with its radar screen that didn't work, and above it the flagmast from which the poached egg had now vanished and the Union Jack flew, what was the trouble. The disintegration wouldn't matter if it had been caused by the *end* of the war. *That* was the trouble. For us, and for the undefeated Japanese soldiers all over Southeast Asia, the war hadn't ended. It had just, momentarily, stopped. The tower slid out of view; the symbol of our captivity was gone—but now I could think only of the words of a thousand guards, of Saito himself, of Terai the intellectual who spoke English and wrote plays: "War finish one hundred years."

So, for those of us who had suffered under them, and for the Nipponese themselves, this was just an interlude—the Hiroshima Incident, probably, they would call it. But the war itself, of Asia against the white man, that—under one guise or another: in one place or another—still had ninety-five years to go. The trouble was, of course, that no one at home would believe it.

And with that I brightened. After all, the sea was green and clear: the sun was warm and free: there was food aplenty and no need for anxiety as the old ship ploughed her confident way eastwards, away from Singapore. We were all going Home. That, for the moment, must be enough.

POSTSCRIPT THE GUTS OF THE MATTER

When, before the war, a government official, now Lord Llewellyn, queried Major General Dobbie about the complete absence of fortifications on the north coast of Singapore, though the east and the west and the south bristled with armaments, the general replied simply: "The north needs no fortification. No one could get through the jungle that leads to it."

Unfortunately, the Japanese were never informed of this fact.

"The defences of Singapore are still considerably below standard."

Sir John Dill, May 6, 1941

"I would not tolerate the idea of abandoning the struggle for Egypt, and was resigned to pay whatever forfeits were exacted in Malaya. This view was also shared by my colleagues.

"I am sure that nothing we could have spared at this time, even at the cost of wrecking the Middle Eastern theatre or cutting off supplies to the Soviet, would have changed the march of fate in Malaya."

Winston Churchill: *The Grand Alliance*

"To defend the Northern Malayan Thailand frontier alone 40 battalions and 3 machine gun regiments and 2 anti-tank regiments, with normal tank support, are the minimum required."

Singapore Defence Conference, 1940

In all of Malaya there were only 32 battalions and no tanks at all to resist the Japanese.

"556 first-line aircraft are required in Malaya."

Singapore Defence Conference, 1940

"Relying mainly on Air Power it was deemed necessary to hold the whole of Malaya . . . [but] In no case was the strength of the garrison really adequate for the defence of the aerodromes."

General Percival's Report on Malayan Campaign

In all of Malaya, of all types—Tiger Moths, antiquated bombers, inferior fighters—there were only 141 aircraft, none of them, by Japanese standards, first-line.

"It cannot be too strongly stressed that the object of the defence was the protection of the Naval Base and later of the Air Bases at Singapore."

General Percival's Report

Notwithstanding this "stress," by the time the attack on that Naval Base and later the Air Bases was sprung, General Percival's staff had frittered away the lives and energies and equipment of about two thirds of their most experienced and seasoned troops in the fruitless defence of the Malayan Peninsula itself.

"Our whole fighting reputation is at stake . . . It will be disgraceful if we yield our boasted fortress of Singapore to inferior enemy forces."

General Wavell, February 10, 1942

Five days later Singapore fell!

There are only three deductions that can be made from this last order and its sequel. First, that our British fighting reputation was thereby disgraced. Or, second, that the enemy forces were not in fact inferior. Or, third, that the order was purely propagandistic and not in fact a true appreciation by a brilliant soldier of the position on Singapore Island as it was in the first days of February, 1942.

As to which of these three deductions is the correct one let the reader, having read this book, judge for himself.

"The war will last one hundred years."

Imperial Japanese Army, 1945

"All the critics of the Treaty emphasize that the Japanese population of 86 million cannot possibly be confined to the four home islands."

Sunday Times (on Japanese press opinion), July 15, 1951

This book was completed one year before the signing of the Peace Treaty with Japan. It represents the views of the author then.

Those views have not changed.

R. B.

Lightning Source UK Ltd.
Milton Keynes UK
UKHW021130191020
371842UK00006B/537

9 780343 246020